Regulating Utilities and Promoting Competition

Regulating Utilities and Promoting Competition

Lessons for the Future

Edited by

Colin Robinson

Emeritus Professor of Economics, University of Surrey, UK

In Association with the Institute of Economic Affairs and the London Business School

Edward Elgar

Cheltenham, UK • Northampton, MA, USA

Published by
Edward Elgar Publishing Limited
Glensanda House
Montpellier Parade
Cheltenham
Glos GL50 1UA
UK

Edward Elgar Publishing, Inc.
136 West Street
Suite 202
Northampton
Massachusetts 01060
USA

A catalogue record for this book
is available from the British Library

Library of Congress Cataloguing in Publication Data
Regulating utilities and promoting competition : lessons for the future / edited by Colin Robinson.
    p. cm.
  "In association with the Institute of Economic Affairs and the London Business School".
  Includes bibliographical references and index.
  1. Public utilities—Government policy—Great Britain. 2. Public utilities—Deregulation—Great Britain. 3. Trade regulation—Great Britain. 4. Public utilities—Deregulation. 5. Competition. I. Robinson, Colin, 1932–

HD2768.G74R44 2006
363.60941—dc22

                       2005057706

ISBN-13   978 1 84542 711 5
ISBN-10   1 84542 711 4

Printed and bound in Great Britain by MPG Books Ltd, Bodmin, Cornwall

Contents

Figures and tables

FIGURES

TABLES

Notes on the authors

Sir Christopher Bellamy (b. 1946) is President of the Competition Appeal Tribunal. After qualifying as a barrister, he mainly practised in the fields of competition law, EC law and public law. He was appointed Queen's Counsel in 1986. From 1992 to 1999 he was a judge of the Court of First Instance of the European Communities. He is also authorised to sit as a High Court judge, a judge of the Employment Appeal Tribunal, and a Recorder of the Crown Court.

Alistair Buchanan took up his current position as Chief Executive of Ofgem in October 2003. He began his career as a Chartered Accountant at KPMG. Since then, his working career has been in the financial sector, but closely aligned to utilities. An award-winning analyst, he started at Smith New Court (now Merrill Lynch) where he was one of the central analysts to the privatisations of the electricity industry in the early 1990s, and again in the mid-1990s. From 1995 to 2000, he had a break from UK utilities, and was first Head of Research at BZW, and then moved to New York to run the American Utilities research team for Salomon Smith Barney. On returning to London with DLJ, he looked at European utilities, notably the German companies, which have come to be so important in the UK power scene. Before joining Ofgem he was Head of Utilities Research at ABN Amro and with ABN Rothschild worked with Electricité de France on the early stages of privatisation.

Nigel Cornwall (Cornwall Energy Associates) has had an independent energy consultancy business since 1994. He has worked on energy trading and transmission issues in the UK, having project managed the establishment of National Grid Company (NGC) as a civil servant. Over recent years, his work has focused on the England and Wales pool review and New Electricity Trading Arrangements (NETA) implementation, and he was one of the main negotiators for suppliers during the NETA development process. Since then, he has worked with a range of clients in the UK, including Ofgem, Energywatch, ConocoPhillips, Gaz de France and the Adam Smith Institute. He also maintains his links with overseas clients, and regularly collaborates with the Boston Consulting

Group (BCG). He specialises in issues connected with market design, including the role of transmission and system operations in deregulated markets and the associated legal, regulatory, commercial and governance framework. He takes a strong interest in competition issues, working with a variety of smaller players both in the gas and electricity markets. Besides various technical reports on aspects of energy sector operation, he is also a regular contributor to the industry trade press. The Cornwall Energy Associates website is at www.cornwallenergy.com.

John Fingleton is Chief Executive of the Office of Fair Trading. Previously he was Chairperson of the Irish Competition Authority. He was appointed for a five-year term in May 2000 and reappointed in May 2005. He studied economics at Trinity College Dublin and Nuffield College Oxford, and then returned to teach economics at Trinity College from 1991 to 2000. He has held visiting positions at the Université Libre de Bruxelles (1995) and the Graduate School of Business at the University of Chicago (1998–2000). His academic research focused on microeconomic theory and competition policy. His publications have covered industrial organisation theory, competition and regulatory policy in Ireland, competition policy in transition economies, the Dublin taxi market, and other topics. Before joining the Authority, he engaged in a variety of consultancy work in Ireland and abroad including expert evidence in several Irish High Court cases. He is a member of Ireland's National Competitiveness Council, Vice Chair of the International Competition Network Steering Committee and Chair of the Association of Competition Economics. He also sits on the boards of several journals that specialise in competition policy.

Philip Fletcher was appointed Director General of Water Services on 1 August 2000. From 1 April 2006 he became the Chairman of the successor body, the Water Services Regulation Authority. His previous career was based mainly in central government public service, with an emphasis on financial issues. Ofwat is responsible for the economic regulation of the water industry. Its duties are prescribed by statute, and include the setting of price limits to enable a well-managed company to deliver the required services in a sustainable and efficient way. It has a number of other responsibilities designed to protect the interests of consumers, wherever appropriate through the promotion of competition in the industry.

Stephen Glaister CBE FICE is Professor of Transport and Infrastructure at Imperial College London. He has been a member of the Board of Transport for London since July 2000 and he was a non-executive director of London Regional Transport from 1984 until 1993. He was a member of the Steering Group for the Department for Transport's 2004 National Road Pricing Feasibility Study. Between 1993 and spring 2001 he was an economic advisor to the Rail Regulator. He was a member of the Government's first Advisory Committee on Trunk Road Assessment and he has been Specialist Advisor to the Parliamentary Select Committee on Transport and an advisor to the Commission for Integrated Transport. He has published widely on transport policy and also on regulation in the telecommunications, water and gas industries.

Colin Kirkpatrick is Hallsworth Professor of Development Economics at the Institute for Development Policy and Management, School of Environment and Development, University of Manchester. He is also joint director of the Regulation Programme in the Centre on Regulation and Competition (CRC), University of Manchester. He has published extensively in the field of development economics and policy, and regularly provides advisory services to international development organisations, including the World Bank, the OECD, the UN and the UK Department for International Development (DFID). His most recent research work has been in the area of privatisation and regulation policy, including regulatory impact assessment, in developing countries.

Robin Mason is a professor of economics at the University of Southampton. He graduated from Cambridge University in natural sciences, returning there to complete an MPhil, and PhD in economics. He has held research fellowships at Nuffield College, Oxford and at Cambridge University. He has been the associate director of the Global Communications Consortium at the London Business School, and is currently a research affiliate of the Centre for Economic Policy Research. His main research interests are in the area of industrial organisation in general, and in particular the economics of networks (telecoms, broadcasting and the internet). In a series of published papers, he has examined the extent to which network effects (when consumers' valuations of a firm's product depends on the number of consumers who buy that firm's product) determine the structure of network industries. He is an associate editor of the *Journal of Industrial Economics* and the *Journal of Information Economics and Policy*. He has served as a member of the panel of economic advisers to Ofcom, the UK communications regulator. He has also provided commissioned work for the consortium of UK utility regulators, Bell Labs, British Telecom and the European Commission; and acted as an expert witness in telecoms court cases.

John Michell is director of his own consulting business, Prestbury Enterprises Limited. He is also a director of Eni UK Limited, and a member of the Board of the UK Offshore Operators Association (UKOOA). He was formerly head of the Oil and Gas Directorate of the Department of Trade and Industry (DTI) from 1993 to 1998. This period saw the extension of competition throughout the UK gas market under the framework of the Gas Act 1995 and the accompanying Ofgas licensing regime, negotiation of the First EU Gas Directive, in which the UK took a leading role, and construction of the UK/Belgium Interconnector. Prior to 1993, he held a succession of Civil Service posts over a career of some 30 years in the DTI, the Treasury and the Ministry of Defence.

David Parker is Research Professor, Privatisation and Regulation, at the Cranfield University School of Management and Co-Director of the regulation research initiative at the Centre on Regulation and Competition at the University of Manchester, funded by the Department for International Development. He has published widely on privatisation, competition and regulation issues. Examples of recent publications include the *International Handbook on Privatization* (with David Saal, 2003) and *Privatisation and Corporate Performance* (2000), both published by Edward Elgar. He has provided training and economic advice on privatisation and regulation issues in a number of countries, including the Russian Federation, Trinidad, Germany, India, Bangladesh, Taiwan, Malaysia, the Czech Republic, the Philippines, Slovakia, Estonia, Lithuania, Mexico, Cyprus, Germany, South Africa, Australia, Jamaica, Malawi, Ghana and Sri Lanka. He is a member of the UK Competition Commission and Official Historian on privatisation in the Cabinet Office. His recent work in developing countries has centred on performance in the energy and water sectors and on the application of regulatory impact assessment techniques to improve regulatory governance.

Colin Robinson was educated at the University of Manchester, and then worked for eleven years as a business economist, mainly in the oil industry, before being appointed in 1968 to the Chair of Economics at the University of Surrey, where he founded the Department of Economics and is now Emeritus Professor. His research is principally in the energy industries and the regulated utilities. He is the author of 23 books and monographs and over 150 journal papers. He is a Fellow of the Royal Statistical Society, of the Society of Business Economists and of the Institute of Energy. He was named British Institute of Energy Economics 'Economist of the Year' in 1992 and in 1998 received from the International Association for Energy Economics its 'Outstanding

Contribution to the Profession and its Literature' award. From 1992 to 2002 he was Editorial Director of the Institute of Economic Affairs.

Thomas Sharpe QC taught competition law and regulation at Oxford and was also executive director of the Institute for Fiscal Studies before going to the Bar in 1987, taking silk in 2004. He specialises in cases where law and economics meet and recent interesting cases include acting for Safeway in two Competition Commission references, for the Competition Commission in successfully defending its report on termination charges in judicial review proceedings brought by three of the mobile telephone operators, and acting for electricity generators against Ofgem's attempts to introduce variable transmission losses and the market abuse licence condition. He frequently defends alleged cartelists and abusers of dominant positions in EC Commission and Office of Fair Trading proceedings. He is a member of the editorial or advisory boards of the *European Competition Journal, Concurrences*, and the Centre for Competition Policy, University of East Anglia.

David Simpson was Economic Adviser to Standard Life from 1988 until his retirement in 2001. From 1975 to 1988 he was a Professor of Economics at the University of Strathclyde, and founder director of the Fraser of Allander Institute. He was also for a time a member of the Advisory Council of the Institute of Economic Affairs. He is at present Deputy Chairman of the Water Industry Commission for Scotland and a Trustee of the David Hume Institute. He is the author of several books including *General Equilibrium Analysis* (1975), *The Political Economy of Growth* (1983) and *The End of Macroeconomics?* (1994). His latest book, *Rethinking Economic Behaviour: How The Economy Really Works*, was published by Macmillan in 2001. He has contributed articles, some of them on energy topics, to periodicals ranging from *Econometrica* and *Scientific American* to *The Spectator* and the *Financial Times*.

Sir John Vickers is Drummond Professor of Political Economy at Oxford University. From 2000–05 he was Director General/Chairman of the Office of Fair Trading. Previously he spent two and a half years as Chief Economist at the Bank of England, and was a member of the Monetary Policy Committee. Most of his career has been spent teaching economics at Oxford. He has published widely on privatisation, regulation and competition. He is a fellow of the British Academy, the Econometric Society, and All Souls College, Oxford. He was knighted in 2005.

Leonard Waverman is Professor and Chair of Economics, as well as Director of the Regulation Initiative and the Global Communications Consortium at the London Business School. He is a non-executive board member of GEMA – the UK's electricity and gas market authority. He is a member of the Scientific Advisory Board of the German Institute for Economic Research in Berlin (DIW) and a Fellow of Columbia University's Center for Tele-Information. He has recently been appointed to Vodafone's Advisory Board on the Social and Economic Importance of Mobile as well as to the Advisory Board to Ernst and Young's TCE practice. He is a citizen of Canada and of France and has received the honour of *Chevalier dans l'Ordre des Palmes Academiques* from the French government.

Tom Winsor joined White & Case's London office as a partner in 2004. From 1999–2004, he was UK Rail Regulator and International Rail Regulator, a time of considerable turbulence for the British railway industry. In his period of office, he carried out two major reviews of the financial framework of the British railway industry. He also carried out major reforms of the infrastructure provider's principal instrument of accountability to the public interest, and of the contractual matrix between Network Rail and the passenger and freight train operators. He also sat in arbitration in major legal disputes in the railway industry. As Rail Regulator, he was also the national competition authority for the British railway industry. He was a member of the group of nine economic regulators of the UK, and the senior member of the convention of European rail regulatory authorities. His practice at White & Case embraces infrastructure projects in the UK, Europe and Asia, and includes the development of work advising clients in regulatory dynamics, competition cases, price reviews, investment protection measures and connected matters. White & Case is a global law firm of 1900 lawyers with 38 offices in 25 countries.

George Yarrow is Director of the Regulatory Policy Institute and an Emeritus Fellow of Hertford College, Oxford. His academic career has included appointments at the universities of Warwick, Newcastle, Oxford, California (San Diego), Harvard and London (Queen Mary College). He has written and lectured widely on issues of competition, regulation and privatisation, including in past series of Beesley lectures, and his work has also covered a variety of other areas such as environmental policy, monetary policy, and welfare reform. In addition to teaching and research, he has acted as an advisor or consultant to a range of government departments, regulatory agencies, international agencies, and companies, particularly, in relation to aspects of the conduct of competition and regulatory policies.

Introduction

Colin Robinson

This book contains revised versions of papers presented in the Beesley Lectures in the autumn of 2004, the fourteenth consecutive year of the series which was founded in 1991 by the late Professor Michael Beesley and arranged by him until his death in 1999. His intention was that it should be a forum for discussing utility regulation and competition policy, involving both utility regulators and other commentators. The series is organised by the London Business School and the Institute of Economic Affairs, with both of which Michael was closely associated, the first as a Founding Professor and the second as a Managing Trustee. As usual, the fourteenth series ranged widely in terms of the issues considered and the countries concerned.

The opening chapter is by Tom Winsor who was Rail Regulator and International Rail Regulator from 1999 to 2004. Winsor is highly critical of government policy towards the railways during his period of office. He emphasises that he had to deal with 'some severe assaults on the independence and jurisdiction of the ORR' (Office of Rail Regulation) during his period of office and that there was a 'significant degree of political interference with Railtrack, almost all of it unwarranted'. In his analysis of the 2004 White Paper on the railways, he points out some problems – for instance, the difficulties of taking the functions of the Strategic Rail Authority (SRA) into the Department of Transport and moving rail safety obligations from the Health and Safety Executive to the ORR. Nevertheless, he concludes that his successors have some advantages, particularly now that the SRA no longer exists. They have '(at present) firm political support, significantly better asset knowledge and maintenance and renewal policies and practices on the part of Network Rail'.

Professor Stephen Glaister, of Imperial College, in his comments,[*] argues that the White Paper is a 'terribly weak document'. As in the case of the 1993 Railways Act and the preceding White Paper, ministers were unwilling or unable to write down clearly in advance what they wanted. One outcome of the 2004 White Paper will be a railway more under the direct control of central

---

[*] All of the Chairman's comments in this book were made in Autumn 2004.

government than there has been previously. Glaister has doubts about whether costs are under control and he sees two big questions not even addressed by the White Paper. First is the matter of how much the country is 'willing to pay for the railway of the future'. Second is whether there are incentives to encourage Network Rail to be efficient and to restrain its mounting debt. Competition has not worked as a discipline on the railways, Glaister claims, because the government has undermined competition at every turn.

Nigel Cornwall's Chapter 2 deals with the increasing international trade in gas and prospects for supplies of gas to Britain (which is about to become a net importer of gas as production from its offshore area declines). Cornwall, of Cornwall Consulting Ltd, analyses the world gas market in terms of supply, demand, trade and pricing, pointing to the growing influence of the Continental European gas market on the market in Britain and expressing some concern about the slow transition to competitive gas markets on the Continent. Looking ahead to 'key drivers' of trade he foresees growing demand for gas, a concentration of supply sources on 'technically challenging and politically risky' places, huge infrastructure requirements (including those needed for the trade in liquefied natural gas) and the increasing importance of environmental compliance. European competition policy should be applied 'much more rigorously' in the energy sector, he argues. The best protection for consumers will come from 'liberalised, competitive markets for natural gas, where regulators will monitor developments and introduce or suggest necessary corrective measures'.

In his comment, John Michell, of ENI (UK) Ltd, reinforces Cornwall's argument that more competition in the gas markets of other EU countries is desirable but cautions that Britain has been trying to achieve that result for many years with little sign of success. Ofgem's formal complaint to the EU Commission may not be a 'very productive way forward', especially since the Commission can influence only the purchasing side of the market, not the production sector. Moreover, Michell questions whether market liberalisation is enough, given that there might be market failures. He also raises the issue of political will, which was evident during Britain's energy market liberalisation: how can that political will be encouraged in other EU countries? The British government, Ofgem and others will probably need to go to Brussels and argue the case vigorously and over a long period.

In Chapter 3, Professor David Simpson, of the David Hume Institute in Edinburgh, considers Britain's windpower programme which is aided by 'very large subsidies' from government, funded by a 'stealth user charge'. After examining the scale of the programme, the means used to promote wind energy, the characteristics of wind energy and the relationship of the programme to Britain's energy policy, he concludes that the programme is 'an expensive and ineffective method of carbon emissions abatement that adds little to the security of the nation's energy supplies'. Simpson argues that, instead of the government's 'picking winners' procedure among technologies, it would be better to employ a carbon tax or a carbon trading scheme to reduce the consumption of carbon-intensive energy: market prices would adjust to reflect the environmental damage of carbon emissions and the cost of achieving environmental goals would become more transparent. The government's renewables (and energy efficiency) schemes would then become largely redundant. Simpson ends by saying that wind energy will probably play some part in Britain's future energy supply but it should be done as efficiently as possible.

Alistair Buchanan, Chief Executive of the Office of Gas and Electricity Markets (Ofgem), in his comments, explains the role of Ofgem in the renewables programme. It acts as administrator for the government's Renewables Obligation Certificate (ROC) scheme and it facilitates network development in onshore transmission and distribution and in offshore pipelines. Buchanan also points out the constraints that bind Ofgem. Like other independent regulators, it must not 'cross the boundary of policy at the expense of customers'; it must be accountable for its costs; and, according to its social and environmental guidance from government, any significant financial impact must be dealt with by government.

In Chapter 4, Sir Christopher Bellamy, Chairman of the Competition Appeal Tribunal (CAT), discusses four broad roles of the CAT – to ensure that the system is seen to be fair, to get the law right (given the 'considerable amounts of "grey area"'), to aid transparency and visibility, and to produce dialogue so that the system adapts and develops. In fulfilling its roles, the Tribunal uses working methods that represent modern best practice, including extensive written argument, early disclosure, strict time limits, site visits and extensive use of its website. Bellamy raises some questions for the future that need to be addressed. Among them are whether a 'competition culture' has really taken root in Britain; the importance of regional and local enforcement of competition policy; the benefits of a 'reasonable flow of enforcement decisions'; and the issue of increasing deterrence. Finally, Bellamy points to the need to 'forge a central core of relatively simple rules or presumptions ... capable of being applied by business people or non-specialist advisors in a way that makes the law understandable, accessible and reasonably certain, as well as enforceable at reasonable cost'.

Professor George Yarrow, of RPI Europe, begins his comments on Bellamy's chapter by emphasising the importance of judicial supervision of the use of executive power: 'many of the most important occurrences of conspiracies against consumers, of abuses of power, and of undue concentration of power are to be found within government'. Furthermore, in his view, judges perform a vital function in putting obstacles in the way of presumptions and prejudices built in to economic models. Yarrow argues that static economic analysis all too often leads to intervention when it would have been better to have allowed market participants to deal with the perceived problem. He is less optimistic than Bellamy about the prospects for developing simple rules and presumptions that will speed up procedures, reduce costs and 'do good over the long haul'. The hard part is finding rules that 'have (net) beneficial effects across a wide range of differing market contexts'.

Professor Robin Mason, of the University of Southampton, discusses in Chapter 5 the 'two big reviews' undertaken by Ofcom – one of public service broadcasting and the other of telecommunications. On broadcasting, he doubts whether externalities can justify the present degree of intervention, though there may still be grounds for intervention given the high valuation attached to broadcasting services and their non-rivalrous nature. All public service broadcasting funding should be contestable, he argues – not just part, as Ofcom proposes. As regards telecoms, Mason contends that local loop unbundling may not be effective in developing local loop competition. In any case, the local loop is not the only important issue. There is a general bottleneck problem and 'Ofcom needs to develop a coherent policy towards bottlenecks and vertical integration well in advance: in particular, under what conditions to mandate access to bottlenecks, and to enforce structural separation'.

Chapter 6 is an analysis by Thomas Sharpe QC of the problem of trying to make sense of abuse of a dominant position. He argues that the European courts have been wrongly criticised for 'formalism' rather than economic analysis. The correct distinction is between 'good economics – empirically based and robust – and bad economics – *a priori* and untested by evidence'. Dominance is best expressed in terms of the possession of economic power, a wider concept than market power, giving a firm the capacity to exclude a competitor. Sharpe goes on to explain some of the difficulties involved in dealing with problems associated with dominance such as predatory pricing, price discrimination and loyalty rebates. He concludes: 'There is no general theory, nor should there be'. There is no 'conceptual or intellectual difficulty in assessing motive and effect in the light of the degree of economic power present, and forming a view that the conduct, however justified in terms of short-term profitability or even short-term benefits to consumers, is closely associated with the desire to exclude'.

Sir John Vickers, Chairman of the Board, Office of Fair Trading, agrees with Sharpe about the present uncertain state of the law. However, he disagrees on some of the economic issues. Those who want a better economic basis for the law on abuse are not arguing for the replacement of rules by discretion. Rules are essential but they need to be set in an economic context so that, for instance, rather than prohibiting some form of behaviour, the economic circumstances in which it takes place should be examined. European law on predatory pricing shows that 'practical administrability and economic grounding can go together'. What is now required is to confront the 'fundamental question of what is harm to competition, and to develop practical approaches to other kinds of abuse that are similarly grounded in economic principle'.

In Chapter 7, Dr John Fingleton, Chairman of the Irish Competition Authority when the lecture was given, discusses the role of economics in merger reviews. Economic analysis has, he says, contributed both to the formulation of merger law and to the investigation of economic effects in merger cases. As regards the 'why' of merger policy, the competition test for mergers has become the norm in many countries because of the influence of economics: 'the critical factor is the relationship between competition and productivity growth'. Moreover, in most jurisdictions, economic effects analysis is now common and well established, even if questions remain about standards of proof and evidence. Competition authorities should advocate 'the use of competition tests implemented with effects-based analysis', says Fingleton. In the long term, 'legal certainty is enormously enhanced if merger decisions reflect sound economic analysis'. Solid economic foundations are particularly important 'in a world where merger decisions on the same or similar transactions are taken by different institutions in different countries'.

Professor Leonard Waverman, in his comments, raises the question of whether a consumer surplus or a total surplus test should be used in implementing merger policy. He points out that, despite the efforts to promote convergence in merger policy among countries, which Fingleton mentions, many differences remain even within the EU. Waverman argues that, since there is little evidence that competition authorities make the correct decisions in merger cases, it may not matter if it is difficult to block mergers *ex ante*. More important is *ex post* analysis to determine whether mergers result in increases in consumer surplus or total surplus. He ends by suggesting that economists may find the courts less and less willing to tolerate 'on the one hand' and 'on the other hand' statements by expert witnesses.

Philip Fletcher, Director-General of Water Services, originally commented on a paper in the series – on economies of scale and productivity growth in water – that it has unfortunately not been possible to publish. But, since his remarks on mergers in the water industry and on the place of comparative competition are of interest in themselves, they are reproduced in slightly modified form as a contribution in its own right. He begins by explaining why the regional water authorities were not broken up before being privatised. Quick privatisation meant that their structures could not be changed: structural reorganisation would have meant that there would have been no 'evidence or data to float these companies in the market'. Fletcher points out that although academic commentators tend to argue as though there have been no mergers in water, there have been plenty of takeovers as well as substantial restructuring. He stresses the importance of having 22 companies to compare with each other. In the 2004 price review, 'comparative competition was a crucial and essential part of the regulatory tool kit. Without it the companies could call almost all the shots'.

The final chapter in the book is on privatisation and regulation in developing countries, by Professors David Parker of Cranfield University and Colin Kirkpatrick of the University of Manchester. It was presented in the series by David Parker. The authors argue that insufficient attention has been devoted to the design of institutional structures and regulatory instruments in infrastructure privatisations in the developing world. One problem is the lack of regulatory capacity: for example, the shortage of trained personnel, the absence of sound laws and uncertainty about law enforcement. Regulatory impact assessments (RIAs) might, say the authors, help to improve regulatory capacity. Another issue is whether price cap regulation is suitable in the circumstances of many developing countries – for example, serious information asymmetry, weak regulatory governance and problems in creating effective regulatory incentives. Some survey evidence suggests that there may be advantages in rate of return regulation. Parker and Kirkpatrick conclude that uninformed transfer of regulatory systems has taken place and that more research is required to investigate appropriate forms of regulation for developing countries.

Commenting, Professor Colin Robinson, University of Surrey, agrees with the authors' emphasis on the importance of regulatory institutions and the danger of importing inappropriate regulatory systems from developed countries. He has doubts, however, whether the use of RIAs will bring about much improvement. On price cap regulation, he argues that it is not only in the developing world that price cap regulation has gone far beyond what its originators had intended. He sketches the circumstances in which price caps are appropriate, which normally include separation of the network from the rest of a utility. If these conditions cannot be met, it may indeed be that price caps will not work well, though it is difficult to see that rate of return regulation would be any better. Regulatory systems, once entrenched, tend to grow out of control, Robinson argues.

1. The future of the railways in the light of the government's rail review 2004

Tom Winsor

The third anniversary of Mr Justice Lightman making a railway administration order in respect of Railtrack plc under section 60 of the Railways Act 1993 fell on 7 October 2004. That order is a remarkable document, and the circumstances under which it was procured and the consequences of its procurement have yet to be fully explained and analysed.

In my five years in office as Rail Regulator and International Rail Regulator (1999–2004), there were three pieces of primary legislation in relation to the railways. When I was appointed, the Railways Bill was just that – a Bill. It subsequently became the Transport Act 2000. In 2001 the Secretary of State for Transport, Stephen Byers, intended to introduce a Bill to take my office under direct political control, a matter which I shall mention later. And then there was the Railways and Transport Safety Act 2003. Two of those pieces of legislation were proceeded with during those five years – the Byers Bill was not.

At the Office of the Rail Regulator (ORR) we had to deal with some severe assaults on the independence and the jurisdiction of the ORR. These assaults came from government – particularly the Parliamentary Under-Secretary of State David Jamieson and the Minister of State Kim Howells – and from the Strategic Rail Authority (SRA) and those who were inspired by the SRA. I shall come back to the disfunctionality and the harm that that did.

The Railways and Transport Safety Act 2003 abolished the statutory position of Rail Regulator and replaced it with a seven-member board. This change was brought into effect on 5 July 2004, that is immediately after the end of my five-year term. Ten days later – 15 July 2004 – the government published its White Paper[1] on the future of the railways which said that there would be a Railways Bill ready for the Queen's speech in November 2004. So the government's appetite for legislating in the railways appeared to be undiminished.

In this chapter I shall deal with the White Paper and the collision of politics and regulation, which is part of the context of that document. During my term of office, there was a significant degree of political interference with Railtrack, almost all of it unwarranted. I first witnessed the intensity of that political interference in October 1999 when Bill Callaghan, the newly appointed chair of the Health and Safety Commission (HSC), Sir Alistair Morton, chairman of the shadow SRA, and I were called to 10 Downing Street to have a meeting with the Prime Minister, the Deputy Prime Minister, the Permanent Secretary at the Department of Environment, Transport and the Regions and others to discuss the Paddington rail crash which took place on 5 October 1999. And what happened at that meeting and what happened afterwards and for years afterwards displayed an intensity of interference with a FTSE 100 company, its affairs and its corporate governance which I could never have contemplated. In that five-year period there was also a refusal on the part of some institutions, including government, to acknowledge and accept that Railtrack was accountable to the Rail Regulator (under its network licence) and to its customers (under their access contracts).

When the Hatfield crash took place on 17 October 2000, the integrity of almost the entire network disintegrated and there was a year of very severe disruption. At the same time as Hatfield, I announced my final conclusions in the access charges review 2000,[2] which was intended to establish Railtrack's revenue requirements for 2001 to 2006. On 15 January 2001, the last day on which Railtrack had to make a decision whether or not to appeal my decision to the Competition Commission, I made a public statement[3] that I would be prepared to do an interim review to take into account the long-term consequences of the Hatfield crash – that is, what the aftermath of that crash meant for the condition of the railway network – and made clear that the direct financial consequences of Hatfield were going to be shouldered by Railtrack and its shareholders. In the light of that statement on 15 January 2001,[4] the company accepted my review and did not appeal. However, it unwisely then engaged in secret negotiations with the government throughout summer 2001. It asked for a four-year suspension of the regulatory regime, cost-plus financing – an open cheque book from the state – and the creation of a new class of equity whereby the government would get some of the upside and all of the downside if, during that four-year period, things did not go according to plan. It was not a surprise to anyone except, it appears, the management of Railtrack that the government found those proposals quite unacceptable. Instead, the government devised a different plan.

On 5 October 2001, I was told by the Secretary of State of his intention to apply for a railway administration order in respect of Railtrack, which was, according to the government, insolvent. I was also told by the Secretary of State that if I intervened to restore the company's revenue – as I had publicly indicated on 15 January 2001 that I would – he had the necessary authority to introduce emergency legislation into Parliament to take my office under direct political control. The circumstances of that episode are already well documented,[5] and I am not going to go through them again. But it is necessary to note that there was a failure then on the part of government to appreciate the consequences of its actions or to plan for the future of the infrastructure provider.

On 7 October 2001, the Secretary of State explained[6] why he had applied for the administration order. He said that Railtrack's costs and poor service penalties were expected to exceed the Rail Regulator's October 2000 determination by over £2 billion over the next five years. He said that the West Coast upgrade may now exceed £7 billion. He said that what had been done was not renationalisation. He continued: 'I also plan to legislate when parliamentary time allows to rationalise the present regulatory structure to provide stronger strategic direction while reducing the burdens of day to day interference in the industry and a self-defeating system of penalties and compensation'. And there then followed eight months of considerable uncertainty over the industry's structure and its regulatory regime, with a great deal of disquiet and criticism of what had been done and might be about to be done. That uncertainty came to an end in a statement to Parliament on 12 June 2002[7] by the new Secretary of State for Transport Alistair Darling – the present holder of that office – when he said that the government's commitment to independent economic regulation was virtually unshakable. Well, all I can say is that it did not feel unshakable three years ago.

The regulatory access charges review – independently conducted – which followed Railtrack's going into administration (and which was a crucial factor in the High Court bringing the company out of administration a year later) also had its problems. We had a failure by government to engage with ORR in significant respects, to do its job, to play its part in the review. There was also an intermittent refusal by the government to acknowledge ORR's jurisdiction when it was making public statements. That confused the industry and it confused the market, and it still confuses some people.

So the dynamics of regulation and politics were not as they should have been, and there was a collision. There was a press by government to take control, having assumed, wrongly in my view, responsibility for really quite slight things going wrong on the railway. Things do go wrong on the railway; it is an old network and a lot of underinvestment in the network had to be coped with. Having wrongly accepted that they should answer questions in Parliament about the 7.56 from Staplehurst, ministers then looked around to see what levers of control they could pull to make things better for the commuters on the 7.56. They found none, and so they asserted powers of control which they did not, in reality, possess. By their words and actions ministers distorted the picture and therefore perceptions of the regime and how it operated.

There were criticisms of the existing regime from many quarters. Often these criticisms were born of ignorance, despite ORR's intensive attempts to explain the regime in every public statement, every public document, the ORR websites, leaflets, everything we could possibly do.[8] The motives for some of this criticism arose from the tension created by the conferment of considerable power on the Rail Regulator, by the legislature at the expense of the executive government. That is, as we all know, something that people are unwilling to give up. They also arose – perhaps with even greater intensity – from the fact that, by private law contract, the government had indemnified the private sector passenger train operators against an increase in access charges determined by the Rail Regulator at an access charges review.[9] None of these assaults has so far succeeded, but each has been harmful to industry confidence and industry maturity. They were harmful to the efficiency and effectiveness of the carrying on of regulatory business. They were harmful to investor confidence. And they were harmful to users, the people who pay for railway services. So far I have outlined in very broad terms what some of the difficulties and pressures were in that period. I now turn to see if we can be a little more optimistic about the future.

The government's rail review was announced on 19 January 2004.[10] I do not believe anyone really expected that to be the announcement the Secretary of State was going to make that Monday afternoon. I do not even believe that the Secretary of State expected to be making that statement that day, but that is the statement he made. The review lasted for six months. It concluded with the publication of a White Paper ten days after I left office.

There was a great deal of uncertainty over what the implications of this White Paper were going to be. It had often been said that the decision I made on 12 December 2003[11] in my 2003 access charges review to increase the amount of money for the operation, maintenance, renewal and enhancement of the national railway network to £24.4 billion over five years (2004–09) was the catalyst for the review. I do not believe that it was. I think the catalyst for the rail review was political impatience with the SRA and a perception that the system was overly complex and was not working as it should have been. But it is true that there were many criticisms of the decision that I took to increase Network Rail's income by £7.4 billion over my previous settlement (on 23 October 2000). But it has to be remembered that if Network Rail had carried on spending at the rate contemplated by their 2003 business plan, the increase in state support for the railway would not have been £7 billion, it would have been £17 billion. And so my decision saved the Treasury £10 billion rather than cost it £7 billion, a fact acknowledged only by the Permanent Secretary at the Treasury.

Nevertheless there were criticisms of the decision because it was such a large figure, and because it was made on the authority of an economic regulator and not a politician. On 15 December 2003, the Secretary of State, in a written statement to Parliament,[12] welcomed the conclusions of my access charges review. Subject to smaller interim reviews which I announced at the same time, my 2003 access charges review conclusions will last for five years, so providing Network Rail and, through it, the railway industry, with essential certainty, predictability and stability of income for that period, something which no political settlement could ever do.

Turning back to the government's 2004 rail review, first impressions were that it would be a very wide-ranging review. Nothing would be ruled out. Many commentators and industry players engaged in frothy discussion over vertical integration, renationalisation and much else besides. For my part, as Rail Regulator, I did not see much point in that. There was a need for the government to acknowledge – and it did acknowledge – that this was 2004, not 1994. In 1994, all of the pieces in the railway jigsaw were in the public sector and government could decide to arrange those pieces in any way that it liked because it had not yet sold anything to the private sector. The way in which it arranged those pieces and how they fitted together and how they changed over time – a lot of that was unsatisfactory because it was done in too much of a hurry and there were corners cut and weaknesses built into the matrix, either through ignorance or lack of time or deliberately. But nevertheless it was done that way in 1994, and government could do that. That is not a freedom that government had in 2004 because this is a private sector industry – last time I checked, the names on the title deeds of these companies belonged to private sector companies, whatever people might say about the economic status of Network Rail.

And so on 9 February 2004,[13] the Secretary of State made a statement to Parliament excluding a number of things from his rail review:

1. renationalisation;
2. loss of independence of the regulatory authority (ORR);
3. 'any change to the rights of third parties, which will be protected';
4. weakening the effectiveness of economic regulation; and
5. any 'diminution in the regulatory protection of the private sector investors in the railway'.

Moreover, in his statement to Parliament the Secretary of State said: '[R]egulatory promises will be honoured, and the Government recognises, and is content, that only the Regulator can reopen his determinations'. That included the access charges review of 12 December 2003.

In his statement to Parliament on 9 February 2004, the Secretary of State also said: 'The Government attaches considerable importance to investor confidence and the need to preserve and protect the rights of private sector investors and lenders and their ability to plan and finance their businesses'. Indeed, the purpose of the statement on 9 February 2004 was the reassurance of investors, lenders and others that the rail review would not prejudice their interests and that they could have confidence in the regulatory regime remaining undiminished in all appreciable respects in both its independence and jurisdiction.

It is important to note that one of the things which the Secretary of State excluded was any change to the rights of third parties which will be protected. And he also promised that there would be no diminution in the regulatory protections of private sector investors in the railway. Those were very considerable exclusions from the scope of the rail review. Regrettably this clear statement about what was not in play in the review did not stop people talking about just those sorts of changes, but nevertheless those were important exclusions and there are things that the industry needs to hang on to as the policy is developed. In fact many people assume that those formal assurances of 9 February 2004 will be broken. I think that the most that can be said about that – so far – is that the government has creatively interpreted some of them. But I do not believe that it really intends to break them. A substantial measure of caution is required, however, because in some respects I think that the government is coming very close to the edge. Let us remember, as I said, that this is a private sector industry and the government needs its willing cooperation. So far, the government has had the willing cooperation. The government should not try to impose a settlement on the industry to which it strongly objects, and I think that would be a very wise step for the government to take.

Two weeks before I left office the *Financial Times* published an article I wrote in which I said that the outcome of the rail review – the White Paper – was expected to be incremental change dressed up as radicalism. I said I expected it to be long on generalities and short on specifics. Having now seen the White Paper, I think that both those things turned out to be true. It is necessary to look at a consultation document, published in September 2004[14] by my successors at ORR, for a lot more of the detail and to recognise the nature of what is actually proposed. There is still a lot more that needs to be done, and some policy objectives are still to be developed within the context of the White Paper.

Rather than provide a detailed analysis of everything in the White Paper and the ORR consultation document, I shall focus on the proposed changes to economic regulation and the way in which the industry works. This is because the devil is in the detail, as ever.

The White Paper says that the government is going to be in charge of setting strategy for the railways, including the level of public expenditure and the key outputs. It says that the government and Network Rail will have a binding arrangement which will be developed, with ministers specifying high-level outputs and funding, and that binding arrangement will be enforced by the ORR. It continues: 'Network Rail is to have overall responsibility for operating the network and whole industry performance, including meeting industry planning, setting timetables and directing service recovery'. Network Rail and the train operators are said to be going to work closer together with aligned incentives and rules established in the revised network code. Rail safety will move from the HSC to ORR and there will be a reduction in the number of franchises. The franchise map will be more closely aligned to Network Rail's organisational structure. The franchisees will continue to operate train services; they will focus on marketing, customer service, maintenance, and provision of train crew. Freight and open access will continue as now, and they will pay the incremental costs they impose on the network. The SRA will be abolished with responsibility for strategic planning and franchising transferred to the Department for Transport (DfT) and the Scottish Executive. Network Rail is to be responsible for coordinating route-based planning and the devolved governments in Scotland and Wales and other regional local funders will have increased roles in specification and funding of services reflecting their different circumstances.

Those are the headlines. So what is new about all this? Some of it is undeniably new. A great deal of it is not. What is new is that the SRA is being abolished. I shall come back to that. The railway safety division of the Health and Safety Executive (HSE) is going to be moved into ORR to create a single economic and safety regulatory authority along the lines of the Civil Aviation Authority model. Some of us do not think that is a very good idea, but that is what is going to happen. That has very considerable implications for ORR. Network Rail is going to be responsible for whole industry performance, not just its own performance but also that of the train operators. That also is new. Network Rail will take over route-based planning away from the SRA, so SRA people will go into Network Rail to do that work. There will be a remapping of the franchises and there will be devolution to make local politicians take local decisions and to face the local political consequences of having done so. And that is a very considerable change for them. They do want it, but it is a two-edged sword.

The changes to the SRA, HSE and devolution require primary legislation. The other new features of the government's railway policy can be done using existing powers, powers which are already in the hands of the government. For example, the White Paper speaks about the government 'in future' being in charge of strategy for the railway. The reality is that the government always was in charge of setting strategy for the railways. Section 206 of the Transport Act 2000 says that every strategy that the SRA comes up with has to have the specific endorsement of the Secretary of State. So what is it that the Secretary of State is getting now that he did not have before? The answer is nothing. He always had as much control over strategy as he could ever have wanted, and so, despite the new packaging, in this respect in substance the White Paper announces as new something that is not. There are a great deal of other things in the White Paper of which the same can be said.

The bulk of the White Paper and the ORR consultation document of September 2004 represents a continuation of pre-existing regulatory policy and industry initiatives. It should not be underestimated just how much of this supposedly new programme was already being done by the railway industry and the ORR before July 2004. This represents a welcome political endorsement of what has been done already and is already being done – the things the industry and the ORR were already up to.

The White Paper says that Network Rail is to be in charge of operating the network. It always was in charge of operating the network, and it has always been in charge of handling operational disruption. We hear a lot about the single point of accountability. The Secretary of State said he wanted one person he could ring up on a Monday morning when things go wrong. Apart from the Secretary of State having no appreciable right to try to run the railway on a Monday or any other day of the week, it should be recognised that, under Part H of the network code, Network Rail has the right to stop any train short or to stop it even leaving the depot if it is necessary to do so, having exercised its discretion under the criteria set out in the code, if there is operational disruption. Only in circumstances where only the trains of one operator are being disrupted does Network Rail have to do what that operator says, and even then it is still a single point of accountability because it is one person's finger on the button. That has always been the case; it has not changed now.

Network Rail has a radically reformed network licence when compared with the one held by Railtrack in 1994. A large proportion of the allegedly new accountabilities which were announced in the White Paper are in reality already in that licence. The White Paper speaks about a new unincorporated joint venture between the infrastructure operator and the infrastructure users – Network Rail and the train operators. Of course such a cooperative structure is desirable. That is why such a structure was established in the

ORR's model access contracts for freight and passenger operators.[15] I am glad to see that the government has now said that it is in favour of that structure. We see from ORR's September 2004 consultation document that the model contracts – which are in fact already in force between Network Rail and virtually every passenger and freight train operator – are not to be changed.

On 2 July 2004 ORR reformed the network code,[16] and it continues that programme, announced in December 2003. The reform programme is in two phases. The Phase 1 reforms have already been established and the industry has really engaged with and welcomed them. The Phase 2 reforms – which are about changing the economic architecture of the relationship between track and train – were fully under way in July 2004, and the momentum continues. Of course it is welcome that the government is behind that too. In the network code reform programme – as with the model contracts – we recognised the intensity of the interdependence of the two sides of the track–train interface and the need for a full partnership approach, with a clear specification of what each party has to do and sound, proportionate and effective remedies for when things go wrong, with aligned incentives and a spirit of cooperation rather than confrontation.

There is also nothing new about the need for government to play its part in access charges reviews. On 6 May 2004, ORR published its submission in the rail review.[17] We talked about what needed to change. And a lot of what needed to change was behaviour rather than rules. We certainly did not advocate any legislation except one. As I mentioned earlier, when we did the access charges reviews in 2000 and 2003, the government failed to engage in the process properly. The White Paper talks about how the government 'will take' – future tense – control of public expenditure going into the railway industry. This is phrased in terms as if the unaccountable, unelected regulator, in an offence to democratic principles, has asserted a jurisdiction which he does not possess and should never have. Indeed the House of Commons Transport Select Committee published a report saying that I had overreached my jurisdiction and had arrogated to myself power over public expenditure.[18] This was, of course, completely untrue.[19] I may also mention that a political figure who was a member of the Cabinet in October 2001, and whom I encountered recently, said to me when I asked him about the assault on independent economic jurisdiction:[20] 'Tom, in the seventeenth century Parliament fought a bloody civil war to gain control of public expenditure, and we were not about to give it up to you'. Given the fact that what was in issue was the honouring of indemnities voluntarily given by the state in private law contracts with operators who had entered into them in good faith and made investments on that basis, I found that a remarkable and regrettable thesis.

The fact of the matter is that the government always did have control over the amount of public expenditure going into the railway industry if only it would face up to the consequences of exercising that power. ORR has to have regard to the financial position of the SRA, facilitate its strategies and a number of other things; it has a whole range of statutory duties. Broadly speaking, one of the things that the Rail Regulator did – and the ORR will in future do – when doing an access charges review was determine what were the required network outputs and then price them, set efficiency targets and set the charges and the requirements of the company every five years. In order to know what those network outputs needed to be, we needed to know what were the demands which were going to be made on the system – how intensive was the use to be made of the network by passenger and freight train operators; in plain terms, how much of a hammering was the track and signalling system going to get. In order to know that, we needed to know what was to be the franchising policy, the franchising strategy, of government and its agent the SRA. We needed to know what trains the SRA and the government intended to support, how fast they would go, with what intensity were they going to use the network, where they were going to go, what freight support government was going to put up. And we needed to know from other people who did not require public subsidy – admittedly there were precious few of those – what demands they were going to place on the system. We then put all that information into the melting pot, we worked out what size and quality of network is required in order to meet those demands, assessed the efficiency and the performance targets, and there you have it. But what was missing, as I have mentioned, was government facing up to the fact that it had to tell us at ORR what it wanted. And I regret to say that government failed to do this. This fact was acknowledged by Sue Killen, the Director-General of Railways at the Department for Transport, at a conference on 6 October 2004.

What ORR said in our 6 May 2004 submission in the rail review was what failed in those two access charges reviews – October 2000 and December 2003 – was an act of will on the part of government to face up to the consequences. Government had to acknowledge and accept that if it did not want access charges to rise, it would have to see some very severe cuts in the operation of the network, in the size of the network, in the number of services operating on the network, in the quality of the network, and in the performance of trains on that network. Government – democratically accountable government – would have to face all of that. And we said that to government in summer 2003. I told the Secretary of State that if the railway were to carry on with the existing pattern of services, access charges (and corresponding grant aid) will rise by between £6 billion and £8 billion over five years – it turned out to be £7.4 billion – and if he did not want that to happen (either at all or as much) he had to tell me then or very shortly afterwards what he was going to do, what he was going to tell the SRA to do – remember that the SRA was the instrument of government – so as to cut back on the franchising programme and turn down the passenger service requirements in the existing contracts, so as to have a less intensive use of the network. These cutbacks would enable me to set lower – that is, cheaper – network outputs and access charges. What I got from government was radio silence. I believe this was because the political consequences of such a step were unpalatable. That much must be quite obvious to all of us. But I do believe that it is not really appropriate then, when the charges go up in accordance with information – indeed, a warning – given to government six months in advance, for government or a parliamentary committee to express surprise and indignation that what was forecast materialised. What politicians have to recognise is you cannot have 100 per cent of the existing network for 50 per cent of its efficient cost.[21] And so we said in our 6 May 2004 submission in the rail review, what failed in that case was an act of will, so maybe what we need now is an Act of Parliament. This would contain a provision that says the Secretary of State shall do something; the Secretary of State shall tell the regulatory authority in good time, in sufficient detail and with sufficient certainty what it is he wants to buy – that is, a statement of the quantity and intensity of railway services the government wishes to use public money to support through its franchising and freight subsidy programme. I think that that is what we shall see in the Railways Bill when it is published. I think it is essential.

ORR's statutory functions and duties remain undiminished; they are going to be added to. This system can be made to work as I have described, but there should be a removal of the unnecessary noise created by the SRA and others. It appears to be clear from the White Paper that there will be no turning back of established regulatory policy. Instead, it is to be confirmed and built upon. Maintaining, continuing and intensifying the initiatives which were already under way, led both by the railway industry and the ORR, is the right thing to do. ORR never did overreach its jurisdiction in the access charges reviews, despite the criticisms (particularly those of the Select Committee on Transport), but others did. And the Secretary of State's statements to Parliament in December 2003 and February 2004 fully acknowledge that fact. But one can underreach one's jurisdiction. That is what the Secretary of State did. I believe that there is now a courageous acknowledgement that that has happened and that we need a legislative fix.

Costs are under control now. They exploded in 2001 when the equity of Railtrack was extinguished when the company went into administration. Performance is now coming back strongly and track quality measures are improving – for example, Britain now has the lowest number of broken rails on average per kilometre in Europe – and are continuing to improve significantly. So things are going in the right direction.

There have been concerns expressed about some of the language and other government statements that have been made around the White Paper. They imply that ORR's role is going to be reduced, especially in access charges reviews and in matters of capacity allocation. I regret to observe that some of the White Paper is phrased in terms of ORR being told what to do by the government. ORR has so far properly rejected this notion. Indeed it is not for ORR to do something just because the White Paper or the executive government says it wants something. ORR has its statutory duties. Much of the work which the White Paper contemplates requires ORR to use its powers in terms of new access charges reviews, reforms to the network code, modifications to the licences, statements on enforcement, and information acquisition and analysis. A great deal of that is in the powers of the ORR, not the Secretary of State for Transport or the Treasury. It would be unlawful for ORR to act in a particular way merely because of political pressure to act in that way, unless that action were also consistent within promoting the statutory objectives of the Railways Act as set out in section 4. And Chris Bolt – the chairman of the new ORR – has acknowledged that.

The White Paper says that the new industry structure will have a triangular shape. The Secretary of State is at the top of the triangle setting overall transport policy and strategy. The train operators are at one of the other corners; they have franchises with the Secretary of State (who takes over the franchising function from the SRA). So there is a direct contractual link between the DfT and the train operators, just as there is now between them and the SRA. Network Rail is in the other corner of the triangle. It is part of an unincorporated joint venture with the train operators, and that joint venture is represented by a line along the bottom of the triangle. That joint venture is established through the access contracts and the network code. And then the final line of the triangle joins Network Rail back to the Secretary of State. This is said in the White Paper to be a binding arrangement with the Secretary of State. This is initially quite a puzzling concept, as it could mean all sorts of things. So where is ORR? ORR occupies the middle territory created by the triangle. This is because ORR monitors, modifies and enforces Network Rail's network licence, including Condition 7 (stewardship of the network), it determines the fair and efficient allocation of capacity, it supervises the development of the network code, it carries out access charges reviews, sets the level of charges, the financial structure and the framework. It enforces competition law and it is the appellate body for certain kinds of network code disputes. In other words it does all the things it does now and has done for quite a few years past.

So what about this binding arrangement? That is the puzzling thing, the part of all this which, at first blush, appears to be new. Franchises are already in place and have been since 1995. The network code and the access contracts have been in place since 1994. The network licence has also been in place since 1994 (although in my term of office I amended it nine times). So what is this new animal, the so-called 'binding arrangement'? Is it a direct agreement? Is it a contract? Is it a protocol? ORR's statement of September 2004 says that it is not a private law commercial contract. But is it going to establish some kind of direct legal nexus between the Secretary of State and Network Rail? If it is, this could amount to an overreaching of ORR's jurisdiction, with the Secretary of State leapfrogging ORR and himself directly setting network outputs. Under the existing access charges review regime,[22] the Secretary of State's input – if he is willing to give it – is a notification of the intensity of use of the system dictated by his franchising and freight support policy (or, rather, a direction from the Secretary of State to the SRA to do this). If, however, the Secretary of State is to go further and himself set the network outputs, that would be an encroachment into the jurisdiction of the ORR. If the Secretary of State takes power directly to set network outputs, this could well establish double jeopardy for Network Rail, a parallel jurisdiction and a parallel accountability. And it could lead to an annualised Treasury control of railway finances, a state which is inimical to private investment and is one of the things which the privatisation matrix had to exclude. So I believe it should not form part of the Railways Bill.

What the binding arrangement should be, in my view, is a statement which formalises the relationship which Network Rail has with the Secretary of State in relation to information flows, communication details and cooperation arrangements. It should not go further than that. It would perhaps be something like the former SRA–Network Rail Co-operation Agreement. The binding arrangement should underscore and support the new process whereby ORR will discuss with government what network outputs cost and government can then take an informed decision as to what it wants in terms of the intensity of demands placed on the system. The binding arrangement must avoid any attempt by government at micromanagement of the affairs of Network Rail. I believe that the binding arrangement must be the latter – the formalisation of communications and so on – and I do not believe it is going to overreach the jurisdiction of ORR. If it were to do so – overreach – such a reform would be quite contrary to government policy in terms of simplification, streamlining and improving the institutional structure and protecting independent economic regulation. It would also trigger a number of changes of law protections in a number of contracts, and government would end up paying for that. Such a step would also break assurances given to Parliament by the Secretary of State on 9 February 2004, a step which the government cannot afford to take.

The arrangement will be properly regarded as binding because it will become a reasonable requirement of one of Network Rail's funders, namely the Secretary of State, under Condition 7 of its network licence. This means that the requirement will be enforceable by ORR under section 55 of the Railways Act 1993. What should not happen is the Secretary of State making an annual statement of what he wants out of the railway and the ORR then carrying out an access charges review every year. If a return to effective nationalisation and annualised Treasury control of railway finances is what is wanted, that is certainly a good way of doing it. What would also happen in such a case would be a driving out of the industry of private investors such as Stagecoach, Virgin, EWS, FirstGroup, National Express and others like them. Such a regime would squeeze out all the commercial talent and entrepreneurial spirit, and the industry would be left with a rump of companies who are happy just to manage a service contract for a fee. I do not believe that the companies of the kind I have mentioned are in the industry for that kind of operation, and I suggest that it is very important that government acknowledges and respects that fact and allows the train operators the commercial freedoms they need to get on with their businesses within the overall context of its transport policy.

The White Paper also contemplates output adjustment mechanisms. That does sound somewhat like the slippery path to annualised Treasury control too, because it would enable year-by-year setting of a railway budget and then the DfT turning up or – more probably – down the outputs demanded of the train operators and, through them, Network Rail. I do not believe it is feasible to save appreciable amounts of money on the railway like that – especially because of the problems of underinvestment which will be stored up for the future – but nevertheless there is a danger that that is what would happen. Such a regime did a great deal of harm in the days of nationalisation. If output adjustment mechanisms were established and operated in this way, the industry would lose the five-year protections and the certainties which are provided by the periodic access charges review process.

The White Paper also speaks of new provisions in the network code relating to network downgrades, and there are some indications that the code's Part G compensation regime is going to be weakened in some way. Part G is the mechanism which provides for full indemnity compensation for train operators from Network Rail if the network gets smaller or gets worse.[23] That appears to me to be a possibly significant straw in the wind for the train operators. There is also a section in ORR's September 2004 consultation document which speaks of adjusting access rights in line with network and route output adjustments. But it also says that the Part G procedures and protections relating to loss of future network capability are going to be widened – which may mean improved – and this is especially important to freight train operators. So it appears that there are some mixed signals in these respects, and I believe that the operators in question would be wise to exercise a fair degree of caution because this could be the thin end of a rather dangerous wedge.

I now turn to the proposed abolition of the Strategic Rail Authority. In the ORR's 6 May 2004 submission in the rail review, we recommended that the SRA should be reined in by means of new ministerial directions and guidance. On 6 October 2004 the SRA was given new directions and guidance by the Secretary of State, but rather than improving its operational effectiveness and drawing it closer to government, they are mainly about closing the organisation down. The government could have achieved all or a very substantial proportion of what it wanted for the future conduct of the SRA simply through amending the Secretary of State's statutory directions and guidance to the Authority. The SRA has always been subject to direct ministerial control; the problem again was that ministers failed to use the powers they had. Now they intend to legislate to dismantle their own creation.

It is true that the SRA was created for ambiguous political reasons. It was a classic modern reaction of government: we have a problem, let us create a new institution. The reality as to why the SRA was created was not because the railway was in desperate need of strategic direction (whatever that was supposed to mean). It was in order to put flesh on the bones of a political catchphrase in 1996 – 'publicly owned, publicly accountable railway'. It was seen as John Prescott's iron fist in an iron glove, and the notion was abroad that being strategic meant telling everyone else what to do. That is of course not what a strategy is, but the harm which was done by that idea through distortions in the dynamics in accountability was considerable. There was an assumption and a pretence that the SRA was omnicompetent, and the eagerness with which that idea was seized upon and promoted in fact laid the seeds of the SRA's destruction.

It should also be recognised that there are real problems with taking the functions of the SRA into the Department for Transport. This is because these are not functions which a central government department is accustomed to carrying out, and there are justifiable anxieties that the assimilation of the SRA's roles will lead to a hiatus in effective despatch of public business. As I have said, the government should play its part in setting overall transport policy and allow everyone else to do their job. This means Network Rail, the train operators, ORR and the rest of the industry. They should have the necessary freedoms. I think if the government does that then it will be doing the industry a great service.

It is regrettable that the White Paper contains language which states or implies that some reforms or accountabilities have just been devised and will be carried into effect in the future when the reality is that they already exist and have been in place for several years. Nor should the White Paper have implied that the ORR is the obedient servant of the government, given that body's legal independence and the importance of that status for private sector confidence. But these are things mainly on the surface. The substance – so far as we can see it and subject to the important cautions I have expressed – is incremental change, building on existing and continuing regulatory and industry policy and initiatives. It is not one of reversing the existing work of the industry and the ORR, which has to date been about simplifying and rationalising the organisational structure of the railway industry, improving the matrix of specifications, incentives and accountabilities. The new ORR has a lot of work to do, and I know it is just as committed as I was to work with the industry.

My successors at ORR have a number of significant challenges, the greatest of which is undoubtedly the acquisition of the rail safety functions and obligations of the HSE. They also have a number of advantages, including (at present) firm political support, significantly better asset knowledge and maintenance and renewal policies and practices on the part of Network Rail, the absence of a public institution which (wrongly) tries to compete with its jurisdiction, and the absence of an infrastructure provider which is determined to thwart rather than work with regulatory policy on accountability to customers and in other respects. At the next major access charges review (in 2008–09), the new ORR will be reducing rather than increasing the amounts of money which go to the infrastructure provider. Of course there will be political pressure to reduce access charges farther and faster than some will judge to be appropriate, but things will be going in the right direction. The cost explosion – brought about mainly through Railtrack's destructive stewardship of the network and the equally harmful loss of equity discipline when Railtrack was put into administration – was brought under control and reversed by the 2003 access charges review. Network Rail's new accountabilities have also led to strong improvements in performance and other asset quality measures. And the matrix of financial, regulatory and contractual instruments has been significantly strengthened, to create and support the true joint venture which the railway is and must always be. It is a sound foundation on which to build and make yet further improvements.

And if that is what happens, then I think the railway industry has a very bright future.

NOTES

1. *The Future of Rail*, Department for Transport, 15 July 2004, Cm 6233.
2. *The Periodic Review of Railtrack's Access Charges: Final Conclusions*, Office of the Rail Regulator, London, 23 October 2000.
3. *Periodic Review: Statement on the Implications of Hatfield*, Office of the Rail Regulator, London, 15 January 2001; see also *Statement by the Rail Regulator*, Office of the Rail Regulator, 24 May 2001 (ORR press notice ORR/16/01) in which the statement of my attitude to the carrying out of an interim access charges review as a result of the Hatfield crash was confirmed.
4. Which was repeated on 24 May 2001 – see *Statement by the Rail Regulator*, ORR press notice ORR/16/01.
5. In relation to the collapse of Railtrack, the constitutional implications of the threat to independent economic regulation and the response to it, see generally *The Relationship Between the Government and the Private Sector: Winsor v Bloom in Context*, the 2004 annual lecture to the Incorporated Council of Law Reporting for England & Wales, given by the Rail Regulator, 5 April 2004. See also oral evidence of the Rail Regulator to the House of Commons Select Committee on Transport, Local Government and the Regions, given on 7 November 2001, Ev 81–94, published in Vol. II, Minutes of Evidence, HC 239-II, The Stationery Office, London, 8 March 2002.
6. News release 2001/0416 issued by the Department for Transport, Local Government and the Regions, 7 October 2001.
7. House of Commons, *Official Report*, 12 June 2002, col 1262W.
8. See in particular *The Accountability of Railtrack*, Office of the Rail Regulator, London, 12 June 2001.
9. See, for example, *DfT Rail Review: Submission by the Rail Regulator*, Office of the Rail Regulator, London, May 2004, paragraphs 21–46.
10. House of Commons, *Official Report*, 19 January 2004, col 1078.
11. *Access Charges Review 2003: Final Conclusions*, Office of the Rail Regulator, London, 12 December 2003.
12. House of Commons, *Official Report*, 15 December 2003, col 121WS.
13. House of Commons, *Official Report*, 9 February 2004, col 1237W.
14. *Implementing the Future of Rail: ORR's Role and Proposed Work Programme*, Office of Rail Regulation, London, 22 September 2004.
15. See: *Developing Better Contracts: A Statement by the Rail Regulator*, Office of the Rail Regulator, London, 23 December 2002; *Model Clauses for Passenger Track Access Contracts: Final Conclusions*, Office of the Rail Regulator, London, 23 December 2002; *Model Clauses: The Template Passenger Track Access Contract – Regulator's Final Conclusions*, Office of the Rail Regulator, London, 25 June 2003; *Criteria and Procedures for the Approval of Track Access Contracts: 3rd edition*, Office of the Rail Regulator, London, 25 June 2003; *Model Freight Track Access Contract: Final Conclusions*, Office of the Rail Regulator, London, 31 March 2004; *Criteria and Procedures for the Approval of Freight Track Access Contracts: 2nd edition*, Office of the Rail Regulator, London, 31 March 2004.
16. See: *Reform of the Network Code: Emerging Conclusions and Proposals for Changes to Address Priority Issues*, Office of the Rail Regulator, London, 4 June 2004; *Reform of the Network Code: Conclusions on Phase 1 and Notice of Changes*, Office of the Rail Regulator, London, 2 July 2004.
17. *DfT Rail Review: Submission by the Rail Regulator*, Office of the Rail Regulator, London, May 2004.
18. *Seventh Report of the House of Commons Select Committee on Transport: The Future of the Railway*, Session 2003–04, HC 145-1, The Stationery Office, London, 1 April 2004.
19. See *Office of the Rail Regulator Response to the Seventh Report from the Committee on the Future of the Railway*, Fourth Special Report of Session 2003–04, HC 1209, The

Stationery Office, London, 27 October 2004, Appendix C, especially paragraph 109. Note that ORR's response was made on 4 July 2004 and published by ORR on that date.

20. When the then Secretary of State for Transport threatened to legislate to extinguish the independence of the Rail Regulator and take that statutory position under direct political control if Railtrack, which was facing an application by the Secretary of State for an order putting the company into administration on the grounds of its alleged insolvency, were to apply for an interim access charges review to demonstrate that it was not insolvent. As to this event, see further.

21. In this respect, see further *Sir Robert Reid Memorial Lecture 2004: The Future of the Railway*, given by the Rail Regulator, Office of the Rail Regulator, London, 10 February 2004.

22. In Part 7 of Schedule 7 of the passenger access contracts, Condition 7 of Network Rail's network licence and Schedule 4A of the Railways Act 1993.

23. See also *Great North Eastern Railway Limited v Network Rail Infrastructure Limited* [2003] RR 2, a legal appeal determined by the Rail Regulator concerning the liability of Network Rail to a train operator for financial compensation as a result of assumed deterioration in the condition of part of its network.

CHAIRMAN'S COMMENTS

Stephen Glaister

I am considerably heartened by Tom's comments because here is somebody who really knows what he is talking about who can see a way through. I was beginning to wonder if there was a way of making it work. Tom has done us all enormous service by writing more than once, clear and as far as I can tell accurate statements about what the law and the constitutional position actually is. I particularly commend his May 2004 statement to the government in the context of the railway review as a *tour de force*. It is a document that we shall be using in teaching and in many other contexts.

I have to say that when I hear Tom talk – and I have enjoyed doing that on many occasions, having worked with him as an advisor when he was Regulator – I understand it, but as soon as he leaves the room I begin to get confused. However, it is evident that it is horrendously complicated. There may be a way through it, but it is very difficult to keep a grip on it all, especially for those of us who are not so familiar with the legal position. So as a mere economist, I do have difficulty. I want to make a few comments about the economic context for the future.

I agree with what I think I heard Tom saying: that the White Paper itself is a terribly weak document. Here is a document about the future of the railway which I think I am right in saying has not one single number in it looking forward. We do not even have the 50 per cent target for passengers and 80 per cent target for freight we used to have; they seem to have gone. Nor do we have the Byers figures about targets for reliability. Who remembers those? They were made one day and forgotten the next. There is no quantitative information in the White Paper about what the government and the population at large can expect from the railway in the future. I am privileged to have seen early drafts of a couple of chapters of a book by Sir Christopher Foster.[1] It is interesting because he gives an inside story of the drafting of the 1993 Railways Act and the preceding White Paper. He describes how the Railways Act was (in my words) not done right for a series of reasons: it could have been better in other words. There was unreasonable rush in trying to do it, and ministers just could not decide what they actually wanted. A consequence was drafting the legislation 'on the hoof', and Tom has referred to that. Who can expect that to produce the right results? But, crucially in my view (and these are my words not Sir Christopher's) was the unwillingness and an inability to write down clearly what ministers wanted in advance. In other words, the inability to write a decent White Paper before the legislation. I say that because it worries me that we are about to repeat history. As Tom has more or less indicated in his comments, that is exactly what is happening now, the White Paper does not tell the story.

I have been thinking about how where we sit today compares with how we might have seen things in, say, 1967. Then we had a very heavily unionised labour force, with real power. Productivity was not improving. I think that is largely the situation we may have now. I have recently done some work[2] and was astonished to find what has happened to unit labour costs in the rail industry: they have shot ahead in advance of general earnings. That has not been the picture of course in all the other privatised utilities. It was not the case for the bus industry when that was deregulated and privatised. Unit labour costs were enormously reduced in other privatised industries but this has not happened in the railway. I do not know why not, but that is an important thing to bear in mind. In the late 1960s we had rapidly rising subsidy and the government was unwilling to pay the price: we have that now. We had little or no transparency, accountability or value for money for the public money that was going in. To a large extent we have that now, and I fear that is about to become worse under the new regime. There was considerable doubt back then about how much things actually cost and we have seen in the last few years similar doubt about how much things are going to cost over the future. Things are not as bad now on that score as they were back in the 1960s. We have learnt a lot, but we still have the problem of really not having as much information about the true long-run cost base of the industry as we would like to have. Finally in my list, and this is really a central point that worries me a great deal, back in the 1960s there was crippling debt. The railways were struggling all the time to deal with the debt that they had inherited. It was distorting economic decisions about the way forward because of the need to repay it. We have walked into a situation over the last year or two of repeating that situation.

In one respect we were much better off in the late 1960s than we are likely to be from here onwards: we at least had a semi-independent board of management. The British Railways Board which in the 1980s demonstrated real power and ability to change the world though asserting its independence. I think everybody recognises that the 1980s was a somewhat successful period for the railways. I am a fan of rail privatisation as it was developed. I worked with Tom's predecessor and with Tom on trying to make it work, and it could have worked very well, for all its faults.[3] But we have to recognise the success in the 1980s of the Railways Board. Now we are going to have a more centralised railway than we have ever had. When I say centralised I mean under more direct control of central government.

Tom has listed many things that have to be sorted out to make the White Paper operational. One is the interpretation of the phrase 'binding arrangement'. He did not mention it explicitly, but it seems to me important

– the working out of what kind of financial performance regime there will have to be for the train operating companies. Because there will still be commercial arrangements, payments will have to be made on performance. The government has said it wants something less complicated and more transparent but I have no idea what that might look like. The procurement regimes, the train operating company franchises, will have to be worked out. As Tom indicated, that was already a problem, but things like contract length and the bundling of the franchises will now all have to be worked out under the cover, as it were, of central government rather than under the slightly transparent mechanism of the Strategic Rail Authority, which we have become used to. Then there is the business about how local authorities are going to get control of the railways. That is of course a particular problem in London. What does it mean in the White Paper to give more control to London over its commuter railway? How much money are we going to get in London? How much discretion are we going to get? That all has to be worked out: at the moment as far as I am aware it is an empty box, it is just words. I am all in favour if it and it is something that Mayor Ken Livingstone has asked for but the practicalities are completely unworked out so far as I am aware.

The regulatory regime for passenger fares will have to be developed: government is now going to be controlling the fares for the first time. I know that there was, as Tom has described, considerable government influence over what the SRA did. But the line between backbenchers and fares control is going to be even more direct than it was in the past, and that is going be a problem.

Then there is the whole business of how enhancements are going to be procured, how special purpose vehicles are going to be made to work (if they can be made to work) and in particular how much genuine risk capital the government can expect to get into this industry now the political risks have been made so much more apparent than they used to be. The Ten Year Plan of 2000 had at least £30 billion of private investment, I am not sure how much has come in so far but I just raise the question, will they get the rest under this new regime?

What do we think is going to happen to productivity and earnings in the future? That is a critical issue. I have already indicated that labour productivity may not have come into line with the market rate in the way that it did in other industries. Do we think under this new regime that there is a better chance of achieving that? For instance, it worries me that bringing rail maintenance in-house will result in engineering companies that were paying maybe something close to market rates for engineering services finding that employees will start to want the rates of pay and terms and conditions essentially that railway employees generally are getting. If that happens the hole in railway finances will look bigger rather than smaller, to put it mildly.

Finally, two big questions that the White Paper did not even ask. One is the simple question – and Tom has alluded to it but did not put it quite as bluntly as this – of how much is the country willing to pay for the railway of the future? And if government is realistic about how much it is going to cost, and when it comes to the honest conclusion that we are not willing to pay the proper cost of keeping the network going at its current scale (I say 'when' because it is my opinion that that will be the conclusion), then we will have to have the debate about what is going to be cut out – this is the debate that really has not been faced up to, and never has been, ever since the war and before. But as long as we go on muddling through the way we have we are not going to get the railways working on a decent basis.

The second big issue – it is actually twin issues – concerns the governance structure of Network Rail and the debt that it is building. I find it very hard to understand the true disciplines on Network Rail to be economic and efficient. When it was set up as a company limited by guarantee it was going to be for profit but not for dividend. The profits were going to be earned in order, among other things, to remunerate capital and to build up a 'buffer fund' in lieu of equity to take the knocks, the day-to-day risks. There was going to be fully commercial borrowing. That was the discipline: you had to be able to borrow on the markets and therefore to be able to convince the markets you could repay the debt. Now we do not have profits. I do not know what has happened to the idea of a buffer fund. Recently, my understanding is that the government has said it will give direct and explicit government guarantee on the Network Rail debt. Therefore there has to be a backstop to provide the ultimate discipline: there has to be a new licence condition which caps Network Rail's debt. That is very much the second best way of providing a discipline. It is, incidentally, an important new role for the Office of Rail Regulation.

Then we have this nonsense about the classification of Network Rail debt. On the one hand the government is still holding to the line that it is not in control of Network Rail and therefore the debt can be off the public balance sheet, but on the other hand it is simultaneously giving a cast iron guarantee on the debt. At the very least I cannot see how that is prudent management of public funds. You are either in control or you are not. And if you not in control why are you underwriting the debts? I do not care personally whether it is classified as public or private debt so long as this issue does not distort the economic decisions in the industry. It risks causing enormous distortion. If it were not for that, the classification dispute would just be good spectator sport for us outsiders. But the worry on debt is, as I indicated earlier, that if we end up with a debt that Network Rail is accountable for, which is open ended because of the lack of discipline, which the Office of the Rail Regulation is not able to limit, then it becomes unmanageable and it becomes a burden which hopelessly distorts the decision making in Network Rail in a doomed attempt to bring it back under control. If that happens we will really lose one of the big advantages that we established under rail privatisation: a debt structure which gave meaningful economic signals about whether forward-looking investment was or was not viable.

A final thought, and I think Tom has actually answered this question, should we not face up to the fact that the idea of using competition as the major disciplining force in the railway has not been able to work? It has not been able to work in my opinion not because it could not work, but because the government kept on intervening to undermine it.[4] If you are going to use competition then you rely on government to promote competition and do all the things you have to do to make competition work. What the government has actually done is at every turn to undermine competition. Therefore competition has failed. So it seems to me that a question for the future is, do we abandon ship on that? And I think Tom has said that we should not abandon ship. But if we did abandon ship then we would have to so something quite different. There is a school of thought that advocates bringing the whole industry back under direct government control and recognise the truth. Under the current proposals we risk suffering the worst of all worlds.

Notes

1. C.D. Foster, *British Government in Crisis*, Hart Publishing, Oxford and Portland, 2005.
2. S. Glaister, *British Rail Privatisation – Competition Destroyed by Politics*, Centre for Regulated Industries, University of Bath, 2005.
3. Ibid.
4. Ibid.

2. International trade in gas and prospects for UK gas supplies

Nigel Cornwall

INTRODUCTION

Gas trading started in April 1990 with the launch of Nymex Henry Hub natural gas futures, with an over-the-counter market developing in the United States soon after. UK gas trading got off the ground in the mid-1990s, picking up towards the end of the decade with IPE launching its futures trading in 1997. The UK gas market is now in a transitional phase, and is set imminently to become a physical net importer. At the same time European markets generally are demanding more and more gas and access to new global gas supplies, and international gas trade is now crucial to the regional energy economy. In fact natural gas is poised to overtake coal as a global energy source. This development reflects the tripling of proven gas reserves and the expansion of European and other markets for gas over the period since 1975. Gas has now become the fuel of choice in many power markets. Further, governments are increasingly looking to low carbon outcomes post-Kyoto. Consequently, the unconstrained availability of growing volumes of gas is not just the key to competitive energy markets but is also a critical ingredient to attainment of wider energy policy goals.

One such policy goal is security of supply. Whether we recognise it or not, gas trade and security of supply in Europe are already synonymous. In 2002, around 46 per cent of gas was imported into the European Union (EU). The Green Paper of the European Commission on energy security of supply foresees that import dependency will amount to 66 per cent in 2020. An important House of Lords[1] committee has taken exception to this and the associated risks, so the issue is very topical.

SCOPE OF THE PAPER

To address the prospects for international gas trade and the prospects for UK gas supplies, I shall address the following issues.

First we shall take a brief look at the anatomy of the global gas market. The focus is the physical rather than the financial gas markets. One such key market is, of course, Western Europe, and we focus on current trading mechanisms and how prices are set. How competitive is the European gas market? What are the main influences on it? Where is trading taking place?

Second, an obvious theme for this chapter is how the market and existing participants are likely to respond as the UK undergoes the transition of moving from significant net exporter to significant net importer. If the lessons of 2003/04 are anything to go by, it is likely to be a choppy ride at least for the consumer, and we shall look at what has been happening in the market and at the October 2004 Ofgem (Office of Gas and Electricity Markets) report into gas prices.

Third, we shall look at a series of wider likely developments and challenges as the European market, including the UK as the largest gas market within Europe, responds to the challenges posed by the shifting import dependency and the agendas of its policy makers, both national and federal. A key consideration in this context is how sustained demand growth fuelled by both gas and electricity sectors can be met. What are the prospects for increased competition? Will enough investment be made in gas transportation infrastructure to deliver the gas to consumers, and what needs to be done to enable such investment?

An important thesis running through my remarks is that competitive markets in gas are relatively new, but nonetheless are at a watershed. If UK participants are to prosper and trade is to continue to develop, continental markets must be opened up much more fully. Incumbent positions need to be challenged both within and across markets through much more aggressive competition policies and liberalisation applied from Brussels.

THE ANATOMY OF THE GLOBAL GAS MARKET

Current Trading Structures

It is worth asking at the outset what we mean by 'international trade'. Gas is traded more as a 'regional' than an 'international' market. As such, the 'international' gas trade is broadly categorised by the three major regional markets of first Europe and Africa, second Asia-Pacific and lastly the Americas.

With respect to the European market, which is our main concern, the physical gas trade is based on both natural gas and liquefied natural gas

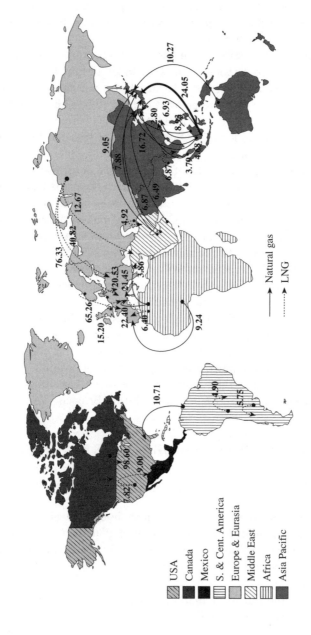

USA
Canada
Mexico
S. & Cent. America
Europe & Eurasia
Middle East
Africa
Asia Pacific

Natural gas
LNG

Source: BP, 'Statistical Review of World Energy 2004'.

Figure 2.1   International trade in gas

(LNG). Figure 2.1, based on BP's excellent 'Statistical Review of World Energy 2004', shows that the main supplies of piped gas into Europe are from Russia, with Norway, Netherlands and the UK being important internal providers. The Middle East, Algeria and Egypt are significant existing players for both LNG and natural gas.

If we look at the national markets within Europe, the UK is Europe's largest single gas market having overtaken Germany in the mid-1990s, thanks to the 'dash for gas'. UK gas demand has increased by 35 percent since then. The UK is also presently Europe's largest gas producer. Some key major markets have yet to experience the phenomenon of the dash for gas, but it is coming. In general, the EU is a well-explored and mature hydrocarbon province. The UK still has a number of small gas discoveries in locations close to existing export pipelines and production facilities that await development. There are no significant new areas for hydrocarbon exploration in the EU, save for the Atlantic margin (West of Ireland) and the West of Shetland.

In contrast, reserves in and around the European market are plentiful, particularly in Russia, the Caspian region and the Middle East, with a total of around 90 trillion cubic metres of proven reserves. Further afield, reserves available to the European market in the form of LNG are also significant. LNG is now a competitive delivery option compared to pipelines because pipeline costs have not fallen as rapidly. LNG also has the advantage of delivery close to demand centres, avoiding costly pipeline access charges to the destination market. LNG is, therefore, already playing an increasing role in the European supply mix, particularly in the Mediterranean markets of Spain, Italy, France, Portugal and Greece.

The Supply/Demand Balance

Table 2.1 sets out the key statistics on market dimensions in Europe.

Belgium, the Netherlands, Germany and the UK together represent Europe's most important gas markets in terms of trading and are also its most self-sufficient and competitive. They will be the markets I focus on. Here and elsewhere, gas supply has historically been provided on an integrated basis with major companies, often with a state ownership involvement, responsible for bulk gas sourcing, for delivery and for supply to customers. The necessity to obtain new custom by encouraging switching from other fuel use, especially oil, encouraged these companies to price their gas at prices competitive enough to encourage customers to change. Thus began the well-established link between oil and gas prices.

Table 2.1   Supply–demand balance

2003 (bcm)	Demand	Production	LNG	Imports	Exports
United Kingdom	95.3	102.7	0.0	7.5	23.4
Germany	85.5	17.7	0.0	86.8	10.5
Italy	71.7	13.7	5.5	55.9	0.0
France	43.8	0.0	9.9	31.8	11.8
Netherlands	39.3	58.3	0.0	12.9	9.7
Spain	23.8	0.0	15.0	8.7	0.0
Belgium	16.0	0.0	3.2	0.0	28.0
Other Europe	77.5	85.3	1.4	57.1	59.0
Total	452.9	277.7	35.0	260.7	142.4
UK%	21%	37%	0%	3%	16%

Source: BP, 'Statistical Review of World Energy 2004'.

Key Market Participants

More recently these companies have undergone a significant degree of restructuring to facilitate the EU drive for market opening. The purest example of this is, of course, the UK, where the former British Gas Board has evolved into a system operator, Transco, and two major supply companies, BG, the offshore producer, and Centrica, which competes to serve end-user customers. Dutch operator Gasunie has split into the Gastransportservices pipeline operator and Gasunie Trade and Supply. In Belgium, Fluxys has been established as the national pipeline operator, and is separately managed from Distrigas. In Germany, the situation is more complex, and separation has to date been less rigorous. Additionally there are a plethora of regional suppliers at the local level in each of these markets.

Table 2.2 shows the major market participants in each of the four countries, and the degree of unbundling that has taken place.

Access to Gas

As we have just seen, market opening has encouraged a variety of new entrants into Europe's gas supply markets, including upstream producers, electricity retailers and independent traders. However, it is easy to overstate the degree of competition at play today in European gas markets, especially on the continent.

Column 2 of Table 2.3 shows that a large proportion of available gas is still controlled by the largest player. In some instances they still control

Table 2.2 Key market participants

	Belgium	Germany	United Kingdom	Netherlands
Wholesale	Distrigas, oil and gas companies, electricity suppliers	Ruhrgas, RWE, Wingas	Oil and gas companies, electricity suppliers, traders	Major oil companies, electricity suppliers, traders
Transmission	Fluxys	9 operators including Ruhrgas, Wingas, RWE Netz	NG Transco	Gastransport-services
Distribution	Local operators	Local operators	NG Transco	Local operators
Supply	Wholesale participants	Wholesale participants	Wholesale participants	Wholesale participants

Source: Cornwall Energy Associates.

Table 2.3 Access to gas

	Companies with at least 5% share of available gas	% available gas controlled by largest	Release programme	Cross-border capacity as % demand
United Kingdom	6	c. 25%	completed	10%
Germany	9	c. 50%	yes	>100%
Italy	3	80%	yes	30%
France	3	64%	yes	30%
Netherlands	3	n.a.	no	>100%
Spain	2	85%	yes	30%
Belgium	1	100%	no	>100%

Source: Third Benchmarking report DG TREN/Cornwall Energy Associates.

access to cross-border capacity. As a result, often smaller and newer players have struggled at one time or other in gaining either wholesale supplies or sourcing a route for it to get to market, and sometimes both. Further, a handful of operators are now emerging as potential suppliers across the four markets. They include BP, Gaz de France and Shell. Additionally Distrigas, E.ON/Ruhrgas, RWE, and Gasunie are able to deal from strong positions in at least one of the four markets.

Because of the control of access to gas enjoyed by the incumbents, release gas programmes have been an important route to stimulate competition, as shown in Table 2.3 column 3, but it is fair to say that these have largely failed to date to exert a significant impact on the development of competition.

How is Gas Priced?

Within these markets, how is gas priced?

Broadly speaking, gas is either traded (that is, priced) indexed to oil or via gas-on-gas competition. The UK is the obvious role model for gas-on-gas competition, but it is important to understand how the concept works. There is no rigid indexation of gas prices to another source, typically oil, but the gas price is free to link and de-link to other energy sources as it sees fit. Driving this 'freedom' in linking or de-linking is the marginal cost of competitive gas. But of course if sellers can identify opportunities for higher margins, they will increase prices.

The converse of gas-on-gas competition is oil-indexed pricing. This approach is presently prevalent throughout mainland Europe and particularly so in France, Germany and Italy. No common index is used with each supplier tailoring its own price index. Most indexations are built around heating oil with typically a 6–9-month time lag, but other primary fuel sources are also used. Germany includes a coal element in its gas pricing, while Italy uses heavy fuel oil. The tendency for gas prices in the UK to go their own way relative to other European gas markets as a result of the different approaches is illustrated by Figure 2.2, which shows the greater seasonality in UK prices.

Oil/Gas Price Correlation

Gas and oil prices correlate, though the strength of the linkage can vary between markets. This observation can be illustrated by mapping National Balancing Point (NBP) prices in the UK versus Zeebrugge or Title Transfer Facility (TTF) prices from the continent, and overlaying them with either Brent or gas oil prices (Figure 2.3).

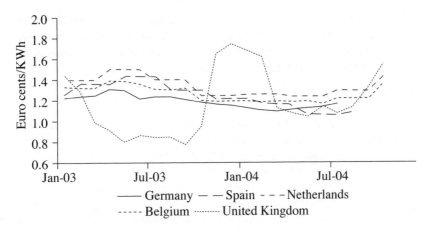

Notes:
Germany: average import price at border as measured by BMWA.
Spain: wholesale price measure SP used in setting regulated tariffs.
Netherlands: GTS neutral gas price.
Belgium: wholesale price measure G used in setting regulated tariffs.
United Kingdom: Spectron month ahead index adjusted for exchange rate.
Conversions from original units by Cornwall Consulting.

Source: Cornwall Energy Associates.

Figure 2.2   How is gas priced?

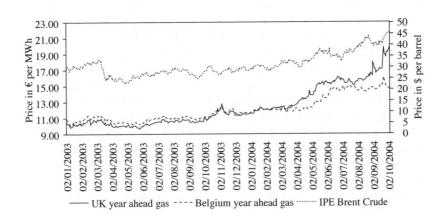

Source: Cornwall Energy Associates.

Figure 2.3   Oil/gas price correlation (NBP vs Zeebrugge vs IPE Brent crude)

What the figure also shows is how the relationship between European gas prices and oil prices has held firm, but UK prices have recently surged ahead, and the traditional discount seen to European gas over most of the year except winter has flipped into a premium.

How is Gas Traded?

Currently gas is traded in a variety of ways in northwest Europe, from long-term contracts that last for decades to short-term trades measured in hours. These different methods are not necessarily consistent, but prices in them tend to be related, if not explicitly.

Longer-term gas supply contracts typically comprise three key elements: a base contract price; a take-or-pay level; and indexation terms. The base price will tend to be agreed in advance of the contract start date, reflecting prevailing views of the value of the gas over the life of the contract. The third element is applied to adjust that base price from time to time according to the movement in the indexation term. Gas contract prices are, in general, determined by the application of 'netback pricing', whereby gas prices to the final consumer are set to be marginally less than the price of competing fuels, typically heavy fuel oil and gas oil. As one moves up the supply chain, the 'wholesale' prices are determined by deducting agreed transport costs from the netback end-user price, thus yielding a price for delivery to a bulk contract point like Waidhaus on the German/Czech border, or Zeebrugge or Emden on the North Sea coast. That is what the triangles stand for in Figure 2.4. 'Bulk contract prices' tend to be influenced mainly by oil prices, but also by local factors such as producer behaviour, market regulation and access to transit pipes, the number of new entrants, and the volume of gas trading.

In contrast traded market gas tends to be priced according to more specific supply and demand conditions, ranging from a fundamental view of the long-term balance to short-term price direction from immediate events. There is a tension between the two, because of the expectation that liberalisation would cause the oil–gas price link to break, as traded gas became a market in its own right. This expectation reflected the British experience, but the oil–gas link has proved resilient, to the extent that it is now seems to be becoming again a major driver of British prices through the growing influence of imports.

As Figure 2.4 shows, *shorter-term gas trading* can be undertaken in a variety of ways:

- it can be landed at the British NBP for onward delivery through the pipeline network, or landed at the Dutch TTF, which fulfils a similar role for the Netherlands – those are indicated by the two boxes in the figure; or

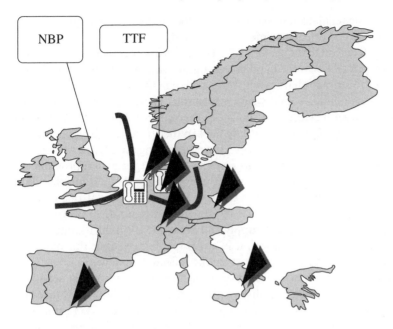

Source: Cornwall Energy Associates.

Figure 2.4   How is gas traded?

• it can be traded at 'hubs' such as Zeebrugge (where the British interconnector lands and where Norwegian supplies presently come ashore), or Bunde (on the German/Dutch border) – those are indicated by the two telephone icons in the figure.

However, liquidity in short-term trading is still very limited, and if anything has begun to decline in response to volatile energy markets driven by $30, then $40 and now $50 oil prices.

UK Gas Price Probe

Gas markets are evolving quickly and in some respects are very dynamic. The events since October 2003 in the UK amply illustrate the effects of a market in transition.

Ofgem is to be congratulated on the thoroughness of its recent gas price probe report. One thing is very clear – it has had a very close look at gas prices to the extent it is able to. The thoroughness is illustrated by the extent to which the regulator has been able to allocate causal explanations to the three periods of price movements considered.

Let us focus on first quarter 2005. Three factors are identified to explain the high prices – increase in oil prices, tighter supply/demand balance and increases to storage charges, implying a change to the forward price of up to 11p/therm under a mild weather scenario. The 1 in 50 winter scenario implies a larger increase of around 24p/therm. On 1 April 2004 the Q1–05 price was nearly 32p/therm. Adding the 11p/therm increase gives an implied price of approximately 43p/therm. However, adding the 24p/therm increase implied by the 1 in 50 conditions gives an expected price of approximately 56p/therm. This level is in fact slightly higher than the first quarter 2005 price at the time the report was written. So far so good – if one believes that we are set to experience a 1 in 50 winter. But do these prices reflect the current fundamentals of supply and demand? Until the trading period moves through to liquidation, it is not possible to answer this question definitively. But two issues at least can be reflected on now.

First it is clear that the suggestion of extreme scarcity that seems to be in the market does not align with Transco's 2004/05 winter forecast and recent confirmations from National Grid Transco (NGT) that it is comfortable about the interactions with electricity even if a severe winter were to occur. The electricity market was 'spooked' in winter 2003/04 by concerns about availability – wrongly in my view – and it looks as if there is the same concern by some parties to talk the problems up in gas in 2004/05. It does not mean that a very cold snap could not occur. It is unquestionable that forecasts of beached gas this winter are lower than previously, and Transco has revised downwards its forecast of peak UK gas supply for winter 2004/05 by 9 per cent.

Second, there is nothing sacrosanct about oil indexation. It is generally accepted that oil prices are some $10–15 above the level implied by fundamentals as a consequence of speculative trading, so why should we assume that these premia should automatically flow into gas and indirectly electricity. On the continent there are strong indications that the indexation arrangements are continuing to provide some mitigation from extreme oil prices – at least for the time being – because of lagging effects, which is one reason why UK prices might have surged ahead. However, Ofgem does not address why traditional relationships between British and European prices have 'flipped', and it is not obvious why market sentiment is a more profound factor in some markets than others. Noting these omissions is not intended as a criticism of Ofgem, but a recognition of the problems we face as we move into uncharted territory involving multiple jurisdictions and changing markets. Ofgem has, of course, taken a complaint about the functioning of the European gas market to the European Commission, and that is very necessary. It is to be hoped that the Commission and other national governments try to execute the type of analysis that Ofgem has just conducted. It asks three particular questions:

1. Did European gas companies withhold surplus gas supplies and prevent more gas flowing to the UK?
2. Did European gas companies withhold transportation capacity on the European pipeline networks and prevent more gas flowing into the UK?
3. Was the decision to place gas into store, rather than sell it to the UK, reasonable given their forecast customer demand and supply contracts for that winter?

But there would seem to be much more subtle influences at work reflecting interaction of the interconnected markets which are becoming subject to different seasonal physical and pricing influences. I would suggest that there are a lot of questions remaining, which fall outside Ofgem's remit, and the learning process has only just begun.

In what can only be described as an embarrassing development for Ofgem and the market since, on the day it published its report prices for January 2005 gas shot up to over 75p/therm, though it is clear that few if any trades went through at such exorbitant levels. In a sense one day of extreme prices can push the monthly average up to this level. During periods of relative scarcity, small changes in supply can have a profound impact on prices – which is why Ofgem is right to have a further look at the small number of contracts – some 5 per cent that may restrict delivery into two subterminals at Bacton. However, the impact of this extreme price volatility is causing immense distress for I&C customers. If 40 per cent increases in the October round in year-on-year prices were not enough, the April 2005 prices now on offer suggest further significant increases. Ofgem's own estimate suggests a £3.6 billion higher gas bill for the economy in the winter of 2004/05 before the latest price surge. BP has just indicated that they are to withdraw from this market, which has already seen a reduction in competition over the past two years, and many customers are openly talking about profit collapse and closure. And virtually all the major domestic suppliers have fed through significant gas price increases based on movements in short-term prices despite the fact that many of them take supplies under long-term contracts.

So I am not at all inclined to agree with Ofgem when it says '[t]he market is working'. The jury is, I believe, out. There is scant liquidity, prices are too volatile and the market has moved significantly away from its fundamentals. The diversity and relative depth provided by Enron, Dynegy and others has not as yet been made good.

In fact I quite liked the following quote from energywatch: 'Ofgem, at the limits of their powers, have not been able to get to the bottom of the critical issues within the market'. This statement is if anything somewhat strong as Ofgem has done a good job in a difficult position with restricted *vires*. The bottom line is, however, that unless the market corrects itself, the pressure for a full competition inquiry or government investigation will be irresistible. In the first instance the Trade and Industry Select Committee are to consider recent wholesale pricing developments, and they announced terms of reference Tuesday. Their report in January 2005 could determine whether gas pricing is nailed or whether it becomes a real political problem as we move forward to the election season. On a lower level, we also need to get away from the anomalous position where different parties are responsible for regulating different parts of the supply chain, and Ofgem needs to be enabled to gather whatever information it considers necessary to protect the consumer interest irrespective of whether this is published.

Competition Status

As I have suggested, a key learning point from events in the UK market is that closer integration with wider European trading is already beginning to exert a profound effect – albeit one that we are just beginning to understand. As we shall see, however, European markets have their own, different problems that raise more fundamental structural issues.

The transition to competitive markets was of course initiated by the 1998 EU gas directive. This required a modest liberalisation with considerable scope for flexibility in interpretation and implementation in individual EU member states. A second EU directive has now meant that, in theory at least, all Europe's business gas users can negotiate for competitive supplies. Of course, the second Gas Directive[2] only came into effect in 2004, and several of the EU-15 have still to transcribe this into national law. The Madrid Forum also has in train much-needed work on access to gas transmission networks, to address a host of issues that are seen as inhibiting progress to a single internal gas market.

However, at the current cruising speed, it is abundantly clear that it will remain some years before the vision underpinning the directives becomes a reality. As is often the case in markets characterised by monopoly suppliers, European gas companies have in general resisted moves to competition through a number of strategies:

- first they have developed significant additional import pipeline capacity, well above current requirements;

- second they have developed significant additional gas storage capacity, again well above their projected needs;
- third they have contracted long-term gas volumes forcing new entrants to bring incremental supplies to market, further increasing contracted oversupply; and
- finally they have developed a pattern of gas supply and transit that reflects individual corporate objectives, rather than wider policy goals.

The Commission itself said with some understatement in its Third Benchmarking report:

> Overall, progress in developing the internal [electricity and] gas market has been steady but, if anything, a little disappointing. ... For gas, it would seem that further progress is dependent on improved conditions for cross border exchanges and the development of a coherent tarification and capacity allocation regime at EU level.

I am not saying anything new here. Ofgem for one has been a strong voice calling for the Commission to devote sufficient resources to considering competition issues in continental gas markets. As we have already noted, it has also presented its gas price probe findings to the Commission. It is to be hoped that the Commission considers carefully the information put to it and takes meaningful steps to consider whether infringements have occurred well before the mid-2006 review date stipulated by the second directive. The Commission also needs to address the wider state of the internal market much more purposefully and set about corrective measures urgently.

Clearly supplier market power is strong, limiting competitive opportunities, especially in Germany, and reinforcing oil–gas price links. Perhaps this was of less concern when the UK was a net exporter. But as a net importer there are real risks that these structural distortions to effective competition will deny opportunities to UK suppliers, limit access to the UK market and perhaps over time undermine competition in the UK market.

ACCESSING FUTURE GAS SUPPLIES AND TRADING IMPLICATIONS

Macro Issues

Looking ahead, a number of key drivers will dominate the international trading landscape.

First, there is the growing demand for energy. Energy demand in Europe is projected to grow by two-thirds between 2001 and 2030. Power generators will continue to favour natural gas as fuel because of its comparative cheapness and its relative environmental benefits, and combined-cycle gas turbines (CCGTs) almost certainly will account for the vast majority of the generating capacity Europe builds in the next decade.

Next there is the widening demand–supply mismatch. The countries with the biggest appetites for energy, including European markets, will be able to supply less and less of their own annual energy consumption. By 2030 their natural gas deficit is expected to rise from 16 to nearly 30 per cent.

Third, there is the increasing reliance on a few energy exporters. There is plenty of gas potentially available, but most of it costs more than existing sources. It is also located in technically challenging and politically risky places such as Russia, the Middle East and North Africa. Europe's vulnerability has been brought into focus increasingly since the European Commission's Green Paper into security of supply in 2000 and the June 2004 report by the Lords' EU Select Committee as well as recently by Brian Wilson, the former energy minister.

Fourth, there is the immense infrastructure needed to ensure delivery of these vast quantities of gas. New CCGTs alone will require annual gas imports to grow from 230 billion cubic metres today to as much as 565 billion cubic metres by 2012. The minimum direct cost to Europe of implementing the Kyoto targets in the power industry alone has been estimated at about €20 billion per year, and total investment needs as a result of increasing gas dependency could reach €110 billion. The International Energy Agency (IEA) estimates that, in all, Europe will need to invest some $16 trillion by 2030 to feed its appetite for energy.

Finally, there is the growing importance of environmental compliance. To comply with Kyoto, it is highly likely that governments will require power generators to be responsible for between 25–50 per cent of the reductions in CO_2 emissions that Europe will have to make. Irrespective of the legal position, the European positions on burden sharing, emissions trading and the large combustion plant directive are already well established. The big question is how governments and regulators decide to allocate – or reallocate – the burden of compliance, especially beyond 2012, and there will be significant winners and losers among stakeholders. And over time, any failure to meet presently established targets is likely to lead to new initiatives, which could create additional challenges for the role of gas.

I now look at some of these issues in more depth.

Supply–Demand Outlook

Natural gas is expected to be the fastest-growing fuel source in Western Europe, with demand projected to grow at an average annual rate of upwards of 2 per cent. However, Western Europe currently holds less than 4 per cent of the world's proved natural gas reserves, and its production is projected to decline. As a result, the region is expected to become increasingly dependent on imports. In 2001, 31 per cent of Western Europe's natural gas supply was imported from outside the region; by 2025 it will need to import about 60 per cent. Some forecasts, such as the Eurogas view summarised in Table 2.4, show even higher dependency levels. By any measure the imperative for rapid growth in trade will increase.

Table 2.4   Supply–demand outlook

BCM	2002	2005	2010	2015	2020
Total demand	367.6	414.7	468.3	503.7	524.0
Indigenous production	210.0	196.1	183.2	159.7	127.5
Net contracted imports	161.8	215.4	239.0	237.9	250.8
Additional supplies to be defined	0.0	3.2	47.2	106.1	145.7
Import dependency	44%	53%	61%	68%	76%

Source: Eurogas Yearbook 2003.

UK Supply/Demand

The United Kingdom is at present both Western Europe's largest producer and its largest consumer of natural gas. Figure 2.5 shows a steady decline in UK Continental Shelf (UKCS) production from over 100 billion cubic metres in 2000 to approximately 90 billion cubic metres in 2007. Thereafter, production is forecast to decline at a greater rate resulting in a 50 per cent import requirement by 2011 even taking into account undeveloped resources. The figure also shows a range of future UKCS production based on high and low reserves scenarios. These indicate UKCS production between 25 and 50 billion cubic metres in 2020 against projected demand requirements of over 130 billion cubic metres. These estimates indicate an import dependency for the UK in 2020 of 60 to 80 per cent, a position reflected in the February 2003 energy policy White Paper.

Global Gas Reserves

So where is this vast amount of gas to come from?

While EU gas reserves and production are set to decline in the near term, there are potentially huge gas reserves that, due to their location, have very limited alternative markets other than pipeline supply to Europe. Proven gas reserves have increased dramatically over recent years, and reserves in

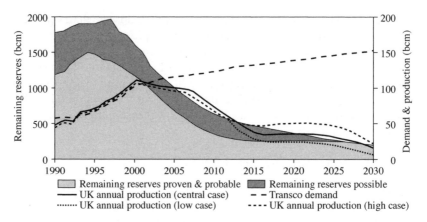

Source: DTI & Transco Forecast included in NGT Transco 10 Year Statement 2003.

Figure 2.5 UK supply/demand

Norway, Russia, the Caspian region, the Middle East and North Africa have the potential to meet both European and domestic demand in producing regions for over 80 years (Figure 2.6). In addition, there is a comparable volume of probable reserves and significant exploration upside in Russia and other key producer markets. Therefore, with no shortage of gas waiting to meet Europe's growing demand, there should be adequacy of supplies over the medium to longer term.

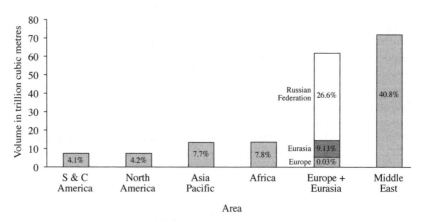

Source: DTI & Transco Forecast included in NGT Transco 10 Year Statement 2003.

Figure 2.6 Global gas reserves (end of 2003, showing % share of international total)

This is of course provided that these new sources are developed, that the infrastructure is available to deliver it, and that EU foreign and external trade policy can secure uninterrupted supply.

LNG

New pipelines are only a part of the picture. LNG is set to make a critical contribution to Europe's gas needs and the structure and location of trading (Figure 2.7). Western Europe currently has 10 operating LNG import facilities with a combined capacity equivalent to about 8 per cent of current gas demand. However, almost half of all new gas supplies to Europe are expected to come from LNG by 2010, and by 2015 the figure could be around 20 per cent of gas demand. Increasing LNG imports will come from Algeria, Nigeria, Iran and particularly Qatar, as well as other, smaller producers. Large amounts of this gas are available, but they would also require substantial investments: major liquefaction facilities at the source of the gas, fleets of tankers, and many new gasification terminals, which convert LNG back into gas and feed it into the pipeline system on delivery. Significant expansion is already under way in Spain, and added capacity is proposed for Belgium, France, Italy, the Netherlands, and of course the United Kingdom.

Potential New UK Projects

The UK will be a major player in these new LNG markets. It will see growth from a position of no use at present to LNG satisfying in excess of 15 per cent of its gas demand by 2008, growing to between 25 and 35 per cent by 2015. Three major projects at Grain and Milford Haven are already proposed or under way and are shown in Figure 2.8. Their combined capacity is equivalent to around one-third of British gas demand. A further 10 billion cubic metres might be developed at Grain in the second half of the decade, depending on user interest.

In addition to the LNG projects, the UK is in the process of developing other sources of supply to meet the projected future need. To give some examples, Centrica has negotiated import agreements scheduled to start in 2005 with Statoil of Norway and Gasunie of the Netherlands. Proposals for new import pipelines are also being considered (likely to include gas from Norway's Ormen Lange field) to Easington, and there is the BBL facility from the Netherlands to Bacton. In addition, plans have been announced to add compression by 2006 that will almost triple the capacity of the existing Interconnector. To provide flexibility in the system, there are also a handful of additional storage facilities flagged in Transco's 2003 Ten Year

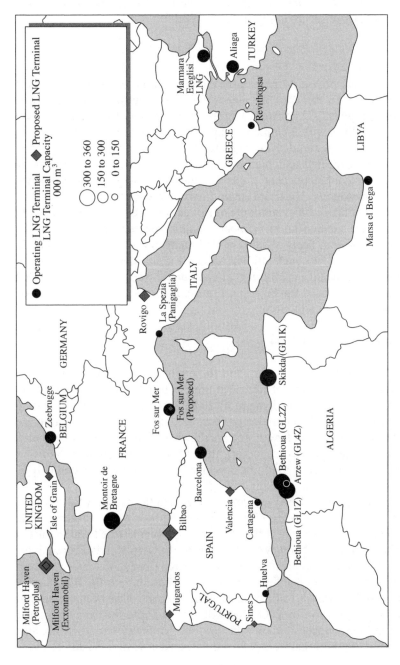

Figure 2.7 European LNG

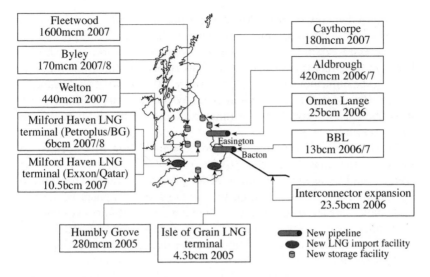

Source: Cornwall Energy Associates.

Figure 2.8 Potential investment projects

Statement. Of course, not all these projects will proceed. But several look very firm now, to the extent that many commentators believe we may see a gas glut in the UK as the decade draws to a close.

Investment Issues

And what will the cost of this immense investment be?

Estimates of the required investment vary for Europe but are uniformly high. A cost of up to €110 billion in upstream field development, pipelines and LNG-regasification infrastructure could be required by 2012. By 2030 the figure could be, according to the IEA, in excess of €10 trillion. Raising such a sum will be daunting.

The investment cannot be taken for granted. Many of the prospective investors have other options. For instance, oil companies may see oil as a better bet because of the long history of high returns for upstream oil investments, which is generally considered less risky than investment in gas pipeline projects. Oil is already a global commodity that can be moved easily around the world, whereas piped gas tends to be tied to the fortunes of one market, or even one customer segment such as power generation.

In addition, it will be difficult to raise the needed capital until several risks and uncertainties are dispelled. One is the rules and structure of the

EU internal energy markets. Moreover, generators will find it difficult to agree to fixed volumes and minimum prices if they face volatile prices. Fitch Ratings last week produced a report that suggested volatile gas prices are here to stay. Other unknowns include how rigorously emissions trading is going to be implemented after phase 1 from 2008 and what environmental targets Europe will adopt beyond 2012. Without clarity on these issues, it will be hard to provide firm estimates of likely demand for gas-related infrastructure.

As I have noted already, stakeholders including investors in gas infrastructure also have concerns because of EU competition policy, which could undermine signature of long-term contracts. The depth of competition is also a factor – if customers can switch suppliers, wholesalers and retailers are less able to commit to buying gas at fixed prices or volumes. As a consequence, it would be difficult to sign long-term contracts with each other unless liquid, cost-effective wholesale markets are developed that make it possible to hedge long-term risks. Given the current concentration of Europe's energy industry, creating such markets is already a challenge.

What Does This Mean for Trading?

What are the implications?

Preservation of the current pricing and contracting regime across Western Europe depends critically on the degree to which the main supply companies can hold on to their market power. E.ON's acquisition of Ruhrgas suggests that they will, and there are already increasing concerns that European competition policy needs to be applied much more rigorously. At the same time the application of competition policy by the Commission is haphazard and the nature of the conditions likely to be imposed are unknown. The same tendency towards further concentration may be becoming evident in the oil sector. Firms such as BP are actively lobbying the European Commission to allow scale players to continue to develop as global players in the interests of ensuring longer-term supply adequacy, and the same argument will no doubt be made in gas. Should the market structure remain as it is, it is likely that gas trading will remain largely a longer-term, asset-based activity. Trading at hubs such as NBP and TTF will continue to be used to balance larger portfolios, and set price direction for contracts for those major users wishing to procure their gas competitively. There are indicators that a more trading-centric approach is evolving. A number of non-commercial players (including hedge funds) are entering the gas market and are starting to inject liquidity in the front end. For many this is a natural extension of their oil trading, given the strong correlation between the two markets. If gas prices continue to be influenced by oil, then these banks and funds will look to trade the oil–gas spread. Any increase in trading this spread will increase gas market liquidity. But if the main focus remains trading around assets, liquidity will continue to struggle, with the associated risks we have become used to of relatively small trades having a disproportionate influence on prices.

However, should market reform be pushed home by member states and the Commission take on a much more aggressive attitude towards competition policy, inherent oversupply could well ensure that European gas starts its life as a traded 'commodity' market with significantly increased liquidity – and, who knows, maybe a price crash. But the prospects for this must be considered very doubtful indeed.

A number of other key variables will influence the way in which trading is likely to develop. International gas trade will increasingly evolve through joint ventures between gas-rich companies (such as Gazprom) and utilities seeking new gas-fired plant build.[3] It is also possible in the long run that Gazprom could lose its monopoly on exports from Russia, opening the way for a competitive free-for-all among Russian gas producers. At present, however, this seems to be a distant prospect.

CONCLUSIONS

Trade in gas internationally is clearly becoming more important, but, outside the UK, wholesale markets are largely illiquid and supply competition is strictly limited. Even in the UK the wholesale market is enduring extreme stress in the light of current geopolitical problems and high oil prices. It is clear that the European market is transitioning from a cost-plus to a commoditised market. However, as long as the fundamental commodity driver is the oil price, this situation will continue to create immense problems in what is a much less mature market with many physical structural rigidities.

There is an endemic tendency among policy makers to assume that there is more competition in gas trading and supply than there actually is, to understate the barriers to its achievement and therefore to create the conditions that will enable trading to thrive. A report from Ofgem and subsequent events suggest that the UK is also not generally immune to problems. That said the following prognosis is much more pertinent to mainland Europe than to the UK. Over the shorter term, the following obstacles to trading and effective competition are likely to endure if there is no concerted corrective action:

- First, for most players, it is simply not possible to buy gas in large quantities, and there is a very strong case for member states and the

Commission to pursue much more significant gas release programmes. Furthermore, many incumbents have long-term contracts with customers, and although there has been a tendency for these to have been modified in the last few years, many customers are still committed to buying the bulk of their gas from incumbent players.

- Second, shipping gas to the end customer has been hampered by the complex rules for third-party access. Although pipeline owners are required by law to make their networks available to potential competitors, pricing systems have been drawn up largely by the incumbent utilities themselves, and it is no surprise that the playing field appears tilted against new entrants. Different arrangements between member states add a further level of complexity and still significantly denude the common carriage concept.
- Third, based on current progress and processes through the Commission and through the Madrid Forum, I would suggest that there will be little prospect that these gas access problems will be solved in the near future.

Therefore, there remain significant structural issues inhibiting international trade in gas within regional gas markets. It is possible that these distortions could impair our ability to access new volumes in a timely and cost-effective manner. It appears also that increased price volatility is here to stay. This will make it very difficult for energy suppliers to provide customers with the broad price stability they have become used to. Rapid energy price changes for householders could also render fuel poverty targets difficult to measure, if not make them meaningless. This instability, against a backdrop of rising markets as they respond to the dual threat of global instability and environmental compliance, is likely to place competition even further on the back foot.

Taking a longer perspective, the drive to environmental improvement and securing energy supplies is encouraging the recognition that vast amounts of money need to be spent upgrading energy infrastructure. Continuing policy impasse on nuclear power, and reasonable scepticism that renewables can play only a modest role in meeting the impending supply gap in Europe, mean the focus of energy policy must be delivery of that gas infrastructure. However, based on the UK experience – which is admittedly limited to date – competitive markets and a variety of players seem poised to deliver significant investment.

What needs to be done to solve the long-term problems of gas security and investment while supporting competition and protecting trading? In addition to removing the barriers we have just noted, I would suggest that there are at least five key ingredients to robust policies going forward:

- First, developing the regulatory framework for the energy market in order to promote incentives for future investment in energy capacities; a critical issue here is of course the need for certainty and stability of regulatory policies and rules. This does not mean that European regulators should do nothing; rather that after a period of decisive reform, we should avoid unnecessary tinkering.
- Second, monitoring the integration into the market of long-term energy policy objectives (for example, environment, renewable generation targets, procurement of primary energy, energy efficiency and so on). The UK has made a good start in this area with the mechanisms introduced under the energy policy White Paper and the Joint Energy Security of Supply (JESS) reporting structure, but while I see lots of ideas from the Commission, I do not see a coherent follow-up to the Green Paper exercise, and subsequent initiatives on holding of strategic oil stocks and treatment of electricity interconnectors look set to stall.
- Third, we need to push hard with the EU and national governments to progress the further development of the internal energy market. The Commission itself has acknowledged disappointing progress, but it is not clear what it now proposes to make good policy failures, towards what remains the right vision. The UK is also not without allies (for example, the Netherlands) in its decision to drive forward the original goals.
- Fourth, competition policy within Europe needs to be applied vigorously to prevent scale issues becoming even worse. The European Commission must address increasing reconsolidation across borders and fuels, an issue for which it presently shows no appetite.
- Finally, much greater effort is required to integrate foreign and trade policy with producer states.

The need for competitive energy markets across Europe is no less important today than in the past, and arguably more pressing than ever if security of supply is to be maintained. The best way to ensure that consumers are protected both in the short and long terms is through the continued implementation of liberalised, competitive markets for natural gas, where regulators will monitor developments and introduce or suggest necessary corrective measures as appropriate. With the growing importance of international transactions to bring gas to Europe, it is more important than ever that the regulatory and political will exists across the continent to bring benefits to customers. This approach will lead to increased international trade and improve prospects for stability in UK supplies.

NOTES

1. House of Lords, Select Committee B, Seventeenth Report 2003/04, 'Gas: Liberalised Markets and Security of Supply'.
2. Directive 2003/55/EC, 1 March 2004, p. 4.
3. Gazprom and E.ON said they had signed a Memorandum of Understanding to develop joint venture projects on gas-fired plant in Europe – Gazprom wants to increase its European exports by 50 per cent in the next decade while E.ON wants to develop into the Central and Eastern European market.

CHAIRMAN'S COMMENTS

John Michell

Nigel has given an extremely comprehensive review – both of what we might call perhaps local, UK issues topical at the moment and also on wider and more medium- and long-term issues. I shall just add one or two comments, but will not comment any further on what Nigel had to say about the recent Ofgem report on the UK price situation. Nigel made quite a number of remarks on that. Some of them as he noted are perhaps controversial. I would just like to add that personally I agree with his comment that the analysis in the Ofgem report was very thorough and I thought genuinely interesting the way they analysed the possible causes of the recent price increases. But I shall say no more about that.

On the longer-term issues, I shall structure my comments around a few questions relating to the more European medium- or longer-term structural issue.

The first question I asked myself, a relatively straightforward one: is there physically enough gas to meet European demand? The answer it appears, is probably yes, and this does not seem an altogether controversial conclusion, although some may want to challenge it. But of course, as Nigel notes, it is in places of varying degrees of abroad, if I can put it that way, some of which, are not particularly liked by some people. And a local issue again, UK indigenous supply is of course forecast to fall. Reports of death may be exaggerated, there is quite a lot of life in the UKCS yet I think, but the figures and tables that Nigel displays are fairly commonly accepted. We should remember perhaps that this is not a new problem, it is not even a new problem in the UK, but other European countries, the likes of France or Italy have been living with this situation for decades so there are many practical places where the UK government, Ofgem or any other players can go to gain experience.

Second question: if there is enough gas available, are there mechanisms in place to ensure reliable supplies to the right places, including the UK of course, at reasonably cost-reflective prices at efficient levels of cost? Doubtful, I think has to be the answer to that one. A number of questions over that have been raised. Both on the production side and also on the, what I might call purchasing side, that is, in our terms shippers and suppliers, the structure of the market is quite clearly still too monopolistic – and Nigel brings that out very well – in Europe, except of course in the UK. With regard to the regulatory regime, the Commission, Nigel used words like disappointing, possibly even outmoded, descriptions of that kind. Is he right about that?

But there is a difference here between the UK and the rest of the EU, which I would like to note. In the UK, the production side of the market, the UKCS producers, were a competitive market in the 1990s to which we added, those of us who were working on these things at the time, a competitive wholesaling and retailing market which of course we now have today. In the rest of the EU generally, they are not facing a situation of competition in the producing sector that they are dealing with. So my third question is: how can this situation be improved? Of course that is the main focus of Nigel's chapter and his first answer is broadly to improve competition within the EU, and indeed that is basically I think the same answer as Ofgem suggest in their report. Of course I do not disagree with it but we have been trying to do this for quite a number of years now and we have not quite worked out the trick of how it is to be done.

Ofgem we learn are taking a formal complaint to the Commission. Maybe that will be effective. I would have to say instinctively that I do not see that as likely to be a very productive way forward; Nigel raises the question of the risks that it would get bogged down in legalistic procedures and so on. It seems to me that you cannot rely only on that approach. The EU Commission in any case is only in a position directly to influence what I call the purchasing side of the market, which is under its direct European jurisdiction within the EU countries, and this I think is why liberalisation has not been seen as attractive on the continent. It is basically no good liberalising your domestic distribution and supply market, if the production sector it is facing still remains un-liberalised. In about the period 1996–97 Clare Spottiswoode (in her position as gas regulator) and I spent quite a lot of time going around Europe, when we had finished creating havoc in the UK, trying to push forward the liberalisation agenda in Europe just as our successors and people like Nigel are trying to do now, and all the time we came up against this argument, 'It's OK for you in the UK with your competitive production sector, but this liberalisation business is no good for us in Europe', and quite frankly we found that a difficult argument to counter and I think it still is.

I wonder whether the present regime, in the Department of Trade and Industry and at Ofgem, have devoted sufficient resources to really get to grips with that issue. I believe the factors for influencing the structure of the producer markets in Russia, Algeria, or whatever, may be in fact quite outside energy policy, and are to do with foreign and international trade policy. There was actually a reference to this in the government's 2003 White Paper but I was never quite clear what the follow-up plan was, and I am still not. Nigel is rather pessimistic about the commitment of the Commission. Is he right to be so?

Could the LNG developments actually be the lever to bring about a more competitive situation within the producing sector of the market?

Nigel's second broad solution is to establish a good climate for investment and infrastructure. He mentioned here regulatory stability; I guess we would all subscribe to that, and once again foreign and international trade policy comes in. Nigel was quite optimistic on the investment front. Was he right to be so? Certainly in the UK there seems to be a long list of projects. What about the rest of Europe?

The next point raised is release gas schemes to ensure that purchasers have access to sufficient supplies. Yes, agreed. But in my view release gas schemes are basically short-term fixes. They are not a substitute for the basic structural reform of the industry which we managed I think to bring about in the UK. We can debate how successful it was, but it has not really yet been tackled in Europe at all.

Ensure integration of demand-side management, Nigel suggested. Yes I think I agree with that; it does not sound like a thing one ought to disagree with. But I am not quite sure what it means, so this needs to be explored further.

Since there has been a great deal of focus on competition, pushing forward the liberalisation issue, is competition enough? Is there any evidence of market failures in parts of the market that might actually need to be addressed by public policy? Possibly storage in the UK? It is just a question.

And lastly, I would like to bring up the question of political will. In the UK in the mid-1990s, and I know Clare would agree with this, it was the political will of people in the British government at that time that was the crucial factor that enabled us to do what we did. There were perhaps three or four, maybe five, key factors at that time which enabled us to push through the reforms that we did then, but the political will was undoubtedly the absolutely overriding one. So my fourth and last question is: how do you get political will, particularly in Europe? One answer is that it just comes by accident, because you have some inspired leader somewhere. That does happen sometimes but it is a bit unpredictable. But there are perhaps ways of stimulating political will by careful graft. And of course the first one is consumer pressure and consumers, in most countries, also equal voters.

Nigel emphasises the need to integrate the consumer view and I think he is very right about that. In the European context, the consumer pressure needs to be bought to bear on government ministers, the Commission or whatever in Europe. One of the key factors in the UK that I mentioned in the 1990s was the timing of the action that we took. It is always easiest for politicians to take controversial action in a relatively early part of their period of power. That means now for the European Commission, because the new Commission has just started in office. Another factor, I am afraid, is not so favourable. In the UK in the mid-1990s the fact that there was at that time downward pressure on gas prices with the supply position very favourable, was a key factor in the choice of timing for the reforms that we brought in, particularly the Gas Act. We suspected that would not last very long and we really pushed to grab that window. That of course is not the situation in Europe now and that undoubtedly is a negative factor. But I think what it comes down to is that the UK government and Ofgem and indeed all the rest of us need to get over to Brussels, probably physically, and argue the case as actively as we can and at all levels and go on doing so for quite a long time.

3. The economics and politics of wind power

David Simpson

INTRODUCTION

I should like to begin by making clear that I am far from being an expert on my subject. Wind power, and energy generally, is an area into which I have only recently strayed. In finding my way about I have relied heavily on the writings of others who are genuine experts, including Lewis Dale, John FitzGerald, Dieter Helm, Eileen Marshall and Colin Robinson, as well as many others too numerous to mention, whose influence I should like to acknowledge. Without their contributions, I should have little to say.

Somewhat to my surprise, I have discovered that wind power is a topic that arouses strong passions, not only among writers of letters to newspapers but even among scientists. Whenever I have mentioned that I have been studying wind power, the response is invariably to ask: 'Are you for it or against it?' People seem to have made up their minds in advance of any economic analysis. There seems to be an unexamined belief that wind power provides clean and cheap energy, but most people appear to have made up their minds largely on aesthetic grounds.

Some people believe that wind turbines are beautiful. Certainly the scale is impressive, with a height of up to 110 metres and a diameter of the rotor blade up to 60 metres. Other people find them ugly. It has been suggested to me that these subjective judgements are largely influenced by a person's age, and that surveys show that the 'crossover' age is 48. Whether or not this is so, it is almost certainly the case that aesthetic judgements about the visual amenity of wind turbines, or the clusters thereof known as wind farms,[1] are influenced by their location. And it is also unfortunately the case that those parts of the country that are the most suitable for wind farms are also among the most scenically beautiful. A map of Designated Areas in Great Britain (that is, National Parks, Areas of Outstanding National Beauty and Sites of Special Scientific Interest) is almost exactly congruent with a map of high-speed wind sites. This has naturally given rise to public concern, which has played an important part in England and Wales in moving wind farms offshore, despite the higher cost. But wherever the turbines are located, it is likely that a large-scale wind programme will require the construction of additional overhead transmission lines. And nearly everyone agrees that pylons and lines are visually unattractive.

Perhaps I should make my own position clear. I have no 'favourite' technologies. Subject only to considerations of safety, amenity and security of supply, I am happy to leave the choice of generating technologies to the market. Accordingly, if a wind farm is profitable without subsidy, and if it fits harmoniously into its surrounding landscape, then I personally have no objection to make to it.

Debate about the advantages and disadvantages of wind power is almost as heated as debate about the related and wider topic of climate change. However, it is not my intention to discuss to what extent our climate is changing, whether man-made carbon dioxide (CO_2) emissions may be responsible and, if they are, what we should do about it.[2] Instead, this chapter accepts as its point of departure the government's stated objective of reducing CO_2 emissions in the UK to 20 per cent below their 1990 level by the year 2010, a target that is slightly tougher than its Kyoto commitment to reduce 'greenhouse gas' (GHG) emissions by 12.5 per cent over a similar period. CO_2 is one of a basket of six gases whose emissions form the target for reduction that was agreed at Kyoto in 1997. The other five are methane, nitrous oxide, hydrofluorocarbons, perfluorocarbons and sulphur hexafluoride. We shall return to the distinction between CO_2 and GHG emissions later. Meanwhile, it may be worth noting that the government has set these targets, not because of any impact they might have on climate change – after all, the UK accounts for only 2 per cent of the global total of such emissions – but in the hope of encouraging other countries to follow their example.

AN OUTLINE OF THE CHAPTER

I shall begin by describing the growth of wind power in this country, that is, the number of wind turbines and their generating capacity. It will be seen that we are now at a point of inflection: starting in 2004, a rapid acceleration in the growth of wind-generating capacity in the UK is under way.

Why is this happening? The simple answer is because of the very large subsidies that are being offered to generators by government. I shall outline what these subsidies are and how they are financed. As we shall see, they are funded by what might be described as a 'stealth user charge' on the electricity bills of households.

The next question which arises is why is wind power being promoted in this way? The official answer is that it is primarily for environmental reasons, but also for reasons of security of supply and employment. The main part of this chapter examines this claim and concludes that expanding wind power in the way now being practised is a costly and relatively ineffective form of emissions abatement that adds little to the security of the nation's energy supply.

If that conclusion is correct, is there a better way of meeting the government's emissions targets? The next section examines the prospect offered by the carbon emissions trading scheme to be launched in 2005.

If economics cannot offer much support for the present wind power policy, then perhaps politics can provide a better explanation. So the penultimate section looks at wind power policy from the perspective of public choice theory. Finally, the future prospects for wind power are discussed.

THE GROWTH OF WIND POWER

In 2004 there were about 1100 wind turbines operating throughout the UK, delivering some 0.4 per cent of the total amount of electricity supplied through the National Grid. It is the aspiration of the British Wind Energy Association (BWEA), the industry's trade association, that by the year 2015 some 8000 turbines should be delivering 15 per cent of British electricity.[3]

Because of the constantly increasing size of the turbines – the current average size has a capacity to generate 1.5 MW of electricity – it is more usual to measure the expansion of wind power in terms of the growth of capacity rather than turbine numbers (see Figure 3.1). At the end of 2003 the total installed wind capacity in the UK amounted to about 0.7 GW (1 GW = 1000 MW). To be on course for the 2015 target it is generally accepted that about 8 GW of wind capacity needs to be in place by 2010. Projections by the Department of Trade and Industry (DTI) show this growing to 25 GW by 2020. In that year about 60 per cent of the total capacity is expected[4] to be located offshore.

Some commentators have pointed out that to achieve 8 GW of wind capacity by 2010 would require the installation of eight 1 MW turbines every day from now until 2010, which they consider an impossibly large undertaking. And indeed capacity projections by Merrill Lynch are more modest: 3.6 GW by 2010 and 11.2 GW by 2020. It is these that are shown on Figure 3.1. The principal reasons for the relatively slow progress to date is the public opposition to wind farms on grounds of amenity, and a degree of financial uncertainty on the part of developers. The main price support arrangement, the Renewables Obligation (RO) scheme, offers developers a generous but uncertain revenue flow.

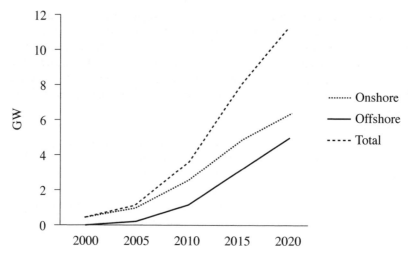

Source: Merrill Lynch 2003.

Figure 3.1   Installed capacity

But government has acted to try to overcome planning objections, and has also extended the RO scheme to 2015. An acceleration in the rate of growth of capacity has now begun. In the year 2003, 61 new turbines were installed with a capacity of 103 MW, while in 2004, 314 were confirmed to go ahead with a capacity of 474 MW.

WHY IS THIS GROWTH OCCURRING?

The rapid expansion of wind power capacity is not taking place as the result of an increase in demand for wind power on the part of individual consumers of electricity. It is occurring for the same reason that periodically rashes of bright yellow crops break out in the countryside and that flocks of sheep and herds of cattle are seen roaming disconsolately on unpromising pastures. Substantial financial incentives are being offered to generators of wind power, and to some other forms of 'renewable' energy. The source of these incentives is the government's RO scheme.

The Renewables Obligation Scheme

Starting in April 2002, the RO scheme set a target for retail power suppliers to source at least a part of their electricity from renewable generators. This target started at 3 per cent of electricity supplied to customers in 2002/03 and increases in steps to reach 10.4 per cent in 2010/11. For the year to 31 March 2004, suppliers could meet their renewables obligation either by producing Ofgem certificates (ROCs) to the value of 4.3 per cent of electricity supplied to customers, or by using a buy-out clause which allowed them to pay £30.50 per MWh for any shortfall, or a combination of both. Generators of electricity from sources designated as 'renewable' are able to sell ROCs to suppliers at a price that varies according to supply and demand. At present the market value of a ROC is about £45 per MWh.

The 'Stealth User Charge'

Electricity from wind and most other renewable sources costs the retail distribution companies more than it costs them to buy electricity generated by conventional sources, so the higher costs are passed on to consumers in the form of higher charges than would otherwise have been the case. At the present time, renewables are thought to add about 2 per cent to household electricity bills. Most consumers are quite unaware that they are paying this hidden levy, and they do not know what they are getting for it.[5] It might reasonably be described as a stealth user charge.

The Climate Change Levy

Wind generators enjoy a further subsidy in the form of the Climate Change Levy (CCL), a tax on energy introduced in April 2001. Households and most renewables are exempt: the value of this exemption is equivalent to £4.30 per MWH of electricity. (Energy from nuclear power and from large hydro schemes is *not* exempt.)

At present (2004), the wholesale price of electricity is about £30 per MWh, and on top of that a wind generator stands to receive an additional £50 for each MWh it sells to a distribution company.

The White Paper of February 2003 estimated that by the year 2010 the combined effect of the RO and CCL schemes would amount to an annual subsidy to the renewables industry of around £1 billion. (For comparison, the annual value of wholesale electricity supplied in the UK in 2004 was about £10.5 billlion.) According to the White Paper, by 2020 the renewables and other schemes would add between 5 and 15 per cent to domestic electricity bills in real terms.

Redistribution of Income

The powerful financial incentive which these subsidies offer to wind developers can be gauged from the rents which developers in turn are prepared to offer to owners of suitable land. In one location in the Scottish Borders with which I am familiar the landowner receives a rent of £10,000 per turbine per annum. With 24 turbines in the 'farm', he is guaranteed an income of £240,000 per annum until at least 2015, representing a substantial gift from the consumer with no outlay and no risk. Elsewhere in the same region, another landowner is being offered between 5 and 8 thousand pounds per MWh per annum for a proposed development of 18 turbines each of 1.5 MW capacity. On the Parc estate in Lewis, the landowner is believed to have been offered £3000 per turbine per annum for each of 125 turbines.[6] So the government's promotion of wind power is having some curious and presumably unintended consequences in terms of income redistribution.

Elsewhere, developers are using some of their potential profits to buy the support of local communities. In Dumfriesshire, for example, Scottish Power has offered to set up a trust fund for a local community based on a payment of £1000 per MW of capacity per annum. The Association of Scottish Community Councils is seeking payments from developers of £5000 per MW of wind-generating capacity per annum. Some people might think that if a community is able to capture some of the rents from its local natural resources, this not only may serve allocative efficiency but also perhaps represents a rough kind of distributive justice. We may be stumbling into a market in property rights. Whether or not that is so, it is clear that the expansion of wind capacity onshore is being driven by strong financial incentives.

WIND POWER AND ENERGY POLICY

How does the government's promotion of wind power (and some other renewables) fit into its overall energy policy?

In his Foreword to the government's 2002 Energy Review, the Prime Minister wrote that he wanted sources of energy that were 'cheap, reliable and sustainable'. These three adjectives refer to the three main objectives of current energy policy, namely economic efficiency, security of supply and a reduction in carbon emissions. Let us look at each of these objectives in turn, and see how wind power measures up.

Costs

Wind is *not* a cheap source of energy. A recent study from the Royal Academy of Engineering of the comparative costs of generating electricity suggested that wind is roughly twice as expensive as gas (Figure 3.2).

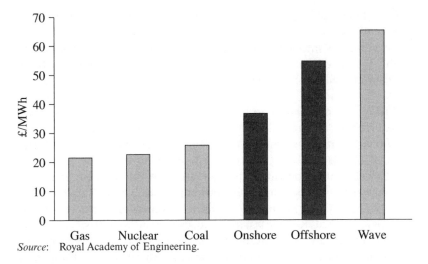

Source: Royal Academy of Engineering.

Figure 3.2   Unit costs of generation

The Royal Academy of Engineering puts the current average generating cost for offshore wind farms at £55/MWh, although North Hoyle, the only one operating so far, is reportedly coming in at £70/MWh. For onshore wind farms, they estimate an average generating cost of approximately £37 per MWh.[7]

And although the generating cost of wind power is expected to continue to fall over time, the authoritative study by Dale and his colleagues shows that this may not be enough, even by the year 2020, to offset its disadvantages. Dale's projections, which also took account of transmission and distribution costs, show that in 2020 a generation portfolio containing 20 per cent wind power will still be more expensive than a conventionally fuelled alternative portfolio, and this conclusion remains true even if gas prices should double between 2002 and 2020.[8]

Of course such comparisons of costs which come from accounting and engineering data can only be indicative, not conclusive. They necessarily leave out of account all the other factors which enter into an investment decision in an actual market, risk, uncertainty, financial, strategic and other considerations, many of which are specific to their context. Nevertheless, the message of the data is clear. Wind is not a cheap source of energy.

Reliability

The biggest disadvantage of wind is that it is not a reliable source of power. It suffers from intermittency. In plain terms, the wind cannot be relied upon to blow all the time. This is a defect that has pervasive adverse consequences, as we shall see.

The problem of intermittency can be divided into two parts: the load factor, roughly the fraction of time that the wind is blowing; and unpredictability – we cannot predict when it will not blow.

1. *The load factor*   The load factor is a measure of how much power a generator will actually deliver in relation to its capacity. It is calculated by dividing its actual output (in MWh) by the product of its capacity and 8760 (the number of hours in the year). In most cases, actual output falls well short of potential: the standard assumption by engineers and economists when designing wind power projects is a load factor of only 35 per cent. Even this may be optimistic. Average load factors actually achieved in the UK in the last five years vary from 26 to 30 per cent.[9] And in West Denmark, where in 2003 wind power accounted for 21 per cent of regional electricity consumption – the target to which the UK officially aspires in 2020 – the average load factor achieved has been only 20 per cent. In Germany, the wind power fed into the national grid in 2003 was, for more than half of that year, less than 11 per cent of the installed capacity of all the wind turbines.[10] If the average load factor in the UK in 2020 should turn out to be no more than that achieved in West Denmark this would almost double the annual cost of the UK wind programme, so that by 2020 it would be costing consumers almost £2.5 billion extra each year. To put the matter another way, the current costings of the Government's wind programme are based on the expectation that when that capacity is built it will deliver 75 per cent more energy for each MW of installed capacity than its Danish counterpart.

2. *Unpredictability*   When the wind blows is unpredictable and, although there is more wind in winter than in summer, it is not otherwise correlated with demand:

> There are significant periods in an average year when demand for electricity is high and wind output is low. For example, in a typical year there will be 23 one-hour periods when the output of wind turbines for the whole of GB is less than 10 per cent of declared net capacity and at the same time the demand for electricity is between 90 per cent and 100 per cent of peak demand'. (OXERA (Oxford Economic Research Associates) 2003, p. 14)

So wind power is an unreliable part of an energy portfolio.

Because of the variable and unpredictable nature of its availability, additional standby generating capacity is required. Estimates of the extent of this additional capacity range from 65 to 100 per cent. At low levels of wind penetration the cost of this standby capacity are small, but when wind power is approaching 20 per cent of the national power supply the costs become prohibitive.

For example, the Royal Academy of Engineering has calculated that if installed wind capacity were to increase from 7.5 GW to 25 GW, that is, a capacity increase of 17.5 GW, the additional conventional back-up capacity that would be required is 15.5 GW, that is, 80 per cent of the increment.

This consideration puts an effective upper limit on the penetration of wind (that is, the proportion of electricity from wind distributed through the grid), in the present UK context to around 20 per cent.

Sustainability

What does it mean?

'Sustainability' is a word which Lewis Carroll's Alice would have loved because it can mean more or less whatever you would like it to mean. In the present context, I think that by 'sustainability', the Government means a measure that does not damage the environment.

It is difficult to disentangle the relationship between government expenditure on wind power expansion and environmental improvement. The reduction of environmental emissions is only one of three justifications commonly offered for supporting wind power, (the others being improving security of supply and promoting technological development and employment in the industry). And the 2003 White Paper cited the promotion of renewables as only one of several elements of its policy directed to the reduction of emissions. Nevertheless, as the subtitle of the White Paper suggests (Creating a Low Carbon Economy), the *main* purpose of promoting wind power appears to be to help to achieve the official target of a 20 per cent reduction in overall CO_2 emissions from their 1990 level by 2010.

Wind power has only limited environmental benefits
The principal advantage of a generating portfolio with a high wind energy content is a reduction in the emission of CO_2 and other greenhouse gases compared to a more conventional portfolio with a higher proportion of thermal generation. But these benefits are limited. Figure 3.3 shows us that electricity generation accounts for less than 30 per cent of CO_2 emissions in the UK. The two other big sinners are road transport and industry.

So, even with a maximum penetration of 20 per cent, wind power could save only 6 per cent (20 per cent × 30 per cent) of total CO_2 emissions. This means that the contribution of wind power to meeting the official environmental target for the UK can only be marginal.

If we had examined the sectoral breakdown of emissions of GHGs rather than of CO_2, a slightly different pattern of distribution would have emerged (see Figure 3.4).

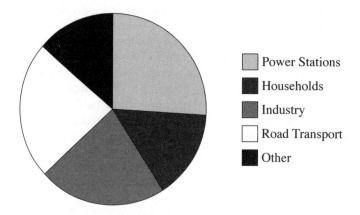

Source: Department of Trade and Industry.

Figure 3.3 CO_2 emissions by sector

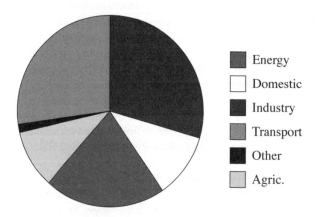

Source: Scottish Executive.

Figure 3.4   GHG emissions by sector

Agriculture is revealed to be as large a polluter as power stations. This raises the question of a comparison of the costs and benefits of reducing stocks of cattle with the costs and benefits of reducing the amount of gas burned in power stations. If marginal farmers in the UK reduced their herds, not only would this lead to a reduction in the emission of GHGs (mainly methane), but there would be a gain to taxpayers, since farm subsidies would also reduce. It might even be that the farmers themselves would benefit, as the value of the marginal product from dairy farming in contemporary Britain may be negative. The Irish Agriculture and Food Development Authority has carried out research showing that, as a result of recent reforms to the Common Agricultural Policy de-coupling payments from output, there has been a significant reduction in GHG emissions in that country.[11]

This finding of the marginal environmental benefit of wind is supported by the recent history of CO_2 emissions from UK power stations (Figure 3.5).

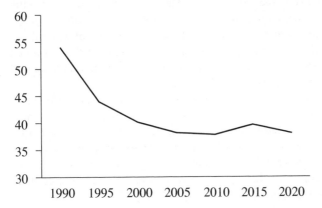

Source: Department of Trade and Industry.

Figure 3.5 CO_2 power station emissions

Throughout the 1990s, CO2 emissions from power stations fell, largely because gas has been replacing coal as the principal fuel in the electricity generating stations. But official projections published in Energy Paper 68 show that from 2005 to 2015 emissions of CO_2 from power stations will start to rise again. Why? Largely because electricity generated by gas will increasingly be replacing the electricity generated by emission-free nuclear power stations. The impact of wind power does not alter this trend.

Therefore, it is not surprising that achieving the official environmental target of a 20 per cent fall in total CO_2 emissions by 2010 is now in doubt.[12]

Back-up requirements are polluting as well as costly
Emissions from power stations are minimised when demand fluctuations are minimised and base load is at its highest. Unpredictable wind power creates additional demand volatility on power stations, and, since nuclear

power is not technically suited to provide back-up supplies at short notice, the use of wind turbines tends to restrict the choice of back-up to fossil fuels, with adverse consequences for emissions.

Cost–benefit analyses

Where projects or programmes of investment are publicly financed, it is quite common to carry out in advance a formal project appraisal known as a cost–benefit analysis (CBA).

In a CBA of wind power one would, in principle, try to bring together on the benefit side not only the value of the electricity generated but also the value of the environmental damage avoided by not emitting polluting gases. On the cost side, one would not only count the normal costs of generation, transmission and distribution, but also the polluting effects of the additional back-up requirements, as well as of such activities as manufacturing and erecting turbines, pylons and transmission lines.

So far as I am aware, there have not been any attempts – official or unofficial – to carry out a formal CBA of the British wind power programme to try to establish whether the value of the environmental benefits outweighs the costs. This is perhaps not so surprising when one considers the formidable difficulties that such an exercise encounters. For example, trying to put a value on the emissions saved by the use of wind power in place of fossil fuels.

First, the value depends on the nature of the fuel actually displaced. If wind turbines replace coal, the value of emissions saved is five or six times greater than the value of emissions saved if wind turbines replace gas. Second, views differ significantly on the monetary value of the environmental damage inflicted by a unit of an emitted gas. Third, estimates do not always account for the use of fossil fuels in the manufacture, installation, and dismantling of wind turbines.

Despite these uncertainties, the Organisation for Economic Cooperation and Development (OECD) carried out a CBA of wind power in Denmark for each year from 1993 to 1998 and came to the following conclusion: 'The renewables programme, now largely based on wind turbines, seems to have incurred costs much higher than any environmental benefits achieved so far'.[13]

An *ex ante* CBA of a proposed wind farm off the coast of the eastern United States – the first offshore wind farm in the US –has reached a similar conclusion. In this case, the overall costs of the 130 turbine wind farm were judged to have exceeded the benefits of the project by $211.8 million.[14]

INTERMEDIATE CONCLUSIONS

The conclusions of the chapter so far must therefore be that wind power is an expensive and ineffective method of carbon emissions abatement that adds little to the security of the nation's energy supplies. The government's preoccupation with renewables and in particular with wind power appears to be a distraction from its stated objectives in the field of energy.

If that is so, two further questions suggest themselves:

1. Is there a better (that is, cheaper, more reliable) way of reducing CO_2 emissions?
2. If the promotion of wind power is unlikely to meet its energy policy objectives, why is the Government pursuing it?

We take up these questions in the next two sections.

THE EU EMISSIONS TRADING SCHEME

Is there a more cost-effective way for the Government to meet its environmental objectives?

Textbook economic theory suggests that there may be. A single economy-wide transparent policy instrument, such as a carbon tax (that is, fixing a price for carbon), or a carbon emissions trading scheme (fixing the amount of carbon emitted and auctioning licences), would encourage us all to reduce the amount of carbon-intensive energy we consume by raising the price of activities that emit carbon. It would allow the mix of fuels for electricity generation to be determined by the market rather than by political decision. The cost of achieving the environmental goals would become more transparent, and pursuit of these objectives by this method would complement, not interfere with, the other energy policy objectives of efficiency and security of supply.

If we were to do this, then, with all our market prices adjusted to reflect the environmental damage caused by carbon emissions, we should probably find that we had more home insulation, and less road and air travel than would otherwise be the case. In electricity generation we might expect to find some wind power, but not very much, and perhaps some nuclear power, (always provided that solutions had been developed within reasonable timescales for the management and disposal of nuclear waste). The problem, of course, for the government's renewables and energy efficiency schemes is that an across-the-board carbon tax or emissions trading scheme has the potential to render them largely redundant.

Nevertheless, the 2003 White Paper endorsed the EU's carbon emissions trading scheme. This scheme is now being phased in as a result of an agreement reached by the governments of EU member states in late 2002. Each member state agreed to limit its emissions of GHGs for the 2008–12 period relative to emissions in 1990, an 8 per cent reduction for the EU as a whole, and a 12.5 per cent reduction for the UK. Unfortunately the version of the scheme that is shortly to be put into effect throughout Europe, including the UK, is flawed: it will impose avoidable costs on many businesses, and an unnecessary burden on households. It starts with CO_2 only, and covers only some industries.

The proposed EU carbon trading scheme has three flaws. As long ago as the early 1990s the EU Commission proposed a harmonised carbon/energy tax. This was rejected by the governments of the member states in favour of a scheme of tradable emissions quotas or permits. While the European Parliament sought to have at least a significant proportion of these permits allocated by auction, the member state governments insisted that at least 95 per cent of the permits be allocated free of charge to the polluting firms. *Flaw no. 1*: by promising a second round of free permits for the 2008–12 period the scheme encourages polluting firms to remain in business: if they shut down they would forgo the free permits.

Furthermore, as Eileen Marshall pointed out in her Beesley Lecture in 2003, ('Energy regulation and competition after the White Paper'), there will be (*Flaw no. 2*) a major windfall gain for shareholders in companies in competitive industries covered by the scheme, for example, electricity. This is because, in a competitive industry, the output price must rise by enough to pay for the permit used in production as well as the price of the fuel used. The windfall gain will occur because the shareholders will receive the permits for free, and at the same time will be fully compensated – through higher output prices – for the permits used up in production. This gain will be paid for by consumers in the shape of higher prices.

Flaw no. 3: a further additional cost to households will arise from the substantial compliance and verification costs, involving a firm-by-firm audit which would not have been incurred by an across-the-board carbon tax.

John FitzGerald has proposed that for the 2008–12 period the present flawed scheme should be replaced either by a common rate of carbon tax across the EU or by the auctioning of all quotas. The only exceptions would be for plants in industries that are both carbon intensive and which face competition from outside the EU, steel being an example.[15]

The lesson of this story appears to be that the governments of EU member states have allowed their environmental schemes to reflect the interests of specific groups of producers rather than the interests of the generality of European citizens. While some of these producers would face genuine difficulties that need to be addressed in any viable scheme, many others will receive major windfall gains. This is not an isolated episode. As we shall see in the next section, the politics of special interest groups appears to have played a major part in determining the British government's promotion of renewable energy including wind power.

THE POLITICS OF WIND POWER

If wind power, as we have argued, is an expensive and ineffective method of carbon abatement, why is it being so strongly promoted by government? It cannot be attributed to wilful ignorance or stupidity. There are dozens of able economists employed in the relevant departments and agencies of government who are well aware of these issues. The only conclusion we can reasonably come to is that policy choices which are apparently 'irrational' when viewed from the perspective of economics may be perfectly 'rational' when viewed from the perspective of politics. In other words, political considerations have overridden economic ones in the formulation of policy towards wind power.

There is, of course, nothing new in this. When one looks at the history of the formation of energy policy in Britain since the Second World War a similar pattern of the dominance of politics over economics is apparent. In his review of energy policy in the early post-war period between 1950 and 1980, Colin Robinson concluded that what successive governments described as 'energy policy' was in practice 'a series of protectionist measures intended to aid British coalmining, with a subsidiary objective of promoting British-designed nuclear power stations'.[16] Robinson goes on to describe the process of policy making in this period as follows:

[Policies were] ... instant responses to apparently pressing problems in the energy field which seemed likely to be of concern to the electorate, and which were therefore capable of swaying votes. Typically, the government of the day reacted to each new problem with a short-term political 'fix'. ... Periodically, the set of short-term 'fixes' which happened to exist at the time would be gathered together in a White Paper ... or a Ministerial speech, described as though it were some analytically sound, coherent whole designed to deal with failures in markets, and dignified by the title of 'policy'.[17]

The arrival of Nigel Lawson at the Department of Energy in 1981 produced a brief return to economic rationality. The wartime planning culture of 'predict and provide' was gradually replaced by the principle of allowing fuel to be priced realistically in competitive markets. Whereas the beneficiaries of the old-style energy policy were producers, the beneficiaries of the new energy policy were consumers. Indeed, with fuel prices being decided in markets there was no need for an 'energy policy' at all; and the White Paper of 2003 was the first White Paper on energy policy for 35 years.

The energy policy of the Lawson era was simple: the main objective was economic efficiency, in other words low costs, and the means was the introduction of competition. The subsequent establishment of wholesale and retail markets in energy led to a prolonged fall in the price of electricity to consumers while at the same time achieving an acceptable level of security of supply.

Helm[18] provides a comprehensive and entertaining account of policy formation in the period from 1997 to 2002. In 1997 the incoming Labour government added a third objective to the existing ones of economic efficiency and security of supply, namely the reduction of carbon emissions. Had they wished to achieve consistency with the existing objectives they might have introduced a carbon tax or a carbon emissions trading scheme. Either of these arrangements should, in principle, have brought about the desired overall reduction in CO_2 emissions at the lowest overall cost.

Instead, the new Government chose to ignore the lessons so painfully learned in the post-war era by governments and regulators all over the world. This is that Governments and centralised planning processes are hopeless at choosing between technologies.[19] The attainment of a physical target for a reduced level of CO_2 emissions for the economy as a whole was arbitrarily divided between an 'energy efficiency programme' and electricity generation. Then, in a re-run of the 'picking winners' procedure, some generation technologies (most renewables, combined heat and power: CHP) were favoured while others (hydro, nuclear) were dismissed.[20] Arbitrary targets 10 and 20 years ahead were set for the favoured technologies, while equally arbitrary incentive schemes (levies, subsidies and exemptions) were put in place in the hope of achieving these targets. As Helm puts it, the ends and means chosen for energy policy were not the result of careful forethought, analysis and planning, but rather the result of reactions to unplanned events mediated by the lobbying of vested interests.

Helm's account of the process by which the energy review was produced by the Cabinet Office's Performance and Innovation Unit (PIU) in February 2002 is clear. What it did *not* do was a carry out an *economic* analysis, which would have involved specifying the objectives, identifying the trade-offs between them, and assessing the efficacy and implications of alternative policies. This would have had the political disadvantage of producing clear losers: any sensible environmental policy would be bad news for the coal industry, new nuclear power stations would offend the Green lobby, too many renewables would impose too high costs, and a realistic carbon tax might upset voters.

The PIU Report instead offered something to each of the several lobbies and interest groups. The business lobby was satisfied with the suggestion that climate change should only be addressed in the UK if other countries did likewise. The Green lobby could take comfort from the target of a 20 per cent Renewables Obligation by 2020, reinforced by an energy efficiency target, although there was no serious analysis of the likely cost of such measures. The idea of a carbon tax was floated, but far enough into the future to avoid creating short-term political difficulties, and the nuclear lobby was encouraged by talk of 'keeping the options open', although no new build programme was recommended.

The problem was that at the end of the review, the government was no nearer having anything which could be described as a coherent energy policy, nor did the review offer clear guidance on how to resolve the tensions between the three objectives of cheap energy, a reduction in carbon emissions and security of energy supply.

PUBLIC CHOICE THEORY

Presumably this process of policy formation in government is not peculiar to energy or the environment. Over the years it has not entirely escaped the attention of economists that decision making in the public sector is heavily influenced by sectional interests. But it was only some forty years ago that this idea was formally recognised in the somewhat confusingly named 'public choice theory'.

From David Hume onwards, economists had assumed that individuals engaged in economic activity were primarily concerned with pursuing their own interests, and explored the consequences of that assumption. Political scientists, on the other hand, assumed until well into the twentieth century that human beings who were engaged in political activity whether as voters, politicians or civil servants were mainly concerned with identifying and following the public interest.

Thus, a man who entered a supermarket was assumed to choose the goods that he believed would benefit him and his family. Yet, when he entered the voting booth he was assumed to vote for those laws and those politicians that he supposed would benefit the nation as a whole rather than those that would benefit him. Likewise, if the same person became a politician, a transformation was assumed to occur so that a broader perspective guided him to make morally correct decisions rather than to follow that course of behaviour that pleased the interest groups that might support his re-election.

Public choice theory put an end to this bifurcated view of human behaviour by developing a theory that amounts in essence to transplanting the broad analytical framework of economics into political science. The shopper in the supermarket and the voter in the polling station are now understood to be the same person. Politicians in a democratic society are seen to be people who make a living by winning elections. They do so by pursuing policies that they think will cause people to reward them with their votes. Since these are presumably the policies that people actually want, then from the standpoint of democracy this is not necessarily undesirable.

The implications of this assumption of universally self-interested behaviour for the understanding of behaviour in the public sector are diverse. They include an explanation of the observed practice of vote-trading among politicians, rent-seeking by business and consumer interest groups, the behaviour of civil servants,[21] and the interaction among all three groups.

The reason why the outcomes of public choices are often different from private choices is not because of differences in the quality or morality or in the behavioural objectives of people working in the two sectors. Rather it is due to the differences in incentives within which those in the two sectors have to work.

What light does this theory of public choice throw upon the government's apparently irrational (from the economic point of view) preoccupation with wind power and other renewable energy technologies? Three possible considerations spring to mind.

First, whatever their economic costs and benefits, wind turbines act as a very visible political signal to voters that the government is taking practical steps to improve the environment. While the hardcore Green vote may not be very large, there must be a huge 'soft' Green vote. How many people would not vote in favour of 'saving the planet'?[22]

Second, there are a small number of large private corporations which together with sponsoring government departments and agencies form an environment–energy complex reminiscent of the defence–industry complex. The financial relationship between these private companies and government is far from being transparent, especially so far as offshore wind developments are concerned. On the one hand, these companies receive capital grants and price subsidies from government for developing wind farms. Some of them are also about to receive windfall gains from the carbon emissions trading scheme. The government is dependent on their goodwill for the realisation of its announced wind power targets. At the same time, many of these companies have been enlisted as unpaid agents for the government's 'energy efficiency' programmes. Together, the companies and the government departments responsible for delivering wind power policy form an extremely powerful producer interest group about whose activities the general public have very little information. The way in which money is transferred from consumers of electricity to the generators of wind power is symptomatic of this lack of transparency.

Third, the 2003 White Paper suggested that in the longer term, carbon trading should be the central plank of emissions policy, but for now the focus of government policy is on what Marshall calls the 'centrally planned' approach to meeting CO_2 goals – half by reducing energy demand, and the other half through renewables and CHP.[23] This is reminiscent of pensions policy, where the short-term 'fix' of means-testing (pensions credit) makes more difficult the achievement of the long-run objective of getting people to save more for their retirement. In both cases, short-termism seems to reflect political rather than economic priorities.

THE FUTURE FOR WIND POWER

Since many of my foregoing remarks have been rather sceptical about the potential for wind power, and particularly for its promotion on a large scale by government, let me conclude on a more positive note.

As we have seen, intermittency is the greatest weakness of wind power. When a cost-effective method of storing energy is eventually developed, wind power, along with other 'intermittent' renewable sources of energy, may at last come in to its own as a supplier of power on a significant scale.

Meanwhile, once market prices reflect the cost of avoiding environmental damage, some individual wind farms should be profitable. And if the proponents of wind power turn out to be right in their contention about the falling rate of costs, in the future an increasing number will be profitable.

There are also significant income benefits to communities where wind resources are located. At the present time these come from subsidies; in the future they may come from the attraction of power-using industries for whom intermittency is not a problem.

Wind power, and eventually other renewable technologies, will undoubtedly play a part in the future of energy supplies in this country. My concern in this chapter has been to argue that this should be done as efficiently as possible. I mean by that not only efficiency in terms of economic costs, but also in terms of the environment and of the reliability of supply.

NOTES

1. Or 'wind factories', as David Bellamy (the botanist and broadcaster) calls them.
2. These issues have been expertly reviewed by Sir Alan Peacock (see Peacock 2003) among many others. For a heretical view, see Baliunas (2002).
3. This is broadly consistent with the government's target of having 15 per cent of electricity generated by renewables by 2015.
4. By Dale, but not by Merrill Lynch. See L. Dale, D. Milborrow, R. Slark and G. Strbac, 'Total cost estimates for large scale wind scenarios in the UK', *Power UK*, March 2003. Merrill Lynch, *Wind Power*, London, 24 September 2003.
5. Following price increases by Powergen and npower in January and February 2004, Scottish Power increased their domestic electricity tariff from 6.873p to 7.328p per kWh, that is, from £69/MWh to £73/MWh, an increase of 6.6 per cent.
6. Encouraged by this prospect, the local crofters appear to be about to exercise their newly acquired right to expropriate their landlord!
7. 'This cost applies however only to the relatively limited areas having the best wind speeds with nominal load factors of 35 per cent', Royal Academy of Engineering, 'Inquiry into the Practicalities of Developing Renewable Energy', Response to the House of Lords Science and Technology Select Committee, October 2003, p. 14.
8. Dale et al., (see note 4, above).
9. Digest of UK Energy Statistics 2003.
10. *The Times*, 20 October 2004.
11. www.teasgasc.ie.
12. Cambridge Econometrics, and House of Commons Environmental Audit Committee.
13. OECD, *Economic Survey of Denmark*, Paris, July 2000, p. 107.
14. 'An economic analysis for a windfarm on Nantucket Sound', submitted to the US Army Corps of Engineers by Beacon Hill Institute, 16 March 2004, available at www.beaconhill.org.
15. J. FitzGerald, 'An expensive way to combat global warming', in D. McCoy, D. Duffy, A. Bergin and J. Cullen (eds), *Quarterly Economic Commentary*, Spring 2004, Dublin: Economic and Social Research Institute.
16. Colin Robinson, 'Gas, electricity and the energy review', Beesley Lecture 26 November 2002, p. 3.
17. Colin Robinson, 'Energy policy: errors, illusions and market realities', Occasional Paper 90, London, Institute of Economic Affairs, 1993 pp. 11–12.
18. D. Helm, *Energy: the State and the Market*, Oxford: Oxford University Press, 2003, chaps 21 and 22.
19. The classic example was the decision in the 1960s to build a series of gas-cooled nuclear reactors (AGRs) with the basic objectives of obtaining cheap power and developing an export industry based on new technology. It was about 30 years before output matched the planned capacity. After incurring about £50 bn of construction costs, the AGRs were sold for £1.9 bn in 1996. Kay observes: 'If the CEGB had been a commercial company, the write-off would have represented by far the largest loss made by any company, anywhere, in business history'. John Kay, *The Truth About Markets*, London: Penguin Books, 2004, p. 92.
20. In a debate in the House of Lords on 6 July 2004, Lord Ezra suggested that the tax privileges available for wind farms should be extended to clean coal, methane gas and CHP technologies. Lord Sainsbury of Turville, the Parliamentary Under Secretary for Trade and Industry, replied: 'If that was the right thing to do, the Government would already have done it'.
21. When Anthony Jay and Jonathan Lynn wrote the scripts for the television series 'Yes, Minister' in the decade after 1977, they had never heard of public choice theory. They later found that it provided an academic corroboration of their personal insights.

22. In fact, the arrival of wind turbines has divided the Green movement. An articulate minority are passionately opposed to the siting of wind turbines onshore, mainly because of the loss of visual amenity.
23. Marshall (2003) p. 7.

REFERENCES

Baliunas, S. (2002), 'The Kyoto Protocol and global warming', *Imprimis*, **31** (3).
Kay, J. (2004), *The Truth About Markets*, London: Penguin Books.
Marshall, E. (2003), 'Energy regulation and competition after the White Paper', Beesley Lecture 11, November.
OXERA (Oxford Economic Research Associates) (2003), *The Non-market Value of Generation Technologies*, June, Oxford.
Peacock, A.T. (2003), *The Political Economy of Sustainable Development*, Edinburgh: The David Hume Institute.

CHAIRMAN'S COMMENTS

Alistair Buchanan

Ofgem's work in the area of wind and renewables falls into three categories: first, administration, second a facilitating role, particularly with regard to the development of networks and third an encouragement role.

I begin with administration. We are the administrator to the ROC scheme. In 2003 alone we carved up £79 million and redistributed that on the back of 5.6 million certificates. That is a huge and complex business. I believe we are highly regarded for the job that we do. In fact in a slightly different area the National Audit Office commended Ofgem for its approach to auditing earlier this year. Administration, though dull, is important because it gives confidence to the marketplace.

Let me move on to the second issue, the facilitation role in networks development. There are three areas that I would like to outline. First, transmission, second offshore and third local networks or distribution networks. In transmission we genuinely seek to be a facilitator but bearing in mind our statutory duties to the customer to ensure that there is value for money. Now, at the last price review for the transmission businesses there was a view that the renewable story was blue sky. Consequently, Ofgem at the time did not seek to deal with the network regulatory aspects of renewables but showed its willingness to do so by offering the comfort letters which were taken up by Scottish Power and Scottish and Southern. We are now doing a series of papers and seeking consultation, ending up in a report in which we will seek to identify through straightforward cost–benefit analysis the costs of constraints. We are also looking at the potential for stranded assets. There are projects which we believe we can allow to go through without having to wait until the next price review.

The offshore regulatory regime has become a very important issue after the passing of the energy bill but I cannot say too much about it because we are discussing with the Department of Trade and Industry what our position will be.

Some areas to which I would draw your attention in terms of our facilitator role are as follows. First, in June 2004 we allocated £5.6 billion to be invested in the local wires networks over the next 5 years. The companies asked for 42 per cent, we gave them 33 per cent in June and since then we have awarded the industry another £182 million. More specifically, as regards wind and renewables, there are two areas I would highlight. First of all, distributed generation where we have given a kick start by allowing 80 per cent to pass through and a more generous rate of return for network businesses, and also through the registered power zones and the innovative funding initiative. Importantly, in the last there is a 'use or lose' requirement on the companies. Then, we are looking at undergrounding and considering our environmental responsibilities embodied in various acts, very carefully: we shall be making a statement on that. So we are acting as a facilitator in networks. Finally, we find ourselves as a 'cheer leader' for energy efficiency which has very important implications for renewables. Here we act as an administrator and an advisor to Defra (Department for Environment, Food and Rural Affairs), and we also have very significant powers by which we can put pressure on to companies.

It may seem that I have gone light on the economics. The reason is that we see our role in this area as primarily one of a facilitator and, of course, Ofgem is not unusual in finding itself in an environment of subsidised power. I have followed the industry since 1987–88 and, in the light of the coal contracts of 1990 and 1994, it is evident that Offer (Office of Electricity Regulation) was in a similar situation. There are three constraints by which Ofgem is bounded. The first is that we need to know our place. Sir John Bourn (Controller and Auditor General) made a very important statement to us in the summer of 2004, which was that independent regulators like Ofgem should be careful not to cross the boundary of policy at the expense of customers. Second, we have to keep our house in order. In 2003, Edward Leigh, as Chairman of the Public Accounts Committee, said that regulators must be more accountable for their costs. Third, and most relevant in this context, Patricia Hewitt (Secretary of State for Trade and Industry) in handing us our revised social and environmental guidance, outlined the scale of Ofgem's input by saying that any significant financial impact must be dealt with by the Government.

It is a challenging mandate to handle these various requirements and one of the things that I am most pleased about with Ofgem is that generally I think we know when – and more importantly when not – to seek to take a policy position. We are, however, very active in transmission: we kick started the review on renewables investment in May 2004 and made a major statement in December. On distribution networks, we will be outlining our full package with what I believe are reasonably innovative aspects taking in aspects related to renewables development. On energy efficiency, possibly more important than ever given the price increases, that we have recently seen, we continue to be highly active.

Another key feature of Ofgem is that we do believe we understand the business environment that we find ourselves in. We are not party to any complex: we are an independent regulator.

In the light of what I have said about policy responsibilities, I am relieved that I am not required to defend policy against David's charge that wind power is an expensive and ineffective method of carbon emissions abatement that contributes very little to the security of the nation's energy supplies.

4. The Competition Appeal Tribunal – five years on

Christopher Bellamy

Five years ago, in 1999, I was appointed as the President of the Appeal Tribunal set up under the Competition Act 1998.[1] It was an unusual position to be in since the Tribunal at that stage had no members, no staff, no premises and no budget of its own. Indeed, it had no jurisdiction since the 1998 Act was not yet in force. What we want, said the Department of Trade and Industry (DTI), is something that is quick, cheap and fair. Here is a clean piece of paper and a pencil. Now get on with it.

At that time, the Tribunal was, as it were, joined at the hip to what was then the reporting side of the Competition Commission. Whatever the pros and cons of that initial arrangement, it certainly enabled the Tribunal to be up and running within a comparatively short space of time.

The Competition Commission very kindly found me an office in New Court. This was in fact the old Monopolies Commission waiting room where, as a young barrister, I had waited nervously for my first appearance before the old MC (later the Monopolies and Merger Commission: MMC) in 1972. To work the treadmill for 30 years and still find oneself in exactly the same room where one started must, I would have thought, be some sort of record.

One little known – perhaps the only – benefit of the crumbling edifice of New Court in Carey Street is that from the former waiting room which became my office there is a fine view out over New Square in Lincoln's Inn. As I sat at my improvised desk in my new surroundings I remembered the *Eagle Star/Sunley* case in the mid-1970s – which was about whether insurance companies should own property developers, which was the kind of thing the MMC investigated in those days. I was waiting in this same room with my client, who was the property developer. The property developer looked out over New Square – arguably the most beautiful eighteenth-century square in the world – and said wistfully: 'There is still a lot of London that needs redeveloping'.

Even by the dismal standards of the 1970s, it was a surprising remark in physical terms; but seen metaphorically, he was undoubtedly right – many

British structures of the time did need redeveloping and rethinking. In the sphere of competition law, however, the wait was a long one. Structures dating essentially from the 1950s were not reformed and updated until the dawn of the twenty-first century.

We can, however, no longer complain about lack of change: in a short space of time we have gone from one extreme to the other. After masterly inactivity for decades, the pace of change since 1998 has been astonishing. There have been four main waves.

First came the 1998 Act, coming into force on 1 March 2000. That brought with it the Chapter I and Chapter II prohibitions, giving new wide powers of investigation and enforcement to the Office of Fair Trading (OFT) (including provision for very heavy penalties) and also gave jurisdiction in these respects to the sectoral regulators. It also saw the introduction of the competition law jurisprudence of the European Community into the domestic competition law of the United Kingdom, thus enabling, for the first time, a coherent body of principles to develop, instead of the 'ad-hoc-ery' for which the former system was notorious. Moreover, the emphasis, in the new system, was very much on economic analysis as a means of enforcing legal rules, another innovation on the domestic scene. Finally there was the setting up of a specialist court, namely the Tribunal, with a multidisciplinary membership, modernised procedures and jurisdiction to decide appeals 'on the merits'.

The second wave was the Enterprise Act 2002 which followed the DTI's 2001 White Paper on Productivity and Enterprise, the aim of which was to create a 'world class' competition regime. The 2002 Act converted the OFT into a corporate body; removed ministers from merger and market investigative decisions; laid to rest 'the public interest' as the criterion for administrative control and introduced the 'substantial lessening of competition' test in merger cases; replaced monopoly inquiries with market investigations; separated the Tribunal from the Competition Commission; made the OFT and the Competition Commission definitive in most merger and market investigation decisions, instead of merely reporting to ministers; gave a judicial review jurisdiction to the Tribunal in relation those decisions under sections 120 and 179; and introduced a criminal cartel offence in section 188.

As regards the Tribunal, apart from its new-found constitutional position (including appointments of the President and chairmen being made by the Lord Chancellor, rather than the Secretary of State) three matters were also important: the simplification of the procedure under section 47 of the 1998 Act in third-party cases; the creation of a damages jurisdiction in 'follow on' cases under section 47A; and the possibility of specified bodies bringing representative claims on behalf of consumers under section 47B.

There was also the power, not yet exercised, to order civil actions involving infringements of domestic and European competition law to be transferred to the Tribunal under section 16.

Following hard on the heels of the second wave, came the third wave – not of interest to everyone here but a major part of the Tribunal's work – the Communications Act 2003, which came into force in July 2003 and reformed the whole of telecommunications law on the basis of four European Directives. Ofcom took over the role previously carried out by six regulatory agencies. Section 192 of that act provides for a wide range of appeals on the merits to the Tribunal from decisions of Ofcom and the Secretary of State in relation to telecommunications, spectrum and related matters. There is a rather convoluted appeal procedure to be followed in price control matters, requiring the involvement of the Competition Commission, under section 193 of the Act. The Communications Act also brought the regime for newspaper mergers into line with the provisions of the Enterprise Act relating to mergers, albeit introducing specific criteria for media mergers with a continuing role for the Secretary of State upon advice from both the OFT and Ofcom. Decisions of the Competition Commission, the Secretary of State, the OFT or Ofcom in this area are subject to review by the Tribunal under section 120 of the Enterprise Act 2002, as amended.

The fourth wave arrived on 1 May 2004, namely the coming into force of the EC Modernisation regime under Regulation 1/2003. That necessitated further amendment to the 1998 Act by an Order made in 2004 under the European Communities Act and the Enterprise Act.

The modernisation reforms abolish notification and allow Article 81 (and the domestic equivalent, section 2 of the 1998 Act) to be treated as one integral whole, so that an agreement infringes only if it falls within Article 81 (1) (section 2) and does not satisfy Article 81(3) (section 9 of the 1998 Act). In addition, national authorities such as the OFT have the power to apply Articles 81 and 82 instead of, or as well as, domestic law. A network of competition authorities across Europe liaise closely on these matters, so we are told. Of some interest also is the introduction of the OFT's power to accept binding commitments in lieu of taking a decision. Under the 2004 Order, decisions by the OFT accepting binding commitments are subject to the possibility of judicial review by the Tribunal.

The 2004 Order also provides for a new kind of appealable decision that is likely to be of some significance for the future: an appeal to the Tribunal against a refusal by the OFT to take an interim measures decision. That, incidentally, honours a commitment to that effect made by the government in the 2001 White Paper.

In all those circumstances, regulators, advisers, business people and others could hardly have had more to cope with over the last four or five years.

Indeed, if I may say so, the Tribunal does not for a moment underestimate the difficulties faced by regulators in setting up and administering the new system, given the complexities of the law, the pace of change, the difficulty of many of the factual issues involved, and the issue of resources. In a system so young and so complicated there are bound to be problems and tensions. In indicating, as I will in a moment, where some possible problem areas may be, I would not for an instant seek to suggest that the other various players are not attempting to grapple effectively with the difficult problems which confront them.

In any such system, especially a new one, there are bound to be, if you like, issues of demarcation and balance. How wide is the discretion of the regulator; what is the proper balance between the administrative and judicial stages; what is the balance between effective enforcement and procedural safeguards; between delay and fairness; between cost and other considerations; on the substantive level, between letting market forces take their course and, on the other hand, seeking to regulate; and so on?

In this complex mosaic, where does the Tribunal fit in?

As I see it, the Tribunal has four broad roles. Its first task is to try to ensure that the system is seen to be fair. In this respect I would not suggest that any regulator would knowingly act unfairly; anyone worth their salt would rightly bridle at any such suggestion. It is simply that since regulators have great power, and combine investigative, prosecutional and decision-making functions, the persons affected by their decisions may feel aggrieved at the way those powers are exercised, or not, as the case may be. Hence a referee is needed. It is a deep truth of any legal system, in my experience, that for the participants the actual outcome is often a secondary consideration: what they really want is a fair hearing. If people can 'have their day in court' they will, although disappointed, often accept an unfavourable outcome as long as it is seen to be fair. A sense of fairness in turn develops public confidence in the system as a whole and should enable it to operate in a balanced way. Systems that are not seen to operate fairly, cannot command authority and do not survive for long.

This does not mean of course that procedural protection should be taken to the *n*th degree, or that companies should be allowed to play procedural games, or that the system should be allowed to deteriorate into an unwieldy, slow-moving procedural morass. Our task, with I hope the help of the parties, is to find the happy medium. Although I would not myself subscribe to the perhaps too candid remark of the Old Bailey judge: 'We at the Old Bailey play it straight down the middle, not too partial – not too impartial either'.

Second, the Tribunal is there to try to get the law right. Surprisingly perhaps, although a number of fixed points are known and understood, there are considerable amounts of 'grey area' still in the substantive law, in relation to Article 82/ Chapter II issues or section 9/Article 81 (3) issues, to give but two examples. In the now devolved world of EC competition law, it seems to me that national regulators have a golden opportunity to seek to fill in the gaps and to some extent proactively mould the future development of Community competition law. My own experience at European level is that the Court of Justice and the Court of First Instance pay close attention to well-argued, sensible decisions taken by expert bodies at national level. It is, I trust, not subversive to suggest that the European Commission does not necessarily have a monopoly of wisdom on all points, or that the case law of the Court of Justice is not necessarily immutable or complete in a number of areas. Those who are concerned with these matters have a unique opportunity to help to shape the future. References to Luxembourg, from the Tribunal, are not out of the question.

The third role of the Tribunal is perhaps to help with the transparency, even visibility, of the system. Although of course regulators seek to be transparent where possible, specific cases in the European system, upon which our domestic system is based, are conducted behind closed doors at the administrative stage, quite unlike the situation in the United States where the system is largely court based. I do not underestimate the advantages of the domestic system, but it sometimes means that transparency is not very great. A simple case closure letter or press release at the end of what has evidently been a substantial investigation does not necessarily tell one much about what has really been going on, and may leave other interested parties with a sense of grievance. The Tribunal, here, it seems to me, provides a safety valve of transparency. The line of cases from *Bettercare* to *Aquavitae*, and now *Pernod-Ricard*, show the circumstances in which 'non-decisions' can be brought before the Tribunal. That is now reinforced by the possibility of bringing before the Tribunal a refusal by the regulator to adopt an interim measures decision. The same will apply, on a judicial review basis, to the binding commitments regime introduced in 2004. I trust that, in one way or another, anyone who has a legitimate interest in knowing how or why a particular case was disposed of will be able to do so, within reasonable limits, if necessary by coming before the Tribunal.

Visibility is not the same thing as transparency, but it is an important element. In my view, a 'closed doors' decision should be subject to the possibility of scrutiny in open proceedings. The Tribunal sits in public, so anyone can come. I am keen to see the Tribunal's proceedings available live online, on the website, and we are currently investigating the technical feasibility of this. All public transcripts are published as soon as possible. We have sat in Edinburgh and Belfast, as well as London, but there is no reason why we should not sit in Birmingham (a recent opportunity to do so eluded us when the appeal was withdrawn), Manchester, or indeed anywhere else. In my view, if you want people to understand the system, they need to see it in action.

The fourth role of the Tribunal is one in which we particularly need the role of dialogue. As we have already seen, we have a new framework, but the framework lacks the details, both of law and of procedure. It also of course needs continual adaptation to meet changing commercial and regulatory circumstances, and to deal with new points and unforeseen issues. There are inherent tensions, already mentioned, arising from the different interests involved, the costs, the competing aims to be achieved. How is all this to be developed, so that the rules are clear but workable; the system kept up to date, and effective yet fair; the costs contained. These issues arise in almost all the appeals to the Tribunal, sometimes in most unexpected ways, whether it is a point of law, or procedure, or a question of ancillary relief or costs. Many of these issues can only be decided in the context of the particular case, but it is necessary to see in a broad sense where a particular decision is likely to lead – what the Duke of Wellington used to call 'guessing what is on the other side of the hill'. To come to a sensible, balanced decision, the Tribunal needs, and greatly benefits from, the dialogue with the parties, the submissions made, the arguments advanced: it is a two-way process, in my view; a Socratic dialogue, if you will; a joint effort. So if you ask me how this system we have is to be developed, by what method, the Tribunal's answer is: we will develop it together with the interested parties, by Socratic dialogue in public forum; and the Court of Appeal is there to put us right if we go wrong.

Those then are the four main roles of the Tribunal as I see them. It is, in this context, of little use if the Tribunal does not seek to set good standards at the outset. After all, good factual analysis, clear reasoning and giving interested parties the opportunity to comment are, in my respectful view, all part of good administration anyway.

One additional point to add to what I have just said. As I think is apparent, what was once seen as a largely administrative process is now part, albeit a specialised part, of the justice system. The main feature of the justice system in the United Kingdom – and it is the same in this respect at European level – is that it is a case law system. Everybody needs to understand what a case law system is. Any court, and particularly a court such as the Tribunal, tries to see the implications of its decision, in a particular case, for other cases – it tries to see 'over the hill'; however, any individual judgment depends on its particular circumstances. It is impossible to understand what a particular judgment decides without seeing that judgment in context. One occupational hazard, from the Tribunal's point of view, is that, however hard one tries, in subsequent cases one is soon told that one has decided something that in fact one had no intention of deciding, or that one has not decided the very thing that one thought one was deciding. In two different cases, the Tribunal's decision on a disclosure application in *Claymore* was cited to the Tribunal in completely different circumstances which were not all the circumstances that the Tribunal was considering in *Claymore*. So it should be borne in mind that context is everything: circumstances alter cases. That said, I hope we never find ourselves in the position of Baron Bramwell in the nineteenth century who reversed one of his own previous decisions, simply saying 'This matter does not appear to me now as it appears to have appeared to me then'.

How then does the Tribunal seek to fulfil its role?

Much of this is familiar. Just as regulators need to operate in modern ways, so too the Tribunal. Our working methods, I hope, represent modern best practice in the judicial sphere and enable us to develop some approaches that are unique to this jurisdiction: extensive written argument; disclosure early in the case; 'hands on' case management; identification of key issues; short and structured oral hearings; strict time limits; informal 'hot tub'-type discussions with experts; site visits (radio base station backhaul circuits in Hampshire, water extraction and treatment processes on Deeside); extensive use of the website; referendaires who not only provide judicial back-up but also, under the supervision of the Registrar, act as 'registrar for the case', so that the parties more or less always have the same point of contact; experienced Registry staff; and multi-disciplinary – and, if I may say so, extremely independently minded – members. If we need to hear witnesses we do so, as in *Football shirts* (15 days), *Toys* (5 days), but also in *Genzyme* and *Napp*.

So far 48 cases have been lodged, of which 18 appeals are or were against infringement decisions under section 46, 16 appeals by interested parties under section 47, 6 interim measures applications, 2 applications for review of a merger decision under section 120 of the 2002 Act, 4 Communications Act cases, and 2 actions for damages.

The Tribunal has so far given about 70 judgments. A number have dealt with substance in competition law: *GISC* (collective exclusive dealing under Chapter I), *Napp* (abuse of dominance by predatory and excessive pricing of pharmaceuticals), *Bettercare (no. 2)* (the concept of an undertaking), *Aberdeen Journals (no. 2)* (abuse by predatory pricing in local free newspapers), *Freeserve* (as to lack of reasoning in relation to alleged predatory pricing and margin squeeze issues), *Genzyme* (margin squeeze abuse) and *JJB and Allsports* (liability on Chapter I infringement. Apart from such cases as *IBA Health* (mergers) and *BT* (radio base station backhaul circuits), many of the Tribunal's decisions have been on procedural issues: whether there was an appealable decision (*Bettercare,*

Claymore, Freeserve, Aquavitae, Pernod–Ricard); confidentiality; disclosure; interest; time limits; the location of the proceedings; and costs; and on more fundamental questions such as the reasoning required on market definition (*Aberdeen Journals (no. 1)*), respect for the Rule 14 procedure (*Argos & Littlewoods*) and the position of complainants (*Pernod*). Major judgments in *BT (Save Activity)*, *Floe Telecommunications* (refusal to supply), *Toys* (Chapter I), *Genzyme* (remedies), *Apex and Price* (Chapter I), among others, are also important.

In the period we are considering it has also been necessary to set up the entire Tribunal apparatus from scratch – for which all possible credit is due to the Registrar and his team. This has included managing the necessary selection boards and recruitment procedures for the staff, designing, fitting out and moving to our new premises in Bloomsbury Square, producing three successive versions of the Rules as each new piece of legislation required, producing the Guide to Appeals now under revision, designing and developing the website, organising and sponsoring the Association of European Competition Law Judges, liaising with the Department of Trade and Industry (DTI), the Treasury, the Department of Constitutional Affairs, the Lord Chief Justice, the Vice Chancellor, the Judicial Studies Board and the Council on Tribunals, discharging the management and audit functions of the Competition Service, giving evidence to committees of the House of Lords, sending delegations to, or receiving delegations from, many foreign countries, supporting the Competition Forum of the British Institute, liaising on law reform issues with the European Commission and fulfilling various speaking engagements. This is a very large programme of work for a body with a staff of five professionally qualified persons and less than 20 in all.

The full Tribunal also meets, every two months, for an intensive training session and to keep up with current developments. This has been done since our original starting point in early 2000. Training is one of our highest priorities, and in my view very necessary in this area. Training consists not only of lectures but also includes case studies and problem-solving elements. The multi-disciplinary character of the membership, appointed from the original 700 candidates, is one of the Tribunal's major strengths, in my view. No one should doubt the detailed analysis which the members bring to bear on the cases before them.

Others I am sure will have identified problems at the level of the Tribunal, but I will share two with you.

Our good intentions, to decide straightforward cases in six months (although we carefully never defined what a straightforward case was) are under pressure – particularly in terms of the production of detailed written judgments. This will I hope be relieved by the appointment to the panel of chairmen not only of Marion Simmons QC but also of the entire Chancery Division bench, of which Mr Justice Lindsay was the first to sit. It is not, however, a problem that can be solved overnight.

Second, we have realised that quite apart from what one might call 'mega appeals', there is a distinct need for access to the Tribunal by small or medium-sized companies as cases such as *Bettercare*, *Albion Water*, *Floe*, *VIP*, *Burgess* and *Powerbond* demonstrate. We need to address how that access can be made as effective as possible, avoiding top-heavy procedures.

I said at the outset that five years have passed; so perhaps it is right to mention briefly where, as I see it there are 'points for discussion' in the system as a whole. For some reason most of these points begin with 'D'. 'D' for debate, for discussion.

My first point is a rather general one, which can perhaps be put under the heading 'Disconnection' or 'Distance'. Whatever may be the aims of competition law, one of them is to protect consumers in terms of lower prices, better quality, more innovation and so forth. Competition law should not become a kind of game, played at public expense between lawyers and large corporations on the one hand, and regulators on the other, while the rest of us look on bemused. My question is: is this new system yet connected with the man in the street; is a competition culture really taking root in this country – as perhaps has occurred to some extent in other countries such as Australia and the United States.

Professor Carl Baudenbacher of St Gallen is fond of relating that, when he spent a sabbatical at the University of Texas, his 12-year-old daughter came home from school excitedly, one day, saying 'Daddy, we've been doing the Sherman Act today'; an incident unimaginable on this side of the Atlantic. Perhaps more focus at local level, using trading standards officers, and the local press, would bring home to consumers what this is all about. Perhaps consumers' associations also have an enhanced role here. We have recently had our first intervention from the Consumer's Association, in support of the appellant in the *Burgess* case.

Related to that there is 'D' for devolution and decentralisation. I have been asked in Edinburgh, pertinently I thought, what the 1998 Act had done for Scotland. One can point, it is true, to *Aberdeen Journals* and *Claymore*, but the underlying message is clear enough; competition is also important at regional and local level. Quite a high proportion of expenditure in the average household is local. Smaller, local cases do matter, and can often raise points of great importance – and will not, I hope, be neglected. In the excitement of the modernisation regime at Community level, let us hope that the less glamorous but equally important aspect of regional and local enforcement will not be overlooked.

That takes me on to enforcement generally and in particular to 'D' for Decisions, to which are linked 'D' for deterrence, D for delay and D for delivery. It is, I would suggest, an important aspect of the edifice we have been discussing that there should be a reasonable flow of enforcement decisions. Without such decisions, deterrence is weakened; and the system is seen as just another level of bureaucracy in a world of overregulation. The system cannot develop without decisions. One has to say – and it is a subjective impression which may be misplaced – that we sometimes seem to be nearer in relative terms to a trickle, rather than a flood, of enforcement decisions, and there appears to be something approaching a complete drought in some of the regulated sectors. Perhaps some kind of study as to whether there is a problem here, and if so what the reasons are, whether anything should be done, and if so what, would, I would have thought, be of some interest.

Linked to the last point is the curiously British phenomenon of the non-decision which seems to have crept into the system. One of the developments which I for one did not expect over the last five years is the number of appeals by persons who say that the regulator did not take a decision, when it should have done, or, more precisely, that the regulator took a non-infringement decision when it should have taken an infringement decision. We get as many such appeals as we do against infringement decisions. This has led in turn to regulators advancing long and expensive arguments to the effect that, contrary to appearances, and after lengthy investigations, they did not in fact decide anything at all, and certainly nothing that was within the jurisdiction of the Tribunal. The irony of some of these largely unsuccessful arguments, coming from bodies one of whose principal functions is to take decisions, has not been entirely lost on neutral observers. Similarly there is a relatively large number of informal case closure decisions. These include, as far as one can tell, over 20 such decisions in suspected resale price maintenance (RPM) cases, including 12 in the past year – notwithstanding that RPM is a potentially serious infringement. This situation does perhaps somewhat raise the eyebrows and raises the issue of balance as between deterrence, enforcement and informal case closures. It would be interesting to understand whether there are difficulties in taking infringement decisions, and if so what they are and how matters can be addressed.

It is not of course particularly comfortable to lose a case. We understand that. But if I were a regulator, I would not worry about it from the point of view of *amour propre*; perhaps it would be better to take eight decisions and lose two rather than to try to 'copper bottom' a smaller number. Deterrence can result from the mere fact of proceedings being brought, irrespective of the outcome.

The question of deterrence seems to me to be an important issue to be thought about, and I am sure is being thought about, in the context of the new possibility of accepting 'binding commitments'. One could perhaps hope that such commitments would be accepted in appropriate cases only, and not necessarily seen as a route to primarily 'soft' enforcement in which the harder and more demanding route of the infringement decision becomes over time the road less travelled.

For some participants, the frustration of the system has been not so much receiving a decision of rejection, but the difficulty of obtaining any decision at all within a reasonable time.

This emerged notably in the *Freeserve* (now *Wanadoo*), *Albion Water* and *Burgess* cases, but there are also echoes of the same problem in *Claymore* and *Pernod*. Although all those are still live cases, and thus I shall say nothing about them individually, still less about the merits, or the course of events in any particular case, I merely point out that obtaining a decision at all, which is then capable of appeal, sometimes causes a difficulty in the present system.

In urgent cases, the new possibility of appealing a refusal to grant interim relief may partially address this gap, particularly for smaller companies where High Court litigation is not a credible option, given the uncertainties involved and the cross-undertaking in damages.

I would also take this opportunity to point out that the procedural system of Community law, provides, as it were, a seamless web. Under Community law, a complainant is entitled to a decision on his or her complaint. He/she is not necessarily entitled to a decision on whether there has been an infringement, but he/she is entitled to an appealable act. If, after a reasonable time, no appealable act is forthcoming from the Commission, he/she may serve a notice on the Commission requesting that such an act be adopted within a two-month period. If, on the expiry of that period, still nothing has happened, Community law presumes that there has been an implied decision of rejection of the complaint; that implied rejection can then be taken on appeal to the Court of First Instance. Whether such a system is implicit in the EC modernisation regime, or should have been introduced under the domestic implementing provisions, is a point that may arise one of these days.

We do not have time to discuss D for damages, and the wider question of the correct balance between public and private enforcement. With regulators necessarily needing to set priorities, and likely always to be short of resources, is a system that depends almost entirely on public enforcement likely to be optimal? If not, what measures, if any, should be taken to facilitate or encourage private enforcement? These very important issues will shortly be the subject of a Green Paper by the European Commission, and merit reflection by all concerned.

Lastly, and perhaps most difficult, C for costs, D for detail and E for economics. Competition law cases can be very heavy in terms of time, resource, economic analysis, and the detail required. Despite our best efforts to the contrary, the Tribunal does not always succeed in reducing cases to manageable proportions. Here is the dilemma familiar to most legal systems – a Rolls Royce procedure, scrupulously fair in which every point is examined in the minutest detail; or a system that is serviceable enough, albeit less detailed? A system of competition law which was still out of reach of many interested parties because of the cost, because the issues had been allowed to become too complex, or because the level of debate or the concepts were simply over the heads of many of the business people concerned would not be achieving its aims. It seems to me that over time it is going to be necessary to forge a central core of relatively simple rules or presumptions, particularly in such areas as dominance or abuse, capable of being applied by business people or non-specialist advisors in a way that makes the law understandable, accessible and reasonably certain, as well as enforceable at reasonable cost. This is probably the major task for the future.

In highlighting these few points for discussion, I would not seek to detract from the considerable vision and achievement of the DTI, and of the Treasury, and the regulators, in the setting up of the new system and in its operation to date. The remaining problems will I am sure be sorted out. In so far as the Tribunal is concerned, I would merely close by saying that we do not see the process of solving the various problems that confront us in adversarial terms, but in terms of a cooperative effort by all interested parties to arrive at good solutions.

NOTE

1. Technically at that stage the appeal tribunals of the Competition Commission to whom appeals lay under sections 46 to 47 of the Act. Since the coming into force of the Enterprise Act 2002, now the self-standing Competition Appeal Tribunal under sections 12 to 15 and Schedules 2 and 4 of that Act.

CHAIRMAN'S COMMENTS

George Yarrow

I shall comment, in an impressionistic way, on a few of the points that Sir Christopher makes in his chapter. I shall not attempt any general assessment of where the Competition Appeal Tribunal (CAT) has got to, since my position on this is akin to one taken by the former Chinese premier Chou en Lai in response to a question back in the 1950s or 1960s. When asked whether he thought the French revolution had been a success, Chou thought for a while and then said that it was probably too early to say. The 5 years that Sir Christopher has been in action is still a rather short period and the number of decisions is still relatively small. I think that, for the moment, it is appropriate to take a 'wait-and-see' approach, and to keep an open mind on performance to date.

I am probably, in some senses at least, a poor choice of Chairman for these proceedings, because for a long time now I have been an advocate of judicial control, or judicial supervision, in competition law and in related regulatory policy areas. When I have given Beesley lectures in the past, that position commanded very little support among economists. It is pleasing, therefore, to say that now that the CAT is well established the number of supporters has increased substantially; and before commenting on some of the specific problems and difficulties identified by Sir Christopher, let me take the opportunity to say why I thought judicial supervision was an important aspect of the system as a whole.

First, as a matter of high-level principle, in a free and democratic society the role of judicial supervision is very important in establishing effective checks and balances on the exercise of executive power. Competition law is directed against conspiracies, abuses of power, and undue concentrations of power: these are the matters that are normally dealt with under Article 81, Article 82, the European Merger Regulation, Chapters I and II of the Competition Act, and so on. However, anyone with reasonable experience both in and out of government will know, empirically, that many of the most important occurrences of conspiracies against consumers, of abuses of power, and of undue concentration of power are to be found within rather than outside government. That is in the nature of things. Therefore, it is also important that the quite extensive executive powers afforded by competition law to the Office of Fair Trading, the sectoral regulators and other administrative agencies are subject to external supervision.

The second set of arguments that have convinced me of the advantages of judicial supervision is more pragmatic. I offer it as a proposition, based on observation, that judges are pretty good at handling complex facts and evidence, and that this skill is less widely distributed among economists and administrators. Sir Christopher pointed out that good factual analysis, clear reasoning, and opportunity to comment are part of good administration everywhere, and later he said that context is everything and that circumstances alter cases. It is probably fair to say that these remarks were made in a way that suggested they were obvious and uncontentious, as no doubt they are to the judicial mind.

On the other hand, an approach that lays emphasis on putting factual material first, developing reasoning around that material, and being ever-conscious of context is not one that comes as second nature to most economists trained over the last few decades. Nor is it one that, from experience, is well embedded in many of the administrative agencies of government. In my view, this is a very important issue. Economic theory does, in a number of areas, point to the sensitivity (sometimes the extreme sensitivity) of outcomes to context – and I think here of a whole body of research in industrial organisation, of which the most widely known is probably the work of Paul Klemperer and others on auction theory – but that appreciation too frequently seems to get lost in the application and use of economics at the coal face. And that is why I have a high regard for judges, who perform a vital (economic) function in putting obstacles in the way of presumptions (or prejudices) built in to economic models and to conceptual biases that may arise from administrative convenience. The courts are (or, where they are not, should be) guardians of factual analysis, clear reasoning, and a sensitivity to context.

Turning to specific issues and problems discussed by Sir Christopher, let me first add another D word to his list, disproportionality. Is all this new activity in competition law proportionate to the effects that it is having and/or the effects that it might have in the longer term? This is a rather basic question – not unlike the one put to Sir Christopher in Edinburgh: what has the Competition Act 1998 done for Scotland? – but it is one that bears asking, and repeatedly; and it is, I believe, closely connected with the other Ds of distance or disconnection. Sir Christopher focused on the distance/disconnection of competition law from the man or woman on the street, but there can also be another disconnection, between legal processes, including associated economic reasoning, and market reality. Since most people are rooted in market realities of one kind or another, the two disconnections are clearly related; and, arguably, together they can be conducive to disproportionality in the application of competition law.

To illustrate, a few months ago I was at a seminar where there was a debate among cognoscenti about the future of Article 82, including its various possible interpretations. I sat through that seminar with a growing sense of alienation. There was only one person from business at the table – the rest were lawyers, economists and government officials – and the words and the concepts and the arguments seemed to be operating in a world of their own, in a language game significantly distant from the everyday world of commerce. It was very difficult to see how any of this could, in practical terms, make material, positive contributions to the functioning of markets, still less how it could credibly be explained to market participants.

I therefore share Sir Christopher's worry about distance/disconnection, but would add that the source of that disconnection may well be the thing itself (competition law and its application) – rather than any failure to explain it to the public – and, in particular, its disconnection from underlying purposes. And those underlying purposes seem to me to be fairly clear: as indicated above, competition policy is concerned with conspiracies, abuses of power and undue concentration of power. These are not esoteric issues, and are not beyond ordinary public discourse.

Let me now consider two points that it might reasonably be expected that an economist would make. First, it is very often the case that an analyst will look at the market and say: there is something going wrong here; the market is not working as effectively as it could because there is some or other obstacle to competition. However, standing back and taking a longer perspective on the issues, it may be discovered that the best resolution of the perceived problem will be to rely on the market participants themselves. There is a great inclination to declare a 'market failure', without recognising that existing inefficiencies (which will always be with us) themselves create incentives for their elimination, because there is money to be made if the inefficiency can be reduced.

This is not an abstract point. Looking back over the history of competition policy, it is not difficult to find cases (and, in my view, all too many of them) where there has been an intervention in the name of competition policy in circumstances when developments in the market were already dealing with the perceived problem. One contributory factor here is the influence of overly-static economic analysis, which tends to substitute presumptions, built into the explicit or implicit economic models that are being relied upon, for facts and context. In many cases, change and evolution are important aspects of (to use a felicitous term of Sir Christopher's) the 'factual matrix', not matters to be assumed away.

My second point concerns the use of the word 'fair' in competition policy. Here it is quite important to distinguish between fairness in process and fairness in outcomes. The big worry is that we know that public policies aimed at achieving 'fairness' in outcomes, however defined, are one of the major sources of distortions of competition. In terms of economic effect, many of the measures that governments have taken to promote fair competition have actually been protectionist measures, taken to shelter one or other interest group from the adverse consequences of competition. 'Fairness', when it appears in competition policy, is therefore one of those words that should signal potential danger. If it is restricted to matters of process and procedures, that is one thing. The danger occurs when an administrative agency starts to think: 'the outcome here doesn't look very fair, competition has gone wrong somewhere, let's find out what and see if we can address the problem'.

In the economics of regulation there are a few broad themes that recur again and again, such as the risk of unintended consequences and of unwanted, secondary incentive effects of intervention more generally. One of those themes is 'regulatory capture'. This is a strong term, but it can be weakened to the notion of 'undue influence', encompassing any situation in which a particular party or interest group acquires advantage by diverting the policy process to serve 'private' ends. Thus, decisions may be procured that contribute neither to competition nor to economic efficiency, but rather redistribute resources at some cost to competition or efficiency.

This tendency is always something to beware of, but resistance to temptation is hard, and competition is often 'unfair' in the outcomes it produces. The temptations are probably greater in the regulated sectors than in general competition policy, since the relevant authority may have a mix of duties. Thus, for example, when arguing for or against measures on competition grounds, life can be difficult when there are opposing arguments based on benefits to the environment, improved safety, 'the poor' and the like. Those much 'softer' words – environment, safety, the poor – have so much more emotional appeal than competition, and can be skilfully used by advocates of interventions that would establish protected (against competition) positions. I am therefore pessimistic about the likelihood of convincing the man and woman in the street of the joys of competition, although I think there is more hope if the stress is placed on the prevention of conspiracies and abuse of power.

In relation to what Sir Christopher said about sectoral regulators – particularly the small number (trickle) of positive decisions thus far and the question of deterrence – I take a more optimistic position. I am not attracted by the strategy of encouraging regulators to make decisions simply in order to acquire more case law and/or to strengthen perceived deterrence. From my own experience, the deterrent effects already exist, at least where they matter most, and the lack of cases is more likely an indicator of the success of parts of competition policy than an indicator of failure.

To be much more specific, let me draw attention to some of what has happened in the energy sector. Following the ending of statutory monopolies in retail electricity and gas markets in 1998/99, there was a remarkably rapid transition to deregulation, unmatched in any other major economy or in

any other sectors, even including telecoms where technological change has
been more rapid (and where the UK was also a pioneer in liberalisation).
A major contributing factor to the speed of deregulation was the introduction of the Competition Act 1998. The energy regulator judged that
it was feasible quickly to let go of control over prices on the basis that, if
things did go seriously amiss and competition did not develop as expected,
then the powers afforded by the Act would allow some of the balance
to be redressed. Particularly given that, in such an eventuality (failure of
competition to develop), the existence of market dominance would be a
fairly obvious fact of economic life, incumbent suppliers were, from the
outset, fully aware of the risks, including financial penalties that would have
very serious commercial consequences in a retail market with thin margins,
associated with conduct that might be held to be abusive. I think it is fair
to say that the relevant companies did a great deal in terms of compliance
programmes and of seeking to determine, in a specific and new market
context, where the boundaries of acceptable conduct might lie. This is not
to say that cases in these markets will not arise, but rather that the absence
of cases should not (so far at least) give rise to major concerns about lack
of clarity as to the implications of Chapter II for retail energy markets, or
about absence of deterrence.

This brings me to Sir Christopher's C and E problems, to costs and
economics. Competition law cases can easily become very costly, complex
and time-consuming processes for the administrative authorities, and, given
this, it is almost inevitable that a regulator will have concerns about whether
or not it would turn out to be disproportionate to be more 'active' in competition law enforcement, particularly given the existence of the options
available for private enforcement.

It can, of course, be argued that, over time, a set of simple rules and
presumptions might be developed, particularly in relation to abuse of
dominance, which will create more speedy procedures and reduce costs. On
this, however, I am less optimistic than Sir Christopher about the prospects
for the future because I think it will be very, very difficult to get relatively
simple rules and presumptions which, if applied generally, would actually
do good over the long haul. It is easy enough to develop a simple set of
rules, the hard part is developing rules that have (net) beneficial effects
across a wide range of differing market contexts. I think it was the American
journalist H.L. Mencken who once said something like: 'For every complex
problem there is a solution that is direct, simple and wrong'.

If context is everything, a simplified rule of conduct may be pro-competitive in one market and anti-competitive in another (and it is a safe bet that
there will be no lack of complaints from competitors about violation of
the rules in the latter case). My own view, therefore, is that, in relation to

abuse, the test must ultimately be based upon harm done, upon the effects of the conduct. This is less simple than a more rules-based approach might become, but I believe the proposition that substantial power should not be used to cause collective harm is a more realistic starting point for policy development. To ask companies in possession of substantial market power to consider wider, potential effects of their decisions (beyond effects on the bottom line) is no bad thing in itself, and, as experts in the relevant markets, such assessment should not be outside their competences.

Indeed, as I have argued before in the context of wholesale energy markets – on the basis of market characteristics that are by no means confined to energy – this approach merits some generalisation beyond the limits imposed by established notions of dominance. I very much agree with Sir Christopher when he says that regulators (and the OFT) should not be deterred from making decisions simply for fear of having those decisions overturned on appeal. It is part of the regulatory task to develop appropriate governance for changing markets, and, since this requires innovation, unwillingness to make arguments and strong aversion to the risk of losing would be particularly inhibiting to market development. In energy just such risks were (knowingly) taken by the regulator in relation to the proposal to introduce a market abuse licence condition. However, the negative outcome in that case points up the fact that success or failure will also be determined by the performance of the CAT and of other appeal bodies, such as the Competition Commission for regulatory licence conditions. While a regulatory advisor might recommend enforcement action aimed at promoting better market governance and conduct, it is difficult not to have sympathy with a regulator who replies: 'But we will have all those lawyers flapping about, and all those legal bills; it will divert resources from other pressing tasks; it will take forever; there is a good chance we will lose on a technicality, to which must be added the possibility that they will make a wrong judgment (these markets are exceedingly complex, after all, which is one reason why they have not existed until recently); and meanwhile the development of competition could be inhibited. Is it worth it? Is there not a better way?' These are not easy questions to answer.

5. A year under Ofcom

Robin Mason[1]

INTRODUCTION

In the first 11 months of Ofcom's existence, it launched over 60 consultations, to add to the responsibilities inherited from the regulators that it has subsumed, plus the extra 135 duties given to it by Parliament. It initiated two major reviews of broadcasting and telecommunications, as it comes to grips with overseeing a media, telecom and communications industry worth £40 billion.

I do not propose to give a review of the whole avalanche of regulatory activity since January 2004. I shall instead focus on the two big reviews that Ofcom has undertaken: on public service broadcasting and on telecommunications. And in particular, I want to see how Ofcom understands broadcasting and telecommunications: how does it see these markets developing? What does it see as being the major regulatory challenges? What does it think it can do about them?

My main conclusions are as follows:

1. There is little evidence that externalities (whether citizenship or some other kind) are important enough to justify the current degree of intervention in broadcasting. If externalities are used as the main argument, then funding of public service broadcasting (and the BBC in particular) is likely to come under increasing pressure. But there are still grounds for large-scale intervention in broadcasting, due to the high valuation that most people attach to broadcasting services; and the non-rivalrous nature of broadcasting, even in the digital era.

2. There is insufficient backing for Ofcom's proposal to make only £300 million per annum of public service broadcasting (PSB) funding contestable. There is a clear theoretical argument for making all PSB funding contestable; and some grounds for dividing the funding pie more finely. Recent empirical evidence indicates some of the problems with these options. The issues need to be balanced within an explicit

theoretical framework that then allows evidence to be collected to assess where the balance should be struck.

3. The local loop continues to be one of the most problematic parts for telecoms regulation. It is the area that has been most resistant to the introduction of competition, and the area that exposes most clearly regulators' attitudes towards the balance between competition and regulation. Recent evidence points to two facts. First, regulation mandating local loop unbundling may be ineffective in developing local loop competition. Second, the presence of a vertically integrated incumbent in a downstream market can limit competition in that market.

4. The local loop is a particular example of a more general issue in telecommunications: the creation and control of bottlenecks. Bottlenecks will be a recurring problem for the regulator. Ofcom needs to develop a coherent policy towards bottlenecks and vertical integration well in advance: in particular, under what conditions to mandate access to bottlenecks, and to enforce structural separation.

THE PUBLIC SERVICE BROADCASTING REVIEW

The Communications Act (2003) calls on Ofcom first to report on how, taken together, the existing public service broadcasters are delivering on the range of public service criteria set out in the act; and second, to make recommendations to Parliament 'with a view to maintaining and strengthening the quality of public service television broadcasting in the United Kingdom'.

In its Phase 1 report, Ofcom concluded that broadcasting on the main terrestrial TV channels has partially, but not completely, fulfilled the requirements of the Communications Act. Ofcom found some significant achievements, but also important shortcomings in effectiveness, partly due to the actions of broadcasters, and partly because viewers have drifted away from the more challenging types of programming. A survey of 6000 individuals, combined with focus group analysis and interviews, indicate that the public like and value public service broadcasting. While Ofcom recognises that the market unaided would produce PSB programming, it concludes that it would not do so in sufficient quantity or sufficient breadth. In its Phase 2 report, Ofcom presents its proposals to maintain and strengthen PSB. At the heart of these proposals is a continued role for the BBC funded by a licence fee; a diminished role for channels 3 and 5; and the creation of a new 'Public Service Publisher'.

In the rest of this section, I review Ofcom's conceptual framework for PSB, in order to lay out its primary argument for continued regulation of broadcasting. I then ask whether it has gathered sufficient evidence to back up this argument; and to make suggestions about what it has to do to gather that evidence. Finally, I question the grounds for its proposals for future regulation: in particular, how much competition should there be in broadcasting?

The Rationale for Public Service Broadcasting

The starting point of any review of PSB in the UK is to define it. In its Phase 1 report, Ofcom proposes its own version: the purposes of PSB are:

1. to inform ourselves and others and to increase our understanding of the world through news, information and analysis of current events and ideas;
2. to reflect and strengthen our cultural identity through high quality UK, national and regional programming;
3. to stimulate our interest in and knowledge of arts, science, history and other topics through content that is accessible, encourages personal development and promotes participation in society; and
4. to support a tolerant and inclusive society through the availability of programmes which reflect the lives of different people and communities within the UK, encourage a better understanding of different cultures and perspectives and, on occasion, bring the nation together for shared experiences.

This is somewhat different from John Reith's (BBC Director-General, 1927–38) 'inform, educate and entertain', but is clearly a descendant of that objective. The Communications Act (2003) is somewhat more prescriptive. It states that the purposes of PSB are:

1. to deal with a wide range of subjects;
2. to cater for the widest possible range of audiences across different times of day and through different types of programme; and
3. to maintain high standards of programme making.

The fulfilment of these purposes is taken to mean that PSB will:

- inform, educate and entertain; and
- support an appropriate range and proportion of production outside London.

The act goes on to specify different types of programming that should be supported (for example, a wide range of 'different sporting and other leisure interests', and 'acts of worship and other ceremonies and practices'). The authors of the Davies report (1999) are more cautious, concluding that 'we may not be able to offer a tight new definition of public service broadcasting, but we nevertheless each felt that we knew it when we saw it'. The report is more explicit when it says:

> [F]orm of market failure must lie at the heart of any concept of public service broadcasting. Beyond simply using the catch-phrase that public service broadcasting must inform, educate and entertain , we must add inform, educate and entertain in a way which the private sector, left unregulated, would not do. Otherwise, why not leave matters entirely to the private sector? (p. 10)

I shall return to this point later. In a speech to the Royal Television Society on 14 October 1998, Chris Smith (the Secretary of State for Culture, Media and Sport who commissioned the Davies report) stated:

> [T]he BBC [and hence PSB] should act as a benchmark for quality, driving up standards across the board; it should provide something for everybody, making the good popular and the popular good; it should inform, educate and entertain, expanding people's horizons with new and innovative programming; it should operate efficiently and effectively and provide value for money for licence fee payers; it should stimulate, support and reflect the diversity of cultural activity in the United Kingdom, acting as a cultural voice for the nation.

The Peacock committee, set up in 1985–86 by then-prime minister Margaret Thatcher, identified the following list of elements which make up PSB: geographic universality; catering for all interests and tastes; catering for minorities; concern for 'national identity and community'; detachment from vested interests and government; one broadcasting system to be directly funded by the corpus of users; competition in good programming rather than for numbers.

So, while there is some common ground to these definitions, there are some significant differences. In particular, opinions clearly differ about the inclusion of certain types of programming, such as arts, religion and some types of regional programming. This point will turn out to be important when I discuss, below, how PSB is to be valued.

Having defined PSB, the next question is: why does the government have to intervene in broadcasting? The definition of PSB in the Davies report raises the question most clearly: why will the private sector fail to provide PSB? Let me rehearse briefly the traditional arguments for government intervention in broadcasting, in order to explain Ofcom's view of the future.

From the start, government has been intimately involved in broadcasting. At several points, there have been calls for the government to take over the BBC (notably during the General Strike of 1926 and the Suez Crisis of 1956). Ofcom has calculated that the full cost of intervention in PSB in the UK amounts to just under £3 billion per annum, or not far off one day's gross domestic product (GDP) for the UK. The government grants licences (via its regulator) to terrestrial broadcasters. In exchange for the right to broadcast, these companies (the BBC, ITV, Channel 4, Channel 5 and S4C) have to fulfil PSB obligations.

I concentrate first on the standard economic arguments for intervention. The basic reason is the existence of *market failure*. There are a number of different possible market failures in broadcasting. The most basic, and least controversial, is that broadcasting uses the scarce resource of electromagnetic spectrum; and without government intervention, the externalities inherent in free use of the spectrum would lead to inefficiencies. The importance of this market failure varies according to technology. Analogue television broadcasting is spectrum-hungry, so that there is room for only a small number of broadcasters within the UK. Digital transmission enables several television channels to be carried in the space used by analogue signals to carry one channel. Smart devices are able to pick up a particular signal from a mix of signals, reducing the problem of interference. Nevertheless, there is likely always to be a coordinating role in the allocation and use of spectrum.

The next argument, in terms of the degree of controversy, is that broadcasting is a *public good*. With a standard private good, only the owner of the good can consume the good (unless he or she agrees to transfer ownership to someone else). Other people can, therefore, be excluded from consuming the good. And once the good is consumed, it is used up. So consumption is rivalrous: either you or I can eat the last biscuit in the tin, but not both of us. Public goods are the exact opposite: they are *non-excludable* and *non-rivalrous* in consumption. The owner of a public good cannot stop others from consuming the good. And consumption of the good by one person does not decrease the amount of the good left for everyone else.

Broadcasting includes many features of a public good – one person watching a television programme does not prevent others from watching the same programme. Because consumption does not reduce the amount available for others, the social value of non-rivalrous goods is given by the sum of everyone's willingness to pay, rather than an individual's valuation. The social value of a TV programme is therefore the aggregated valuation of all those people who might watch the programme, not just those that do. But non-excludability means that it is very difficult to persuade anyone to pay for the good, since they can access freely. There is a strong incentive to *free ride*: enjoy the benefits of consumption without paying, in the hope that others will foot the cost. Of course, if everyone thinks like this, then no one pays and the public good is not provided. But this is socially inefficient: it is optimal for the public good to be produced (every one gains from consuming it). Hence, provision of such a good by the private sector is likely to be inefficient.

A further potential market failure arises from the economies of scale in broadcasting The making and broadcasting of television programmes has exceptionally high fixed costs and very low marginal costs – it costs no more to make a programme available to extra people (within range of a given transmitter system). This cost structure has tended to limit the number of firms that enter the broadcasting market (at least, the sectors dealing with commissioning of new programmes and transmission). The result is a highly concentrated industry, with a small number of vertically integrated broadcasters. The lack of competition in this structure can lead to both productive and allocative inefficiencies.

The most controversial market failure involves content. Here, two arguments are usually presented. The first is that, in the absence of direct funding (for example, through a licence fee) or subscription pricing (made possible by conditional access technology), broadcasters must rely on advertising income. With pure advertising funding, a broadcaster's aim is to maximise audience size in order to maximise advertising revenues. Some argue that this form of funding leads to too little diversity in programming (from a social perspective). As Anderson and Coates (2005) and Dukes and Gal-Or (2003) make clear, however, the issue is complicated: they show that advertising-funded broadcasters may *overprovide* programming. But there is support from these studies for the general conclusion that funding through advertising involves inefficiencies.

The second argument is that the consumption of broadcasting content is subject to externalities. Externalities are spillover effects that occur when the social costs and benefits derived from some activity are different from the costs and benefits derived by the producers and consumers of the products. Externalities can be positive or negative and can arise from production and/or consumption. Externalities lead to market failure because the full costs and benefits of an activity are not borne by the same people.

Externalities may exist in broadcasting. Suppose that television has some influence on the behaviour of the people who watch it. If viewing violent programmes tends to make people more violent, then the negative effect of more violence in society will not necessarily be factored in correctly by programme makers, whose objective may be to maximise the size of the viewing audience rather than pursuing the wider social good. Typically, markets overproduce activities that involve negative externalities. Similarly, certain types of programming might help to induce greater tolerance and inclusiveness, constructive engagement in the democratic process, 'network' externalities (see, for example, Brookes 2004) and other behaviour that are beneficial to society as a whole. The positive externalities involved are unlikely to be incorporated fully by broadcasters when making commissioning and transmission decisions. Typically, markets underproduce activities that involve positive externalities.

Ofcom uses the phrase 'citizenship externalities', perhaps to persuade those who object to the market failure rationale for intervention. But this label should not obscure the basic fact that this is a very standard form of market failure. There is nothing new or revolutionary in the concept: it is familiar to A-level economics students and economists have been thinking about it for over one hundred years. (The term 'external economies' seems to appear first in Alfred Marshall's *Principles of Economics*, published in 1890.) The value of seeing Ofcom's 'citizenship externality' as just another type of externality is that it allows the body of work developed by economists over many years to be brought to bear on the problem. Broadcasting in the UK is not the only market ever to suffer from externalities. The precise form of the externalities may be particular to UK broadcasting (perhaps that is all that the qualifier 'citizenship' is meant to mean). But the general inefficiencies arising from externalities have been encountered in fields as disparate as the environment, education, health and marriage.

It is often stated that broadcasting is a 'merit good'. In the case of a merit good, society deems that the good is undervalued by consumers in normal market exchanges. Exactly *why* the good is undervalued does not have to be specified, and will anyway depend on the case in question. More often than not, the argument is that individuals are imperfectly informed about the benefits from consuming the good. This lies behind making school education compulsory for children. For adults, the Davies report (p. 203) stated:

> [T]elevision has the capacity either to restrict or expand the knowledge, experience and imagination of individuals. If all television is provided via the free market, there is a danger that consumers will under-invest in the development of their own tastes, experience and capacity to comprehend because it is only in retrospect that the benefits of such investment become apparent.

This is a tricky line of argument. When the notion of a merit good is clearly defined, the argument smacks of paternalism; when it is not, the argument is indistinguishable from market failure through externalities.

Public Intervention in the Digital World

These, then, are the standard reasons given for intervention in broadcasting. How do these reasons stand up to the onset of digital broadcasting? Ofcom's view is, largely, that most of the market failures will be eliminated.

The arguments go, briefly, as follows. Digitisation means that broadcast signals can easily be encrypted; only viewers who have been given a 'key' (for example, a viewing card or PIN number) are able to decrypt the signal and watch the transmission. If they could not encrypt their signals, pay-TV providers would struggle to make any money. But they can, and they do. Technically, this means that broadcasting is no longer a pure public good: while it is still non-rivalrous in consumption, it is no longer necessarily non-excludable.

What about market concentration? The economies of scale in broadcasting are still there. New digital technology has helped to reduce programme production costs significantly. Rather than recording on to a tape or DVD, programmes filmed digitally can be saved straight on to a computer hard disk. Once there, they can be transferred easily to the many different units around the country that are involved in production. (Previously, a man in a van had to drive the tapes or DVDs to their destination.) Other tasks, such as retrieval of information and sub-titling, is also easier digitally. But even so, the fixed costs of programming and broadcasting are still enormous compared to the marginal costs.

Spectrum scarcity, on the other hand, which restricted the number of terrestrial analogue channels in the UK to five, is largely a thing of the past. The better use of the spectrum that digitisation allows means that the number of channels is, if not limitless, then enough to be getting on with. This means that while the number of firms that commission original programming and run broadcast facilities may remain small, the number of firms involved in bundling old programmes into packages to appeal to various audience groups (such as comedy, cooking, DIY (do-it-yourself) and home improvement) can be very large. The amount of competition at the level of channels can be very large, even if the amount of competition in commissioning is limited by the large costs involved.

Ofcom also argues that advertising-funded programming will become more diverse. The proliferation of channels allowed by digital technology means that niche audiences can be targeted by broadcasters, and hence advertisers. There is no evidence (either theoretical or empirical) that the outcome will be efficient in any sense; but, Ofcom argues, at least the range of programming available should broaden.

That leaves externalities and merit goods. These sources of market failure, if they exist, are unaffected by whether our TV pictures get to us by analogue or digitally: what matters is what happens when they get there. Ofcom has identified these market failures, which it summarises in the phrase 'citizen externality', as the core of continued intervention in broadcasting. To quote from the PSB Phase 1 report, Ofcom's argument is that 'programming that has wider social value, and which most of us would like to see provided, would either be under-provided or not provided at all [by an unregulated market]' (p. 75 of the Phase 1 report). Hence Ofcom concludes that 'the rationale for a continued investment in PSB is that only with such an intervention would TV serve UK citizens adequately' (p. 75).[2]

As the rationale for intervention changes due to digitisation, so the sustainability of the current regulatory regime becomes questionable. The current public service broadcasters in the UK receive, in exchange for their PSB obligations, privileged access to spectrum. As the audience using the analogue spectrum declines, the value of this privileged access will decrease until, eventually, it will fall below the costs of meeting public service obligations. Ofcom estimates that ITV1, and channels 4 and 5 currently receive approximately £400 million a year in implicit subsidies for PSB. By the time that the analogue broadcasting signal is switched off, these implicit subsidies will be close to zero. If PSB is to be maintained and strengthened, Ofcom argues, then a new arrangement must be devised.

In summary, Ofcom has concluded that the broadcasting market fails due to externalities; and that explicit funding (rather than implicit, through gifted spectrum) must be provided to correct the market failure. To quote from the Phase 1 report:

> As digital take-up progresses, with multichannel provision, encryption systems and a wide variety of different models of consumption, the market failures associated with consumers not being able to watch the programmes they would willingly buy are diminishing fast. We believe that in the future, public service broadcasting will no longer be needed to ensure consumers can buy and watch their own choice of programming.
>
> There may remain concerns about the market power of some broadcasters, but in our view these are better dealt with by the application of competition law than through a large public intervention. ...
>
> Bridging the shortfall between what a well-functioning broadcasting market would provide and the wider ambitions of UK citizens is our definition of the enduring purposes of public service broadcasting. It constitutes a continuing rationale for PSB, one which, for the time being, retains widespread public support. (p. 9, Phase 1 report)

The Evidence: How Important are Externalities?

Public funding of broadcasting in the UK comes to not far off one day's GDP. Can the market failures identified in the previous section justify this degree of intervention? In particular, are externalities really that large? In this section, I argue that there is little evidence that externalities are that important. So, if Ofcom comes to rely on this argument alone to justify PSB, it is likely that the scale of funding, particularly of the BBC, will come under increasing pressure. But there are still, potentially, grounds for significant intervention in broadcasting, due to the high valuations that most individuals attach to television; and the non-rivalrous nature of broadcasting, even in the digital era.

What is the evidence that externalities are worth £3 billion per annum? How large are externalities in broadcasting? There is very little evidence on this question, which is perhaps why so much pure theory is written. (For example, Brookes (2004) contains no quantitative measure of the extent to which a free market in broadcasting would underproduce social capital.) This measurement question is difficult to answer, of course, since the usual places that economists would look (that is, markets) are largely missing. To answer the question 'How important do individuals think X is?', an economist will usually look at a market in which X is traded to see what price has been paid. In a competitive market, the prevailing price will equal the willingness to pay of the marginal individual who buys X, and the incremental cost of the marginal seller of X. In a sense which the economic theory behind competitive markets makes precise, the price measures the value of X. When there is no, or an imperfect market for X (because, say, X is an externality, such as 'social values' or 'diversity'), there is no such (reliable) measure of value.

I am aware of three possible sources that can be used to form a rough estimate. The first is the Mori analysis commissioned by Ofcom in the Phase 2 report. The primary objective of the study was to examine '[h]ow much value (both monetary and evaluative) viewers place upon PSB output once costs are attached, within a framework of benefit to society as a whole rather than individual personal preference'. Six groups of 20–25 participants were asked to evaluate five different programming schedules, which varied according to the degree of 'public serviceness'. Participants were first asked to rank the five schedules according to their own, personal preference, with no information given about the price of the schedule. They were then asked to rank the schedules, again with no price information, based on their opinions about what would be the best schedule for society. Then varying degrees of price information were given, including the actual price of the schedules, in terms of an increase or decrease in the licence fee.

The analysis contains a great deal of interesting data, but falls short of giving enough information to assess the monetary value of externalities. The only instance when the participants were asked for their personal (rather than their social) preference was at the outset, without price information attached. The majority of participants chose what was in fact the least-cost schedule with the lowest degree of 'public serviceness'. This schedule would require an annual licence fee of £91. In contrast, a weak majority of participants chose a schedule with a licence fee of £121 (that is, the same as the current fee), as the socially preferred schedule when price information was given. These figures suggest, but only very vaguely, an externality value (the difference between personal and social valuations) of £30 per annum. Put differently, approximately one-quarter of the current licence fee can be attributed to externalities; the remaining three-quarters relates to the personal preferences of selfish individuals. This calculation should be treated with extreme caution, however. The figure of £91 is unlikely to be an accurate measure of personal valuations, since at that stage of the survey, the participants did not know the schedule prices. In addition, there are too few data points to form accurate or precise estimates.

A second attempt to estimate the values of externalities uses the data from the recent BBC and Human Capital (2004) report. In this analysis, the BBC looks to measure its value. Some 1136 people were asked to state their opinions about the total, social value of the BBC, while a separate sample of 1121 people were asked to state the value of the BBC to consumers only. For the first sample, the alternative was total closure of the BBC; for the second sample, the alternative was exclusion from watching the BBC. Hence, any calculations relate to the externalities generated by the BBC alone, rather than (public service) broadcasting more generally. The study found that, on average, the 'consumer value' of the BBC was between £220 and £224 per annum, while the 'social value' was between £248 and £282 per annum. (The ranges come from different methods of eliciting valuations from survey participants.) The average value of externalities – the gap between private and social values – was therefore between £28 and £58 per annum; or between 11 and 21 per cent of social value.

Again, there are obvious holes in this calculation. In particular, it identifies the BBC's current scheduling as being the appropriate public service broadcasting benchmark, from which the gap between private and social values can be measured. This restricts the choices of the survey participants, who might, for example, choose two different schedules for their private and social preferences. It is not possible to say, however, whether this leads to an under- or overestimate of the value of externalities in this calculation.

One last attempt to arrive at the size of broadcasting externalities comes from a study of the Canadian Broadcasting Corporation (CBC) by Finn et al. (2003). These authors used contingent valuation and contingent choice techniques[3] to estimate use and non-use values of the programming services provided by the CBC. They received 577 responses from a mail-survey sample of 2404 households conducted in September 1998. They estimated a total household value for the CBC of $5.03 per household. Of this, $3.70 was the value of the average respondent's own household having access, and $1.33 was the value to the average household of other Canadian households having access to the services. This represents an aggregated yearly value of $664 million for the total value of the CBC, with about $488 million (or

74 per cent) coming from private effects and $175 million (or 26 per cent) coming from external effects.

There are major problems with all of these calculations and they should all be treated with great caution. One clear message, then, is that more work needs to be done to quantify externalities. But from these calculations, there is limited evidence that externalities are all that large in broadcasting. Private (or consumer) valuations appear to make up between 75 and 90 per cent of social valuations. If these figures are remotely correct, then they suggest that a large portion of the funding of broadcasting can be left to the free market meeting the demands of consumers. Additional funding to meet 'citizens' needs' would be a relatively modest component of the total.

In fact, I do think that there are grounds for more extensive intervention in broadcasting, precisely because individuals' private valuations for television are so large. The basic point can be seen in a simple example. The example involves just two individuals. I shall use figures from the BBC/Human Capital study; and from that study, the 'service valuation' and 'national voting method' figures for private and social values.[4] Figure 5.1 reproduces figure 8 in the BBC/Digital World report. The figure shows for example, that a third of respondents state a private willingness to pay of £20 per month that is, £240 annually (around twice the current licence fee) for BBC services. The median private willingness to pay is around £15 per month, that is, 50 per cent more than the current licence fee. The figure also shows the corresponding social willingness-to-pay statements, which, on the whole, are quite similar.

To convert these data for my two-person example, consider the top 25 and 75 per cent of participants, in terms of stated willingness to pay. A simple calculation shows that the top 25 per cent of participants, in terms of stated willingness to pay, have a private valuation of at least £293 per annum, and a social valuation of at least £329 per annum. The top 75 per cent of participants, in terms of stated willingness to pay, have a private valuation of at least £123 per annum, and a social valuation of at least £137 per annum.

So, suppose that person A's private valuation of the schedule is £293, and person B's is £123; and that their social valuations are £329 and £137. Table 5.1 shows the socially efficient and private provision outcomes, according to the cost of providing the programming schedule.

As the table makes clear, the free market (private provision) is inefficient whenever the cost is between £294 and £329, or between £124 and £137. Generally, too few people are provided with programming, because the free market does not incorporate the (positive) externalities.

This example assumed implicitly that broadcasting is a private good: both excludable and rivalrous. But in fact, even in the digital era, broadcasting is

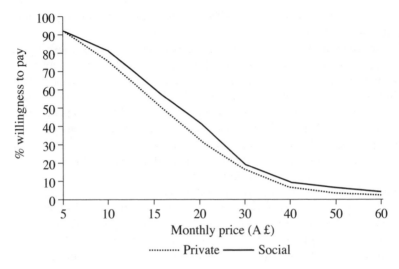

Source: BBC/Digital World study.

Figure 5.1   Private and social willingness to pay

non-rivalrous. To see the consequence of this, suppose that externalities are zero; but note now that the social valuation from the programming schedule is the *sum* of the private values, that is, the social valuation is £416.

Table 5.1   Social and private provision with externalities

Cost per person (£)	Efficient provision: to	Private provision: to	Inefficiency (£)
Over 329	No-one	No-one	0
294–329	A	No-one	0–35
138–293	A	A	0
124–137	A and B	A	0–13
Less than 120	A and B	A and B	0

Table 5.2 shows the socially efficient and private provision outcomes in this case.

Inefficiency is greater in this case, in two senses: (i) when inefficiency occurs, its value is greater; (ii) the range of costs over which inefficiency occurs is wider. Why is this the case? The reason is that private valuations are much larger than the value of externalities. In the first example, externalities are worth £36 for person A and £14 for person B. In the example, the inefficiency is never greater than the externality experienced by an individual; and hence the inefficiency is never greater than £36. In the second example, social and private valuations differ by as much as the private valuation of person B; since this is large (£123), the inefficiency is large.

Table 5.2   Social and private provision with non-rivalry

Cost (£)	Efficient provision: to	Private provision: to	Inefficiency (£)
Over 416	No-one	No-one	0
294–416	A and B	No-one	0–122
247–293	A and B	A	123
Less than 247	A and B	A and B	0

It is often argued that the non-rivalry argument has no bite, since there are many industries in which it is relatively costless to supply additional individuals. For example, David Elstein (2004) has noted:

> The marginal cost of producing an extra copy of a newspaper is virtually zero, yet unsold copies of newspapers with a cover price are not given away. At the end of the day, newsagents wrap them up and return them to the publishers, who pulp them rather than hand them out. Likewise, empty cinema seats are not offered to freeloaders, just because the cash demand for them has been exhausted and they would otherwise go to waste.

This is a reasonable point, and one that can only be answered fully by appealing to evidence. The trade-offs are the following. Intervention has costs, inevitably. For example, collecting the mandatory licence fee costs around £120 million per annum; running a regulator is not cheap. These costs have to be compared to the benefits from intervention: the value of the inefficiencies which are corrected. I have argued that the inefficiency that arises from non-rivalry in broadcasting is large, since individuals' valuations appear to be large. This means that the gap between the social value (that is, the sum of all private values) and private values is significant. Other markets may also have non-rivalrous features (or at least, a low marginal cost). The question then is: how large are private valuations? In the example that I gave above, if the private value of person B is £20 rather than £123, then the extent of inefficiency is a lot less. If these valuations described, for example, the movie market, then the conclusion may well be that movies should be provided by an unregulated free market. For other markets with higher individual (and hence total) valuations (broadcasting, for example?), intervention may be justified.

It is tempting to conclude that all of this is beside the point. Provided that there is some sort of market failure, there is a continued rationale for intervention in broadcasting. But identifying the source of the market failure has implications for the scale and future of intervention. To justify the scale of intervention, it is necessary to quantify the size of the market failure. If the market failure is small, then it will be difficult in the long run to maintain the position that intervention is necessary: that inefficiencies outweigh the inevitable costs of regulation.

In addition, intervention can be rendered obsolete. For example, if new technology allows broadcasters to price discriminate more effectively, then they may be able to mitigate the market failure that arises through non-rivalry. In the limit, when price discrimination is perfect, inefficiency can be eliminated altogether. This limit can rarely be met in practice, and the question of how much of the efficiency gap can be closed by price discrimination is open. In contrast, technology is less likely to eliminate externalities (which may be why Ofcom finds them to be so important).

Ofcom's Phase 2 Proposals

In this section, I shall take the scale of intervention in broadcasting as given, and consider how intervention should be structured: especially, how much competition should there be for public service funding? The proposals set out by Ofcom in Phase 2 of its review are quite detailed. I want to concentrate on just one aspect of them (as it happens, the aspect that seems to be attracting the most attention): the creation of a Public Service Publisher (PSP). In summary, Ofcom proposes to leave the BBC largely intact (subject to possible asset transfers to Channel 4). The budget of the PSP will be approximately £300 million per annum. With this budget, the PSP will commission and distribute content on other digital distribution systems such as broadband, networked personal video recorders (PVRs), mobile networks as well as cable, satellite and digital terrestrial broadcasting. The right to set up and run the PSP would be awarded after competition between rival organisations; the right to operate the PSP will be granted for a set period of up to 10 years. Only the BBC is barred from gaining the franchise; and the winner will have to demonstrate clear separation between its PSP and other (commercial) activities. The review makes some suggestions about how the PSP can be funded (from general taxation, a £12 supplement to the licence fee, or a levy on other broadcasters), but the final decision on this is beyond Ofcom's control.[5]

Is this degree of funding contestability sufficient? In its Phase 2 report, Ofcom weighed up the pros and cons of establishing a fully contestable PSB fund. On the pro side, Ofcom states that:

- it maximises the amount of competition for PSB provision because competition occurs between many suppliers and on a continuous basis;
- the high degree of competition for funding should add to the quality of PSB programming and should also drive innovation; and
- the central funding body would be able to use the bidding process to exercise control over costs and to avoid duplication, derivative PSB programming and aggressive scheduling.

On the con side, Ofcom notes that:

- the introduction of a PBA [Public Broadcasting Authority] could duplicate many costs;
- multiple commissioners in different organisations would reduce the chance that innovative programmes are funded because only safer programmes would stand a reasonable chance of receiving approval from both organisations;
- PSB programming would become fragmented across a wide range of channels, making it harder for viewers to find and diminishing its contribution to PSB purposes;
- it would be difficult to secure agreement with commercial channels for the distribution of programming that was not a good fit with the rest of their schedules; and
- there would be a serious risk that the efficiency of funding would be compromised by subsidising content that would have been produced anyway.

Ofcom therefore concludes that 'the risks in establishing a fully contestable PSB fund outweigh the potential benefits' (pp. 60–61, Phase 2 report). This judgement is backed up by New Zealand's not-entirely-successful experience of running an 'arts council of the air'. Instead, Ofcom opts for an approach 'that blends the two approaches above by introducing competition for PSB funding for the first time, but attempts to minimise the bureaucracy and deadweight costs associated with programme-by-programme contestable funding and the lack of a distribution mechanism' (p. 63), through the creation of the PSP.

Let me start first by putting in some sort of context the structure that Ofcom is proposing for PSB funding. Each point in Figure 5.2 represents a different communications industry. For each industry, the number of firms in the industry is shown on the horizontal axis; the 'concentration index' (technically, the Herfindahl index) is shown on the vertical axis. The top left-hand corner corresponds to a pure monopoly: one firm with a 100 per cent market share. The bottom right-hand corner corresponds (roughly) to a perfectly competitive industry: a large number of firms (set to 100 in the figure) each with a very small market share. Typically, industry structures that lie closer to the bottom right are preferred by policy makers to those closer to the top left. For example, the US Department of Justice (DOJ) views concentration indices between 0.1 and 0.18 to indicate 'moderate' concentration; and indices above 0.18 to indicate concentration. The figure shows that the newspaper and ISP[6] market is moderately competitive; all other industries in the figure are highly concentrated. Compared to the other industries, Ofcom's proposal for the structure of PSB funding is acutely concentrated.

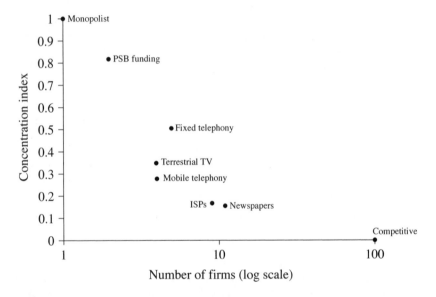

Figure 5.2   Industry structure for different communication sectors

In the light of this observation, I want to raise two questions in this section:

1. What are the arguments for choosing a 90/10 structure (in which the BBC receives £3 billion per annum and the PSP £300 million per annum)? How should alternative splits (for example, 75/25, or £2.5 billion and £800 million) be evaluated?
2. Should the roles of both the BBC and the PSP be opened to competition?

One limitation of Ofcom's Phase 2 report is that it provides no framework for answering these two questions.

Ofcom sees increased innovation as one of the major benefits of competition. The Phase 2 report makes this view explicit: 'the lack of competition in broadcasting PSB programming risks leading to complacency, inefficient production, lack of innovation, lower quality programming, a narrowing of perspectives and the loss of PSB programming for certain groups' (p. 59). In a recent speech, David Currie (2004) has stated that the PSP 'has to do enough, as a catalyst, to keep the BBC on its mettle and act as a continuing spur to innovation in the BBC and Channel 4'.

Figure 5.3 illustrates the model of competition in innovation that is implicit in this statement. The vertical axis measures the BBC's 'effort' or spending on innovation; the horizontal axis measures the PSP's innovation effort. The BBC is assumed to respond to innovative effort by the PSP by increasing its own effort. Hence the dotted line, which represents the BBC's choice of effort, slopes upward: the greater the PSP's effort, the more the BBC responds with higher effort. A similar point holds for the PSP; when the BBC exerts more innovative effort, the PSP responds by also making more effort. The PSP's reaction to the BBC's effort level is shown as the dashed line. When there is no PSP, the BBC makes some effort toward innovation: the point is marked 'monopoly effort'. Alternatively, when the BBC faces a well-funded PSP, the final outcome of competition in innovation is for the BBC to exert the 'competitive effort 1'. Combined with the PSP's effort level, the result (point 1 in the figure) is substantially more effort in total than the monopoly level. This, then, is the basic argument behind Ofcom's belief in competition spurring innovation.

The same figure can be used to assess the implications of awarding different budgets to the BBC and the PSP. In the figure, I have assumed that the PSP's funding of £300 million (marked by the thick black line) is so low that it lies below the 'competitive effort 1' level that a PSP with large funding would expend. With this funding constraint, the BBC exerts less effort: its effort level falls from 'competitive effort 1' to 'competitive effort 2'. And obviously, the PSP's effort level falls, from 'competitive effort 1' to the budget level. The total amount of innovative effort falls.

There are then two cases to consider. In the first, the combined funding of the BBC and the PSP is large enough to support point 1. In this case, the total amount of innovative effort can be increased by increasing the PSP's funding at the expense of the BBC. In the second case, the combined funding is not enough to meet the efforts required at point 1. In this case, reallocation of funding between the BBC and the PSP makes no difference to the amount of innovation.

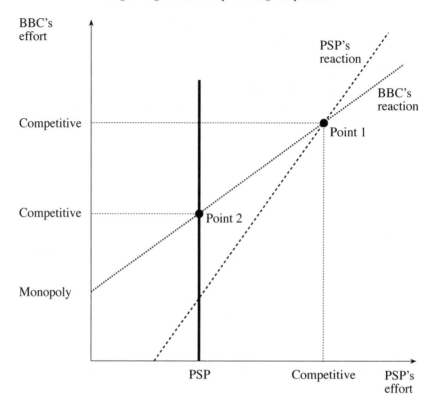

Figure 5.3   Competition and innovation

Finally, it may be that a small amount of competition induces a large increase in effort levels. (In Figure 5.3, this means that, for example, the BBC's choice of effort is very steeply sloped.) And it may be that the amount of innovation that occurs when the PSP's budget constraint bites is enough: the benefits from the extra effort to get to higher effort levels marked '1' may be small. These are questions that require quantitative answers, for example, assessments of how responsive broadcasters are to rivals' innovations. But the basic point remains: making the funding of the two organisations more equal will not decrease the amount of innovation, and may well increase it.

Should funding be allocated directly to the BBC, which is then subject to regulation that describes the functions that it performs and the services that it supplies? Or should other organisations be able to bid to perform the functions and supply the services of the BBC? The basic message of economic theory is clear: competition outperforms regulation. More explicitly, the competitive process does a better job of revealing the organisation that can provide the services more efficiently; and ensure that the services are provided at lower cost to the taxpayer. In order to see why this is the case, it is helpful to view the funding of PSB as a procurement exercise, in which the identity of the public service broadcaster and the amount of funding it is awarded is to be determined. The exercise can be conducted in one of two ways: either by negotiation with a single organisation (such as the BBC); or by allocating the role to the organisation that declares that it can perform the role for the lowest amount of funding. Viewed in this way, the analysis of Bulow and Klemperer (1996) tells us what to do. Bulow and Klemperer show that a seller of an object can typically do better by attracting one more bidder into an auction, than it can by restricting the number of buyers and negotiating with the smaller number.[7] Their result suggests that the value of negotiating skill is small relative to the value of additional competition. Specifically, negotiation with the BBC over the level of the licence fee will cost licence payers more than allowing competition between the BBC and just one other organisation for the supply of the BBC's output. And the more serious bidders there are for the BBC's position, the greater the benefit to licence payers. This argument lies behind statutes such as the Federal Acquisition Regulations (FAR) in the US, which strongly favour the use of auctions in public sector procurement.

The next step is to evaluate the option of splitting the total PSB funding into more than two (that is, £3 billion to the BBC, £300 million to the PSP) units, with competitive bidding for each unit. There are, of course, many issues to be addressed in thinking about this option. How many units? How big, in terms of funding, should each unit be? What obligations should be attached to each unit? (For example, should one unit be reserved for news and current affairs, another for drama, and so on; or would this limit cross-genre innovation?) But some progress can be made thinking about the issue. The more general problem, to which this belongs, is that of designing *package auctions*: competitive bidding situations in which the seller/procurer must decide not only how to sell to/buy from and for how much, but also how many units to sell/buy. This problem is familiar from the sale of spectrum, where an important sales decision is how many licences of what size to make available for sale. Milgrom (2004) analyses the trade-offs in the packaging decision. A key factor is whether there are *complementarities* between units. For example, are there benefits to broadcasters to providing both current affairs and drama (if units are defined by programming genre)? Or more generally, to providing more hours or programming rather than less? There are several reasons why this might be so. There may be economies of scale or scope in broadcasting, so that having two units of provision rather than one reduces average costs.

There may be learning-by-doing effects, where lessons learned, for example, in drama can be used to improve, for example, documentaries. Milgrom shows that offering a larger number of units when some bidders find some unit complementary creates an 'exposure problem' that can depress bidding. (The exposure problem comes about when a bidder fails to win the units that it most wants, and ends up bidding more aggressively on a complementary unit that it does not value all that highly.) Offering units in large packages, however, can make it hard for small bidders to participate, limiting the amount of competition for the units. In order to determine the optimal number of units, or equivalently the right amount of packaging, these two factors have to be quantified and balanced.

These recent advances in auction theory provide very useful frameworks for thinking about the issue of procuring PSB television; and they also point to some strong conclusions about the benefit of more competition. Of course, there are important qualifications to be made. Bajari et al. (2003) test Bulow and Klemperer's theoretical prediction – that competition is better than negotiation – using data on private sector contracts (the building construction industry in Northern California from 1995–2001). They present three findings. First, more complicated projects are more likely to be awarded by negotiation than by auction. Second, auctions are used more when contractors have more idle capacity (that is, there are more potential bidders). Third, negotiated projects tend to be awarded to larger, more experienced contractors. Their work suggests a number of potential limitations to the use of auctions. Auctions perform poorly when projects are complex, contractual design is incomplete and there are few available bidders. And so they find that in the private sector, more complicated projects are more likely to be awarded by negotiation than by auction. They also find that auctions stifle communication between buyers and the sellers, preventing the buyer from using the contractor's expertise when designing the project.

These arguments provide partial support for an approach that splits PSB funding. Recognising the difficulties (noted earlier) in describing PSB, some part of funding can be allocated directly to an organisation (such as the BBC), with negotiation over the scale of funding and the services to be supplied. Recognising the benefits of competition, some part of funding should be made contestable, to ensure that PSB is supplied by the most efficient provider to the benefit of licence payers. Ofcom's proposal has the merit of this pragmatic mixture. But, as I have tried to show, these issues need to be balanced within an explicit theoretical framework that then allows evidence to be collected to assess where the balance should be struck.

THE TELECOMMUNICATIONS STRATEGIC REVIEW

A second major task for Ofcom is a strategic review of the telecommunications market. The Phase 1 report, published in April 2004, examined the current position and prospects for the telecoms sector. In that report, Ofcom posed five general questions for the review:

1. What are the key attributes of a well-functioning market?
2. Where can effective and sustainable competition be achieved?
3. Is there scope significantly to reduce regulation?
4. How can the regulatory framework encourage efficient and timely investment in next-generation networks?
5. Are structural or operational separation of British Telecom (BT) or the delivery of full functional equivalence still relevant questions?

(There were a further 16 questions, specific to the Phase 1 report.)

The Phase 2 report, due to be published in early September 2004, has yet to appear.[8] Consequently, this section is shorter than the previous one. In the rest of the section, I argue that a key challenge for Ofcom is to develop policy that makes compatible the very different approaches of competition policy and telecommunications regulation. The differences between these two approaches are nowhere clearer than in their treatment of access. I consider three topics: the local loop; bottlenecks; and vertical integration and separation.

Natural Monopoly and the Local Loop

Regulation of telecommunications is motivated by the presence of market failures, particularly large fixed and sunk costs that lead to natural monopoly. (Externalities and public good provision also arise, in the form of universal service.) Economies of scale are an inverse function of consumers served per line, and so should be strongest in the local part of the network where, in the extreme, there is a single consumer per line. More generally, the lower the network density and the shorter the call distance, the more likely it is that natural monopoly prevails.

Given the familiarity of this argument, it is surprising how little hard evidence there is of the technological conditions required for the existence of natural monopoly. Fuss and Waverman (2002) provide a comprehensive survey of econometric analysis of telecommunication cost functions. (See also Gasmi et al. (2002), chapter 3, for a review of econometric studies of local exchange networks.) They find that the evidence about costs of long-distance services, where natural monopoly is least likely to prevail, is mixed: some studies find increasing returns to scale in this part of the network; others find constant returns to scale. Studies of local services are correspondingly more undecided. (See Appendix 1 of Fuss and Waverman.) Fuss and Waverman argue that this situation arises due to lack of adequate data and suitable econometric technique. Existing studies typically concentrate on production of a single firm (usually, AT&T in the US); and concentrate on whether there are scale economies in the aggregate, across all services. A key question, however, is whether there are scale economies in individual services (that is, long-distance or local). Moreover, since competitive provision levels are likely to be quite different from monopoly levels, it is unreliable to draw inferences from observed data about costs when there are multiple service providers. These criticisms lead Fuss and Waverman to conclude that 'econometric evidence of the type surveyed in this chapter should not, and has appeared not to, influence regulators' decisions regarding permissible market structures' (p. 170).

An alternative approach, pioneered by Gasmi et al. (2002), uses a combination of engineering and econometric analysis to tackle the question of whether and where natural monopoly exists. In this approach, an engineering model of a local exchange network is allied to an economic model of regulation and firm behaviour to assess the impact of alternative regulatory approaches. Their cost proxy LECOM model is used in simulations of different networks to generate cost (pseudo-)data; these data are then used to estimate a translog functional form to give a smooth representation of the telecommunications cost function. Gasmi et al.'s model displays economies of scope for switched services; but returns dis-economies of scope for other parts of the local exchange network. As they note, however, the engineering approach does not model labour inputs (such as managerial effort and expertise) very satisfactorily. In addition, the model is static, omitting important forward-looking aspects of technology choices.

Finally, Correa (2003) analyses whether scale economies exist in the UK telcommunications industry. She includes data on fixed-link public (that is, copper-wire-based), cable and mobile companies – all operators who had local loop or access infrastructure – over the 1990–97 period. Analysis of this unbalanced panel (rather than just time-series) data indicates that there are overall constant returns to scale in the fixed and cable sectors. Her results suggest that there are no significant economies of scale in the local loop in the UK.

So, there is no conclusive econometric evidence of natural monopoly in telecommunications networks. But market outcomes seem to provide clear guidance: despite deregulation in a great many countries, with many different policy regimes, incumbent firms have remained dominant in most markets, and in nearly all local telephony markets. Entry in the latter, where it has occurred at all, is very slow. But, as Woroch (2002) points out, the reason for this may not be technological, but strategic. Economies of scale and scope may still exist at the local level; but there are new technologies that have cost characteristics that may support competition. What remains unchanged, however, is the possibility that incumbent suppliers enjoy strategic advantages that tend to fortify any initial advantage they have acquired.

Hence the local loop continues to be one of the most problematic parts for telecoms regulation. It is the area that has been most resistant to the introduction of competition, and the area that exposes most clearly regulators' attitudes towards the balance between competition and regulation. There are two major policy questions:

1. Is competition between infrastructure providers in the local loop necessary for effective competition in the telecommunications market?
2. Does a lack of competition in the local loop lead to lack of competition in downstream markets?

Infrastructure competition is typically contrasted with service competition (that is, competition between providers of services that all make use of the same monopolistic network). The question is then: which of these forms of competition is to be preferred? The dilemma is summarised well in Bergman et al. (1998), (p. 38–9):

> Where it is thought that natural monopoly elements are important, it is often argued that competition is best accommodated via service providers being granted access to a monopoly network infrastructure. Although this type of competition may deliver benefits in the short run as prices move closer to costs, it may undermine *ex ante* investment incentives on the part of infrastructure firms, particularly if access is granted on relatively favorable terms. The diminished significance of natural monopoly elements in network industries means that competition is now recognized to be a more powerful means of achieving both efficiency and equity objectives than monopoly. Differences in opinion about the form competition should take do arise, however. If policy makers encourage competition via service providers, terms of access must be set so as not to undermine *ex ante* investment incentives. This is especially important in dynamic network industries like telecoms.

Unsurprisingly, opinions differ. Broadly speaking, Oftel (Office of Telecommunications) was of the view that only infrastructure competition would bring benefits to consumers. Oftel therefore implemented a policy in line with this view: access to existing infrastructure in the UK has been relatively difficult, or expensive, so that market players have had an incentive to construct alternative infrastructure. In the US, on the other hand, there has been strong reliance on service competition. There, access to existing networks has been easy (because of unbundling requirements, the entrants pay only for what they use) and relatively cheap (that is, it is cost based and the costs are calculated in a favourable way). These two approaches essentially take opposite views on whether competition requires that the incumbent's bottleneck facilities be bypassed or shared. The regulatory systems of other countries lie between these two extremes, and there is considerable variety in approach.

There have been few empirical studies of how access requirements affect the incentives to invest in facilities. Most recently, Crandall et al. (2004) argue that resale and unbundling does not seem to have acted as a stepping stone for new entrants to get a start in the market, followed by a build-out of their own facilities. The authors find that facilities-based line growth relative to unbundled network element (UNE) growth is faster in US states where the cost of UNEs is relatively high. This finding does not rule out altogether the possibility that entrant networks are in a transition stage, currently renting with a view to investing in facilities later. But, given the amount of time over which unbundling has been mandated in the US, this possibility is becoming increasingly unlikely. Eisner and Lehman (2001) conclude that each one dollar increase in the statewide average UNE rate results in 3741 new competitive local exchange carrier (CLEC) facilities-based lines. (Bourreau and Dogan (2004) give a theoretical explanation of these findings.) On the other hand, Chang et al. (2003) find that a lower access price promotes greater deployment of digital technology among US incumbent local exchange carriers. Hence they find that access regulation affects investment decisions, although in this case, it is the investment of incumbents, rather than entrants, that is investigated.

Similarly, there is little empirical work on whether competition in local loop and downstream markets is related. Faulhaber (2003) analyses intrastate long-distance services in the US to assess this hypothesis. Following the restructuring of AT&T, Regional Bell Operating Companies (RBOCs) are restricted to telephone operations within Local Access and Transport Areas (LATAs) boundaries. All traffic between LATAs (interLATA traffic) has to be handed off to an interexchange carrier (IXC).[9] But RBOCs are permitted to carry intrastate intraLATA long-distance calls. Faulhaber (2003) finds that for intrastate long-distance calls, in the intraLATA markets in which RBOCs were permitted to compete, there was little entry by non-incumbent IXCs (despite various regulatory attempts to prevent discrimination by RBOCs against IXC rivals). In the interLATA markets, in which RBOCs were not permitted to compete, competition was implemented almost as soon as equal access became available. In short, Faulhaber finds that competition in long-distance markets is less successful when an incumbent is allowed to operate in the (potentially) competitive market.

This empirical evidence is not encouraging for Ofcom. There is no conclusive evidence of natural monopoly, even in the local loop. Economies of scale and scope inherent in networks have not vanished. But the strategic dominance of incumbents is an equally likely explanation of continued concentration in the local loop. The evidence also suggests that regulation mandating local loop unbundling may be ineffective in developing local loop competition. And it suggests that the presence of a vertically integrated incumbent in a downstream market can limit competition in that market.

These findings stop short of forming a policy conclusion, primarily because they say nothing about the consequences of vertical relationships between the local loop and downstream markets. In order to reach a policy conclusion, it is useful at this point to step away from the specific issue of the local loop, and consider the broader class of situations to which it belongs.

Bottlenecks

The local loop in fixed-line telephony is one example of a more general issue in telecoms – the problem of bottlenecks: the market power associated with them, the social welfare losses that occur due to market power, and the appropriate regulation of the price and other terms of access to the bottleneck. In this section, I discuss two issues: what creates a bottleneck? And what are the policy approaches to them?

What exactly is a bottleneck? An engineering definition is that it is a system capacity constraint that may result in reduced data flow during peak load conditions. Competition policy uses the notion of an 'essential facility': that is, any input

1. which is deemed necessary for all industry participants to operate in a given industry;
2. which is not easily duplicated; and
3. for which there is no objective reason (such as limited capacity) for the owner to deny access.

There are several versions of the essential facility doctrine, depending on jurisdiction. In the US, the leading essential facilities case is *MCI Communications Corp. v. AT&T* (1983), in which the Seventh Circuit identified four necessary elements:

1. the control of the essential facility by a monopolist;
2. a competitor's inability practically or reasonably to duplicate the essential facility;
3. the denial of the use of the facility to a competitor; and
4. the feasibility of providing the facility.

The European Commission has defined an essential facility as 'a facility or infrastructure, without access to which competitors cannot provide services to their customers, and which cannot be replicated by any reasonable means' (Notice on the Application of the Competition Rules to Access Agreements in the Telecommunications Sector (1998), 5 C.M.L.R. 821, p.838). Under UK competition law, the fundamental characteristics of an essential facility are:

1. competitors must have access to the facility because it is essential for the provision of goods or services in that related market; and
2. it is not economically efficient, or may not be feasible, for new entrants to replicate the facility.

These definitions have been thrown into some doubt by two recent court rulings. In the US, the Supreme Court rejected a refusal-to-deal claim in the case *Verizon v. Trinko* (January 2004). Curtis Trinko, an AT&T customer, filed a class action lawsuit against Verizon Communications. Trinko alleged that Verizon, the incumbent monopoly local service provider in New York City, had filled rivals' (and AT&T's) orders on a discriminatory basis as part of an anti-competitive scheme to discourage customers from becoming or remaining customers of competitive carriers. Trinko alleged that this refusal violated Verizon's obligations under the Telecommunications Act of 1996, and thereby also amounted to anticompetitive and exclusionary conduct. The Supreme Court said:

> Verizon's alleged insufficient assistance in the provision of service to rivals is not a recognized antitrust claim under this Court's existing refusal-to-deal precedents. This conclusion would be unchanged even if we considered to be established law the essential facilities doctrine crafted by some lower courts. We have never recognized such a doctrine and we find no need to recognize it or to repudiate it here.

In Europe, the decision of the European Court of Justice (ECJ) in the 1998 *Bronner* case has set a higher standard for the application of the essential facilities doctrine. The case concerned a claim by an Austrian newspaper publisher, Bronner, that the refusal of its competitor, Mediaprint, to grant

Bronner access to its newspaper home delivery network constituted an abuse of dominance. The Court held that it was necessary to show that:

1. refusal of the service would be likely to eliminate all competition in the daily newspaper market;
2. the refusal was incapable of being objectively justified; and
3. access to the service was indispensable to Bronner's business, in that there was no actual or potential substitute for that home delivery scheme.

The ECJ argued that it was necessary, at least, to establish that it was not economically viable to create a second home-delivery scheme for the distribution of daily newspapers with a circulation comparable to that of the newspapers distributed by the existing scheme. It was not enough to argue that such a scheme would be less advantageous. Hence the ruling emphasises that the essential facilities doctrine is applicable only in exceptional circumstances; and that the purpose of EC competition policy is to protect the state of competition in the market, not individual competitors.

The legal basis of the essential facilities doctrine is, therefore, being questioned by the courts: what does 'necessary' mean? How costly must duplication be before an input is essential? What objective reasons are acceptable for access exclusion by the owner? This in turn raises the fundamental question: is a bottleneck to be defined purely in technological (for example, cost) terms? Is a bottleneck simply a natural monopoly in one market where there are complementarities between markets? What are the causes of bottlenecks? What conditions create them?

Bottlenecks in telecoms often involve infrastructure and hence are caused by scale economies. The classic example is the local loop for narrowband voice telephony; similar arguments are developing for broadband access. See also the Federal Communications Commission's (FCC's) recent orders regarding fibre-to-the curb and fibre-to-the-home loops (FCC 04–248).

But there are other sources of bottlenecks in electronic communication networks. A second source is economies of scale *on the demand side*, that is, network externalities. Consider communication networks involving instant messaging (IM), in which different networks have proprietary and incompatible protocols. Is the names-and-presence directory of each network a bottleneck? In principle, yes: it would be difficult for a competitor to achieve the consumer coordination required to replicate the directory; there is no real cost for the owner to give access to the directory; and a small IM network may need access to a large network's directory in order to be viable. This was the argument of FCC chairman William Kennard, when he said letting the AOL–Time Warner merger go forward without specific IM constraints was 'tantamount to allowing a single entity to control the nation's phone system'. (See also Faulhaber 2002b.) The same argument has been applied in the US to voice mail services and subscriber lists for telephone directories. It is likely to arise in the UK in a number of diverse situations, for example, with mobile networks' portals on 3G; pay-TV; control over content; and conditional access systems.

A more complex situation involves the bottleneck of termination with competing networks. To illustrate this, consider call termination on mobile networks. In this case, there are typically several alternative networks. Access to the network does not, therefore, constitute a bottleneck, since the user can choose between several alternatives and the fixed (and sunk) costs of access for the user are low. But the pricing structure on these networks creates *de facto* bottlenecks. In countries where calls are paid only by the calling party (the calling-party-pays, or CPP, principle), the receiving party has little incentive to change providers when the price of terminating calls goes up. The only way to reach a particular end user is to call and terminate the call on the network to which that user is subscribed. If the end user were paying for receiving the call, it would react to a potential abuse of monopoly power by changing providers; but the fact that it does not pay for that service generates an inelastic demand and an outcome equivalent to a bottleneck. Hence the EU Guidelines allow the potential definition of two separate mobile markets, one for call origination and one for call termination, and recognise the problems of low incentives to compete on prices for terminating traffic. UK regulation has gone further, concluding that call termination on each mobile network is a relevant market where price regulation is needed due to the existence of insufficient competitive pressures.

There are a number of possibilities for the source of the bottleneck in this situation. First, there is some cost to duplicating connection: with mobile networks, most users have one subscription; only one SIM card can be slotted into a phone; multiple SIM card hand-sets are not (yet) on the market. Once a mobile network has been chosen, it is typically costly (in time and effort) to switch supplier; and so users are 'locked in'. But these considerations apply just as well to call origination. Are there factors particular to termination? It has been noted that there is an externality between callers and receivers, so that one side of the call does not take into account fully both the benefits and costs (including the price) incurred by the other side. Under the CPP, this can create incentives for high termination charges: competition shifts towards attracting subscribers; profits from termination are used to subsidise subscription (See, for example, Jeon et al. 2004.)

Finally, and probably most importantly, there is a distortion created by asymmetric regulation. In the case of mobile termination, in most countries the majority of the calls for which termination charges are levied come from fixed network operators (FNOs) rather than from other mobile operators.

In the UK (and many other countries) the termination charges levied by the fixed operators (such as BT) are regulated and capped close to cost. If the mobile operators set their termination charges above cost, and the fixed operators do not, there is a net flow of revenue from the fixed network and its customers to the mobile networks and their customers. This may more than compensate for the loss of business from higher charges. Hence, in these circumstances, high termination charges are potentially profitable for mobile operators. (See Littlechild (2004a) and Jeon et al. (2004) for more on the CPP and receiver pays principle; and Gans and King (2002) for a formal model of this story.)

This digression on call termination bottlenecks on mobile networks has served to highlight a key issue: it is important to identify the *source* of the bottleneck before concluding that a bottleneck exists. Not all bottlenecks are caused by standard economies of scale: some may arise because of demand-side scale economies. The different types of bottleneck have different implications for the form of competition and hence the regulatory approach that should be adopted. (See, for example, Faulhaber 2002a.) But also not every bottleneck is actually a bottleneck. I would argue that the mobile call termination 'bottleneck' is not in fact a bottleneck, but an artefact of particular pricing structures (CPP plus regulated fixed-line termination charges).

How does the notion of essential facility, and the competition law approach to access, relate to telecommunications regulation? The latter is set by the New Regulatory Framework (NRF) for electronic communications networks and services, brought into effect in 2003 by the European Commission. The NRF specifies that, if in a given country a company is found to have significant market power (SMP) in the supply of a service included in the list of wholesale markets, then the national regulatory agency (NRA) may impose on the dominant operator an obligation to provide that service to third parties: '*inter alia*, in situations where the [NRA] considers that denial of access or unreasonable terms and conditions having a similar effect would hinder the emergence of a sustainable competitive market at the retail level, or would not be in the end-user's interest'.[10]

The conditions under which access must be granted in telecommunications are therefore significantly broader than those specified by competition law. (See Oldale and Padilla (2004) for further discussion.) Since a pure bottleneck has, by definition, no good substitutes in use, and cannot be reproduced easily, it is likely to constitute a separate market under the market-definition approach of the Commission's SMP guidelines. It could, therefore, be concluded that any firm with a bottleneck has SMP in the bottleneck market. Hence SMP is central to the granting of access in telecoms networks – in contrast to the essential facilities doctrine, which requires objective justification of the need for access.

Why does this difference between competition policy and telecoms regulation matter? Because it points to the central tension in access: the trade-off between *ex post* competition and *ex ante* innovation incentives. As Advocate General Jacobs stated in the *Bronner* case (quoted by Oldale and Padilla 2004):

> [I]n the long term it is generally pro-competitive and in the interest of consumers to allow a company to retain for its own use facilities which it has developed for the purpose of its business. For example, if access to a production, purchasing or distribution facility were allowed too easily there would be no incentive for a competitor to develop competing facilities. Thus while competition was increased in the short term, it would be reduced in the long term. Moreover, the incentive for a dominant undertaking to invest in efficient facilities would be reduced if its competitors were, upon request, able to share the benefits,. Thus the mere fact that by retaining a facility for its own use a dominant undertaking retains an advantage over a competitor cannot justify requiring access to it.

At the same time, the courts recognise that *ex ante* incentives are relevant only when investment is required to create the bottleneck. There is an important difference between firms which have invested and firms which have obtained the right of using a certain facility without having borne the risk of its creation or having paid for it.

This trade-off is recognised, of course, in telecoms regulation – it is precisely this concern that forces a choice between service- and facilities-based competition (see the previous section on the local loop). It is notable, however, that competition policy tends to come down on the opposite side of the debate to telecoms regulation.

A second area in which competition policy and telecoms regulation differ is in their attitude towards vertical integration.

Separation and Vertical Integration

The Phase 1 Telecommunciations Strategic Review (TSR) report raises explicitly the question of the structural separation of BT. Stephen Carter, Ofcom's chief executive, has referred to this issue as 'elephant in the corner': the perennial question that has hung in the air ever since the start of privatisation of BT in 1984. Despite hopes to the contrary, it has become the question that has generated the most debate. (It is, after all, the most specific and direct of the five questions in the Phase 1 report.)

The arguments for and against vertical separation can be found in many other places, so I do not repeat them here. See Rey et al. (2001) and

Farrell and Weiser (2003) for useful summaries of the arguments; and, for example, Littlechild (2004b) for a recent call for vertical separation. Instead, I should like to look at the question from a slightly different angle: when does a vertically integrated firm have incentives to make an efficient decision towards separation?

If an upstream monopolist, or owner of a bottleneck, chooses not to compete in the downstream market, then it prefers that downstream products – the complements to its product – be supplied cheaply, innovatively and efficiently. Thus, in choosing how to interact with downstream firms (for example, in providing access to its upstream product), such a firm has a clear incentive to choose the pattern that will best provide its customers with end-products. That is, the upstream firm has an incentive to internalise the complementarities between the markets.

What about when an upstream monopolist chooses to integrate downstream? The policy concern in this case is the ability of the upstream firm to establish a dominant position downstream. This policy concern is mitigated by the fact that, in certain circumstances, the upstream monopolists will act efficiently in deciding whether or not to integrate downstream. In these same circumstances, the vertically integrated firm will welcome innovations by downstream rivals. In other words, given the right circumstances, vertical integration does not raise economic policy concerns.

A simple numerical example (taken from Farrell and Weiser 2003) illustrates the point. Suppose that the upstream monopolist could integrate into the downstream market, and by participating in that market improve the value of the upstream product to users from £100 to £105, while breaking even on its downstream product. Then, it will certainly profit from vertical integration; and this is (socially) efficient, since integration increases value.

Suppose, on the other hand, that the upstream monopolist contemplates integrating downstream, monopolising that market, and making a profit of £20 per user there while users value the upstream product at £70 rather than at £100. Because the £20 profit is less than the £30 harm created by this action, the integrated monopolist will lose by such a strategy. And such a move would not be socially desirable either, since overall value is lower. Of course, if the monopolist could make a profit of £40 per user in the downstream market, rather than £20 in doing so, then it would choose to integrate and monopolise the downstream market. But, in this case, this would be efficient.

So, in this example, the monopolist's profits follow social welfare; and hence the monopolist makes efficient decisions about integration into and monopolisation of the downstream market. The upstream monopolist cannot increase its overall profit by monopolising the downstream market, because it could always have charged a higher price in the first place; it has no incentive to take profits or inefficiently hamper or exclude rivals in the downstream market because it can appropriate the benefits from better or cheaper downstream products in its pricing of the upstream product. Farrell and Weiser (2003) refer to this situation as 'ICE': the incentives of an upstream monopolist to internalise complementary efficiencies. See also Rey et al. (2001) for a similar analysis.

This argument is closely related to the 'one monopoly profit' theory made famous by the Chicago School and Posner and Easterbrook (1981, p. 870): 'there is only one monopoly profit to be made in a chain of production'. But there is a distinct difference between the two. The traditional Chicago School argument would maintain that the upstream monopolist cannot gain by inefficiently leveraging its market power into the downstream market. The argument here is that, in addition, the upstream monopolist gains from an efficient downstream market – whether it involves perfect competition, integration and monopolisation, granting access to a limited set of downstream firms, or whatever. In the strongest form of this argument, competition law and regulation need not worry even if a vertically integrated firm engages in exclusionary behaviour in the downstream market.

This paints a very stark picture of incentives towards vertical behaviour. There are several qualifications to this basic story: ways in which the upstream monopolist's incentives can depart from efficiency. A primary reason is that regulation, imposed for whatever good reasons, at the upstream level encourages the monopolist to seek additional, and perhaps inefficient, profits in the downstream market. A second reason is that the upstream monopolist may view downstream rivals as potential competitors *in the upstream market*. Consequently, it may eliminate downstream competition to eliminate the possibility of upstream competition. This argument is behind the provision in the US 1996 Telecommunications Act, restricting entry by local telephony providers into the long-distance market. A third reason is that the degree of complementarity between upstream and downstream products may be variable. I have so far assumed (implicitly) that one unit of the downstream product requires one unit of the upstream product. But in some cases, the downstream product may be sold without the upstream input; for example, a product for one platform – say, broadband transport – may also be sold over another – say, narrowband transport. Whinston (1990) shows that in this situation, the broadband transport provider may try to control the downstream market. See Rey and Tirole (forthcoming) for further discussion, as well as an argument that integration and foreclosure can save the upstream monopolist from Coasian dissipation of profits.

Despite these qualifications, modern competition law generally supposes that, with limited and fairly easily diagnosed exceptions, dominant firms face efficient incentives towards vertical choices. In contrast, telecommunications policy has moved increasingly towards mandating access. A key issue for future policy, then, is: which stance is appropriate in telecommunications? Are the conditions for efficient vertical behaviour the exception or the rule in telecoms? In traditional telecommunications markets, the upstream market was heavily price regulated, and so there was good reason to doubt the efficiency of incentives. Existing unbundling obligations in the US and Europe can, therefore, by justified. But in new markets that are not price regulated, what are the remaining arguments for open access regulation?

Summary

I have not tried in this section to anticipate the conclusions of the Phase 2 TSR report. My aim has not been to come to any particular policy conclusions, but instead to sketch a framework to understand what is going on in competition in and regulation of telecommunications, especially in the area of access regulation. I have emphasised three questions:

1. what constitutes a bottleneck?
2. how should access to bottlenecks be treated?
3. should bottlenecks be separated from (potentially) competitive markets?

In general, competition policy and telecommunications regulation give different answers to these questions. How these approaches are reconciled will have important consequences for *ex ante* incentives for innovation and *ex post* competition.

This trade-off is familiar, not only from telecommunications, but also intellectual property (IP). In IP, monopoly rents are granted to successful innovators. Despite the *ex post* deadweight loss that this entails, it improves *ex ante* incentives to innovate. When the balance is struck correctly, this system is welfare improving. An important issue, then, is how much profit to award to the innovator, in terms of the scope of IP protection (for example, the length and breadth of a patent). Note that all criteria of essential facilities are often met by IP: IP is costly to duplicate; there is no real (*ex post*) cost to the owner granting access to IP; and when IP is highly innovative, it often confers monopoly power on the innovator. It is interesting to note that the same sort of debate is occurring in that field also. Many commentators are calling for ideas to be 'open source': see, for example, Lessig (2001). Others (for example, Landes and Posner (2002)) advocate extended property rights, to improve both *ex ante* incentives and *ex post* management of the IP.

Still, the question of what to do about the historic local loop remains. In many ways, this is the simplest question to answer, given the preceding discussion. BT, the dominant operator in the UK, has inherited a bottleneck (the local loop) from its days as the sole nationalised telecoms operator. The price regulation to which is has been subject has distorted its incentives towards downstream markets. Its strategic advantage, derived from its incumbency, allows it to retain its dominance in a number of markets. This situation will continue while BT is subject to access price regulation and while it is vertically integrated. Local-loop unbundling has yet to prove sufficient to tackle this issue. The benefits from continued vertical integration, in terms of investment coordination and incentives, are low and unlikely to outweigh the cost of decreased competition. Structural separation of BT, or the equivalent, is necessary.

The much harder question is: how should access to new networks and bottlenecks be regulated? What should be the access regime for BT's new '21st Century Network'? These questions require the trade-off between *ex ante* investment incentives and *ex post* competition to be decided.

CONCLUSIONS

The scale of the task facing Ofcom at its outset was daunting. Much progress has been made in getting to grips with two of the biggest monoliths in the UK: the BBC and BT. Ofcom's picture of broadcasting has come into focus. It is broadly coherent, although still lacks the evidence required to back up the hard quantitative decisions. The telecommunications picture is much less clear, and we await the next report to see the direction that Ofcom has planned, especially for the structure of BT. The challenge for Ofcom is to extend policy from the current problem of the copper-wire local loop, to develop a consistent framework for the treatment of bottlenecks.

NOTES

1. I acted as an external economic advisor to Ofcom during its first 12 months. The views expressed in this chapter are entirely mine. This chapter was written before Ofcom published its Phase 2 report of the Strategic Review of Telecommunications.
2. There may also be a distributional concern: 'there is an argument that where the market delivered programming of quality, range and balance, much of it would probably be provided on a pay-per-view basis, only for those who could afford it' (p. 75).
3. Contingent valuation studies attempt to place a monetary value on non-marketed goods by asking individuals to state a willingness to pay in hypothetical choice formats. See Delaney and O'Toole (2004) for a recent example estimating the value of Irish public service broadcasting.

4. These figures happen to return the lowest externality value: the private value is £18.70 per month and the social value is £20.70 per month. This is unfortunate, since this is not the reason why I use these figures: it is just that the report contains the most information about these calculations. I need the information to calculate the valuations of the marginal individuals in each of the quartiles.
5. The idea of a publisher is not entirely new. Over the course of its three-year inquiry, the Annan Committee (1974–77) emphasised the importance of greater pluralism (beyond the duopoly of ITV and the BBC) in broadcasting. It proposed an Open Broadcasting Authority that would act as a publisher and draw programming from a new independent production sector, which would be a fount of diversity and of new ideas. In further details spelled out by the Home Secretary, William Whitelaw, the new Channel 4 was to bring innovation, extend the range of programmes, serve minority and specialised audiences, and provide educational programming. It was not to engage in ratings rivalries. The largest possible proportion of programmes was to be secured from independent producers. The fourth channel was to be paid for by a levy on the ITV companies, and the size of its budget was independent of the revenue raised by advertisements shown on the channel. See Born (2004) for further discussion.
6. In the ISP (internet service provider) market, the top eight providers have been identified separately; all other providers have been grouped into one firm, called 'other'. Data are taken from the Ofcom October 2004 Quarterly Update on the Communications Market.
7. To be exact: a seller with no bargaining power who can run only an English auction with no reserve price among $N + 1$ symmetric bidders will earn more in expectation than a seller with all the bargaining power, including the ability to make binding commitments.
8. In fact, the report was published on 18 November 2004.
9. More recently, RBOCS are allowed to enter the interLATA market if their local market is sufficiently competitive.
10. Directive 2002/19/EC of the European Parliament and of the Council of 7 March 2002 on access to, and interconnection of, electronic communications networks and services, OJ 24.4.2002, L108/7, Article 12.

REFERENCES

Anderson, Simon and Stephen Coates (2005), 'Market provision of broadcasting: a welfare analysis', *Review of Economic Studies*, **72** (4), 947–72.
Bajari, Patrick L., Robert S. McMillan and Steve Tadelis (2003), 'Auctions versus negotiations in procurement: an empirical analysis', NBER Working Paper 9757, National Bureau of Economic Research, New York.
Bergman, L., C. Doyle, J. Gual, L. Hultkrantz, D. Neven, L.-H. Roller and L. Waverman (1998), 'Europe's network industries: conflicting priorities (telecommunications)', CEPR Discussion paper, Centre for Economic Policy Research, London.
Born, Georgina (2004), *Uncertain Vision: Birt, Dyke and the Reinvention of the BBC*, London: Secker & Warburg.
Bourreau, M. and P. Dogan (2004), 'Service-based vs. facility-based competition in local access networks', *Information Economics and Policy*, **16** (2), 287–306.
Brookes, Martin (2004), *Watching Alone: Social Capital and Public Service Broadcasting*, London: BBC and The Work Foundation.
Bulow, Jeremy and Paul Klemperer (1996), 'Auctions versus negotiations', *American Economic Review*, **86** (1), 180–94.

136   *Regulating utilities and promoting competition*

Chang, Hsihui, Heli Koski and Sumit K. Majumdar (2003), 'Regulation and investment behaviour in the telecommunications sector: policies and patterns in US and Europe', *Telecommunications Policy*, **27**, 677–99.

Correa, Lisa (2003), 'Natural or unnatural monopolies in UK telecommunications?', Working Paper no. 501, Department of Economics, Queen Mary College, University of London.

Crandall, R.W., A.T. Ingraham and H.J. Singer (2004), 'Do unbundling policies discourage CLEC facilities-based investment?', *Topics in Economic Analysis and Policy*, Berkeley Electronic Press, **4** (1).

Currie, David (2004), 'Television and the digital future', R.T.S. Fleming Memorial Lecture, London, 11 October.

Davies, Gavyn (chairman) (1999), *The Future Funding of the BBC*, Report of the Independent Review Panel to the Department of Culture, Media and Sport, London.

Delaney, Liam and Francis O'Toole (2004), 'Irish public service broadcasting: a contingent valuation analysis', Mimeo, Department of Economics, University of Dublin.

Dukes, Anthony and Esther Gal-Or (2003), 'Minimum differentiation in commercial media markets', *Journal of Economics and Management Strategy*, **12** (3), 291–325.

Eisner, James and Dale E. Lehman (2001), 'Regulatory behavior and competitive entry', Paper given at the 14th Annual Western Conference, Center for Research in Regulated Industries, 28 June.

Elstein, David (2004), 'Building public value: a new definition of public service broadcasting?', 19th Institute of Economic Affairs Current Controversies Paper.

Farrell, Joseph and Philip J. Weiser (2003), 'Modularity, vertical integration, and open access policies: towards a convergence of antitrust and regulation in the internet age', *Harvard Journal of Law and Technology*, **17** (1), 85–134.

Faulhaber, G.R. (2002a), 'Access $\neq$ ACCESS$_1$ + ACCESS$_2$', Discussion paper, Available at http://rider.wharton.upenn.edu/ªfaulhabe/Access.pdf.

Faulhaber, G.R. (2002b), 'Network effects and merger analysis: instant messaging and the *AOL–Time Warner* case', *Telecommunications Policy*, **26**, 311–33.

Faulhaber, G.R. (2003), 'Policy-induced competition: the telecommunications experiments', *Information Economics and Policy*, **15** (1), 73–97.

Finn, A., S. McFadyen and C. Hoskins (2003), 'Valuing the Canadian Broadcasting Corporation', *Journal of Cultural Economics*, **27** (3/4), 177–92.

Fuss, M.A. and L. Waverman (2002), 'Econometric cost functions', in M.E. Cave, S.K. Majumdar and I. Vogelsang (eds), *Handbook of Telecommunications Economics*, Vol. 1: *Structure, Regulation and Competition*, Amsterdam: North-Holland, Ch. 5, 144–77.

Gans, J.S. and S.P. King (2002), 'Regulating termination charges for telecommunications networks', *Australian Journal of Management*, **27**, 75–86.

Gasmi, F., D. M. Kennet, J.-J. Laffont and W.W. Sharkey (2002), *Cost Proxy Models and Telecommunications Policy*, Cambridge, MA: MIT Press.

Jeon, D.-S., J.-J. Laffont and J. Tirole (2004), 'On the receiver-pays principle', *RAND Journal of Economics*, **35** (1), 85–110.

Landes, W.M. and R.A. Posner (2002), 'Indefinitely renewable copyright', Olin Working Paper No. 154, University of Chicago Law and Economics, http://ssrn.com/abstract=319321.

Lessig, Lawrence (2001), *The Future of Ideas: The Fate of the Commons in a Connected World*, New York: Random House.

Littlechild, S.C. (2004a), 'Mobile termination charges: calling party pays versus receiving party pays', Department of Applied Economics Working Paper 0426, University of Cambridge.

Littlechild, S.C. (2004b), 'Why BT needs to be carved up', *Financial Times*, 5 October.

Milgrom, Paul (2004), *Putting Auction Theory to Work*, Cambridge: Cambridge University Press.

Oldale, Alison and A. Jorge Padilla (2004), 'From state monopoly to the "investment ladder": competition policy and the NRF', Mimeo, LECG Europe.

Posner, R. and F. Easterbrook (1981), *Antitrust Cases, Economic Notes and Other Materials*, 2nd edn, St Paul, MN: West Publishing.

Rey, Patrick, Paul Seabright and Jean Tirole (2001), 'The activities of a monopoly firm in adjacent competitive markets: economic consequences and implications for competition policy', Report, Institut of Éconmie Industrielle (IDEI), Toulouse.

Rey, Patrick and Jean Tirole (forthcoming), *A Primer on Foreclosure*, Forthcoming *Handbook of Industrial Organization III*, edited by Mark Armstrong and Rob Porter, Elsevier.

Whinston, M. (1990), 'Tying, foreclosure, and exclusion', *American Economic Review*, **80**, 837–60.

Woroch, G. (2002), 'Local network competition', in M.E. Cave, S.K. Majumdar and I. Vogelsang (eds), *Handbook of Telecommunications Economics*, Vol. 1: *Structure, Regulation and Competition*, Amsterdam: North-Holland, Ch. 15, 642–716.

6. *Trying* to make sense of abuse of a dominant position

Thomas Sharpe

INTRODUCTION

The title was chosen with some deliberation. I am *trying* to rationalise matters which many economists seem to regard as irrational. I am not here to expound a new general theory of dominance, abuse and economic efficiency but I am well aware of the current debates on so-called 'modernisation' of Article 82 and the apparent dichotomy between 'ordo-liberal' form-based theories, where 'economic efficiency' is seen as secondary or as a byproduct of economic liberalism, and the alternative approach, said to be based on economic analysis, the enhancement of 'consumer welfare' and the efficient allocation of resources.

The current situation, often classified as 'formalism', is in contrast to an 'economics-based' evolution which, it is said, 'will clarify underlying principles in terms of actual and potential economic effects, develop practicable administrable rules and methods explicitly on the basis of those principles and apply them to cases'.[1]

My conclusions are: (a) this alleged dichotomy has been hopelessly overblown. Economic analysis of varying quality has been central to EU competition cases since virtually the beginning of the Community and some of the earliest cases emphasise the necessity to analyse agreements and conduct within their economic context; (b) it is no surprise that political liberals tend to espouse economic liberalism and tend to prefer Austria to Chicago (though to many the distinction would be invidious, if not ridiculous) but this does not lessen their devotion to 'economic efficiency'; (c) the European courts are wrongly condemned for 'formalism' rather than economic analysis. To this, it should be recalled that courts apply laws or rules: a case is not a free-ranging seminar in the latest economic theory. Some cases win *some* economists' favour, as, for example, those connected to predation; others relating to, for example, aggregated or loyalty rebates, seem to attract no consensus. The evidence and case law does not support the mindless application of form over economic effect. The courts favour new entry and are very hesitant indeed to accept as valid economic *theories* on behalf of dominant undertakings which justify conduct, in the form of exclusivity, fidelity rebates or unfair pricing or anything which would increase competitors' cost of entry, on the grounds of efficiency or 'disciplined' market entry: they are rightly hesitant in my view; (d) the real dichotomy is between good economics – empirically based and robust – and bad economics – a priori and untested by evidence.

Few would argue with John Vickers's statement, above. 'Ordo-liberalism' is doubtless a neo-Cathar heresy to serious economists but it is of no particular relevance to serious participants in this debate.

The blending of law and economics has great power and has generated very useful insights to economists and jurists. It is obvious to me, especially when founded, modestly, on economic 'principles' rather than economic 'theory',[2] that economics can be used as a means by which practical rules suitable for general advice and adjudication can be generated. No doubt the rules generated will, if useful, be regarded in due course as a new 'formalism', as, for example, the 'Areeda–Turner/Joskow–Klevorik'[3] formulations for predation can be viewed. This is an example of economic theory and legal process coming together and concretising a legal rule in an important way.

In the end, however, competition policy must be framed in legal terms. The application of that policy can have profound impact on property values and freedom to trade, with the corollary that policy intervention must only be taken with due regard to evidence based upon facts rather than 'theory' (though which facts are deemed relevant may well be contingent on whatever underlying economic theory is being employed from time to time), the consequences of such intervention and the rights of the party or parties involved to be heard properly. The right to protection from such interference is enshrined in common law, good administrative practice and ultimately in the European Convention on Human Rights. But, in relation to the application of economics, as John Kay put it, 'The economic approach to competition policy has invited economic engineering—a belief that the courts can make cost–benefit analyses of alternative industrial structures'.[4]

This statement cannot be dismissed as merely a reference to mergers policy, as was suggested to me. It is in fact a cautionary warning against employing quite elementary theories of economic behaviour to complex business conduct and relationships. These are matters which few economists are remotely qualified to understand and equally, where businesspeople are occasionally hopelessly inarticulate in justifying the business rationality of their conduct, other than on the basis of instinct and inclination (neither of which would invalidate the decisions themselves). In other words, there is a mismatch between economic theories and understanding the rationality of business decision making, and this is far more important than any alleged dichotomy between 'form' and 'substance' in the law.

Competition lawyers have to make sense of Article 82 and its UK analogue, the chapter 2 prohibition. But, as with other practitioners, I am seldom in a position to advise on Article 82 questions without caution. And that (widespread) infirmity is both reflected and caused by the paucity of substantive[5] case law in the EU and in the UK. While little litigation will take place if the law (and its application to particular facts) is certain, it is equally true that if the degree of legal uncertainty is appreciable, little litigation will take place either. It is therefore unsurprising that there should have been so few cases because few parties would risk litigation when faced with radical uncertainty about the outcome. This is quite apart from the factual, evidential and presentational problems, and expense, that any abuse case creates.

Case law on Article 82 is therefore overwhelmingly the product of official enforcement, and once again any advice to clients in relation to possible official action has to be tinged with caution. That legal caution slides easily into commercial caution, the so-called 'chilling' effect. 'Chilling', of course, has two dimensions: it may frustrate innovation by undertakings in a dominant position in, for example, pricing, rebates and bundling and lead theoretically to an 'inefficient allocation of resources'. Viewed in a different light, it may sustain or encourage opportunities for entry (albeit, in accordance with the current economic orthodoxy, 'inefficient or undisciplined entry'), or for experimentation with alternative business strategies, or to offer greater consumer choice and pluralism possibly, but not inevitably, at the expense of an 'efficient allocation of resources'. In a world of uncertainty, it is not irrational to veer towards the latter course: diverse strategies, market pluralism and the information generated by competitors (which would not be obtainable anywhere else) are tangible and useful; 'inefficient allocation of resources', by contrast, has fairly precise meaning to economists but is less easy to identify or measure. Indeed, where the attempt is made, it seems to be inferred from cost and incomplete data sets. I am also reminded of the danger against which Professor Eleanor Fox warned years ago:[6]

> The use of economics in judicial decision-making is not dangerous at its core, but it holds a great potential for misuse in ways that are relatively undetectable, and those who use economics generally tend to do so in ways that are transparent. The tools of Economics may be neutral, but we who must select and use them are not.

The decisional practice of the Commission (and the OFT), as well as the decision to take a decision, is governed by many factors, some of which

I shall discuss. But, as I hope to show, the relatively few cases which have been brought seldom if ever deserve the opprobrium heaped upon them by some economists, still less the charge that the European courts follow a form-based agenda or are indifferent to economics-based approaches or economic evidence.

As I stated above, the 'formalism' of the courts and the claims for an 'economics-based' approach run the risk of creating a false dichotomy. The courts are not deaf to economics and (more or less) consciously deploy economic principles in evaluating competition disputes. With some temerity, I suggest that the real tension lies between different conceptions of economic reality. I mean between those, on the one hand, who apply the brilliant insights into the theory of the optimal allocation of resources and apply the rationality of profit-maximisation and those, on the other hand, who see markets as performing many roles, not only in the efficient allocation of resources at any moment in time, but also in generating information leading to innovation and experimentation. In this tradition, entry, choice, innovation, variety, competing technologies and rivalry in research and development, are each to be valued and encouraged and public policy should lean in their favour. Markets generate information which would not otherwise exist, allocate risk, identify future needs, and create some sort of spontaneous order in the production of new goods and services over time.[7] There is little room for marginal principles in such an approach, still less in the calibration of what is efficient/disciplined entry or inefficient entry. It is plain that for the protagonists of this view the market performs more functions than the efficient allocation of resources. It therefore follows that competition law will play a different role.

There is, however, rightly, a widespread notion that the time has come for some fundamental rethinking about Article 82. The EU Commission has embarked upon this process[8] though a treaty amendment is unlikely. Any change is likely to take the form of EU Commission guidelines and, over time, the pattern of EU discretion in deciding to take certain cases and not others. I presume the same process will be followed in the UK, indeed, in two thoughtful and important contributions by Dr Vickers, that process is under way in the UK already.

A CONTRAST

I continue with a contrast. The application Article 81, and its analogue, the chapter 1 prohibition, dealing with agreements between undertakings, now enjoys a significant, if rare, transatlantic consensus.

- Horizontal cartels should be detected, suppressed and punished by very severe financial penalties. More controversially (in the UK) some individual protagonists of cartels will face criminal penalties.
- The prize for revealing details of an illegal cartel is leniency. The prize for non-cooperation and recidivism is even higher financial penalties. The risks of being in a cartel have materially increased.
- Horizontal agreements dealing with cooperation and technological transfer are subject to regulations and guidance and are usually lawful.
- Non-price vertical agreements are similarly subject to regulation and guidance and those which meet certain conditions are lawful.
- The national courts are capable of assessing whether an agreement is anti-competitive, pro-competitive or just neutral, and enjoy competence in parallel with the UK, EU and US competition enforcement authorities.

Some say that this is the product of 'Chicago' ('new',' modern') thinking in economics, largely in the US, and spurred by the pioneering legal scholarship and revisionism of (would-be Supreme Court judge) Robert Bork and Judge Richard Posner.[9] There is something in this but it is perhaps too easy to follow John Maynard Keynes and attribute policy changes simply to defunct economists. It is salutary to remember that:

- The Sherman Act, on which Article 86 (now 82) was based, owed nothing to explicit notions of efficiency and everything to distrust of concentrations of economic power.[10] *Sylvania*,[11] which vastly liberalised the law relating to non-price vertical restraints was superimposed on those foundations thirty years ago. This case reflected orthodox business thinking about the benefits of product differentiation, advertising, the provision of incentives to local distributors and the avoidance of 'free-riding' and inter-brand competition. In the end, there is an *ex post* economic rationale for these changes but common business practice preceded that realisation (by some considerable period).[12]
- So far as the UK is concerned, it is occasionally overlooked that nearly all non-price vertical restraints were lawful under the Restrictive Trade Practices Acts 1956–76.[13]

Another reason for the changes has been the sheer inefficiency flowing from overenforcement, and the cost of advice and compliance, including the opportunity cost of diverting anti-trust enforcement from dealing with more damaging issues. This was particularly marked in the EU which, following a centralising continental tradition, virtually required notification to the EC Commission of all important agreements and, in practice, saw the notification of many more. The fact that notification was usually followed by a long period of inaction and silence and seldom culminated in a formal Decision on which parties could rely, provoked the policy rethink. This has had the effect of, first, identifying and minimising the formal areas of concern; and second, devolving enforcement to national competition authorities and to the national courts. All this is very welcome.

By contrast, when one turns to Article 82 (and the chapter 2 prohibition, for which understandably, there have been few cases since 2000, but one (*Napp*), of substance is discussed below) the position is very different. The most obvious points are:

- Compared with Article 81, there are remarkably few Article 82 cases of substance.
- They constitute 'a wilderness of single instances', most explicable by their peculiar facts and history, often revealing evidence of naked intent to exclude or destroy competitors.
- The cases which do matter all have the effect of *expanding* the scope of Article 82. There is no equivalent of *ENS*[14] in which the Court of First Instance (CFI) set out the appropriate approach to the analysis of 'restriction' and reined in the Commission's practice.
- Unlike Article 81, there is some divergence between EU and US law: see, for example, the differing treatment of the 'essential facilities' doctrine in the *Trinko* case,[15] the *IMS* case[16] and the *Microsoft* decision.[17]

ARTICLE 82 – 'NARROW, SHALLOW AND INCOHERENT'?[18]

The legal test of dominance is usually expressed in terms of an undertaking's ability to behave independently and to a large measure to be in a position to act without taking into account competitors, purchasers or suppliers. This is the classic formulation in the *United Brands* case:[19]

> The dominant position referred to in this Article relates to a position of economic strength enjoyed by an undertaking which enables it to prevent effective competition being maintained on the relevant market by giving it the power to behave to an appreciable extent independently of its competitors, customers and ultimately of its consumers.

The paradox in this definition is that it focuses on the exploitation of a dominant position where an undertaking has the power to operate independently yet, when the case law of Article 82 is considered, the abuses examined by the Commission and the European courts deal with exclusionary abuse. These do not take place in situations where an undertaking could operate independently of other competitors. Indeed, the paradigm is where the dominant undertaking's conduct indicates the opposite: it is precisely because it cannot operate with the commercial discretion it wishes owing to the threat of the competition that the dominant undertaking seeks to eliminate or weaken a competitor.

The court's definition is more appropriate to the older, pre-*Continental Can*[20] notion of abuse, where an undertaking *exploits* its dominant position by, for example, overcharging, in the knowledge that no competitor could enter or offer effective competition to it.

In my view, dominance is better formulated in terms of the possession of economic power. The more interesting question is: does an undertaking have the capacity to destroy competitors rather then the ability to ignore them. This is why, at the risk of apostasy, I elevate 'economic power' as the important concept rather than 'market power'. This *may* be a distinction without a difference but, in embracing situations beyond a specific product market or geographical market, and allowing for deep financial pockets and product 'portfolio' effects and other indicia of *economic* power, I believe it makes better sense of the case law.

There is some evidence that this is precisely what the European Court of Justice (ECJ) actually means: in *Hoffmann–La Roche*:[21]

> Such a position (of dominance) does not preclude some competition, which it does where there is a monopoly or quasi-monopoly, but enables the undertaking which profits by it, if not to determine, at least to have an appreciable influence on the conditions under which that competition will develop, and in any case to act largely and disregard it *so long as such conduct does not operate to its detriment*. (My emphasis).

Thus if an undertaking possesses economic power it has the capacity to exclude a competitor, including one of greater efficiency or one offering a superior product.

The European courts have steadily widened the scope of Article 82.

- The abuse does not have to be causally related to the existence of a dominant position[22] (in contrast to the US and regimes such as that in New Zealand where section 36 of the Commerce Act 1986 refers to the 'use' of a dominant position for the purposes of the abuses, defined essentially in terms of market exclusion, which are set out in the act.

- Article 82 does not confine the notion of dominance and abuse to the same geographical or product markets so that an undertaking may be dominant in one market, commit what would constitute an abuse in a separate market, yet still fall within Article 82.[23]
- Undertakings may commit an abuse unintentionally: it is an 'objective' concept. It is clear that intent is neither a necessary nor a sufficient condition for an abuse to exist but proof of intent plainly influences the Commission in its decision to investigate; it is central to allegations of predation if costs lie between marginal and average total cost; and it is important in setting financial penalties. Most, but not all, abuse cases have much more than a whiff of using *economic* power specifically to eliminate or discipline a competitor. Typically, such conduct would not otherwise have been profitable or rational in the absence of the prospect of the competitor exiting or competitor acquiescence to the dominant undertaking's wishes.
- Article 82 has been extended to situations of 'collective dominance', recently in the *Compagnie Maritime Belge* case,[24] where parties present themselves on a particular market as a collective entity. As the ECJ held in this case, it would depend on an economic assessment, in particular, of the structure of the market in question. This opens up the possibility of examining non-collusive but parallel behaviour in an oligopolistic market.
- The notion of collective dominance has been extended from 'horizontal' to 'vertical' relations[25] and the CFI declared that it was not necessary for all undertakings within the collectively dominant position to commit the same abuse. As disparate action by the parties might well call into question the validity of the finding of 'collective dominance', this extension of the law is perhaps especially problematic.

ABUSE IN GENERAL

My understanding of the 'modernist' position is that the fact of dominance is a neutral fact in relation to the degree of actual or potential competition in any market.[26] Accordingly, it is illegitimate to draw any presumption from dominance: it is the effect of conduct on competition in the market or on consumer welfare which must be examined. By contrast, 'ordo-liberals' are said to promote the belief that if an undertaking is in a dominant position, the conditions of competition in a relevant market are abnormal. This has the consequence that any commercial response in that market by that undertaking designed to respond to the competitive pressures which remain will, inevitably, have an impact on the overall market situation and even on market structure. The ECJ has declared, therefore, in an important statement, that undertakings in a dominant position have a special responsibility not to allow their conduct to impair *genuine undistorted competition* on the common market.[27] I take this to mean not the competition which would exist in a hypothetical situation of perfect competition but the competition which does exist in the market in question, namely, one in which there is an undertaking in a dominant position. In *Hoffman–la Roche*[28] the Court of Justice offered a definition of anti-competitive abuse which emphasised the nature of the abuse:

> The concept of abuse is an objective concept relating to the behaviour of an undertaking in a dominant position which is such as to influence the structure of a market where, as a result of the very presence of the undertaking in question, the degree of competition is weakened and which to recourse to methods different from those which condition normal competition in products or services on the basis of the transactions of commercial operators, has the effect of hindering the maintenance of the degree of competition still existing in the market or the growth of that competition.

The notion of what constitutes 'genuine undistorted competition' and 'methods different from those which condition normal competition' is not defined. This is not necessarily a source of uncertainty, circularity or imprecision. Law is full of broad formulae designed to allow judicial discretion and creativity: for example, the law of negligence is based on 'reasonableness' and the law of damages on 'foreseeability'. More specific rules derive from specific applications, and Article 82 is no exception. The problem arises in the belief that the European courts, by drawing inferences about the nature of remaining competition where a market is dominated, adopt form-based prohibitions based upon assumptions about the harm which follows from specific conduct without an adequate economic analysis of the market.

The cases which have given rise to the greatest criticism from economists have involved pricing and the impact on new entrants. Recent judicial decisions are said to be: 'formalistic' and 'represent a major set-back to the introduction of a more economic-effects based enforcement regime'.[29]

PREDATORY PRICING

I start with perhaps the least controversial body of case law. This is the most developed area of case law and (accordingly?) the one less vulnerable to criticism. I recall that a distinguished American antitrust professor compared predation to witchcraft: frequently suspected but never seen.[30]

Judges are less sceptical today. The European courts have embraced the work of leading economists in applying tests which mirror current notions of economic rationality.[31] A dominant undertaking which makes a loss on each unit of sale and makes no contribution to fixed costs is presumed to be acting abusively. Even if a contribution is made, this may be predatory when combined with evidence of intent to exclude. This is near to being a *per se* ('form-based'?) rule owing, presumably, to the inability of the incumbent to offer any credible business justification for the practice other than a desire to eliminate competitors. In my view, there is great power and economy in a judicial test of abuse based upon the absence of a legitimate business justification, where (to avoid the charge of a 'definitional stop') 'illegitimate' means where the objective and primary intention is to exclude or destroy a competitor and/or to establish a reputation for a willingness to do so, and is thus likely to inhibit future entry.

There are, however, significant difficulties in analysing an allegedly predatory situation. First, what cost base should be considered? Are we considering historic cost, replacement cost or some variation of modern equivalent asset? For some industries, average variable cost is very low indeed. Is this a good reason for having a higher standard in, for example, telecommunications? Second, average cost is difficult to apply in the presence of common and/or joint costs. If there are common or joint costs it is difficult or impossible to divine a unique average cost because the costs span more than one product and so there is no unique number to apply to the calculation. Third, what is the timeframe? The case law does not formally set a time limit. The 'economically operative' time period will vary. In some cases, as was argued successfully in resisting Ofgem's request for a licence amendment conferring summary competition law powers on the regulator, it will be very short, if opportunism is present.[32] I doubt whether this could or should be codified.

A current debate is whether proof of the ability to recoup the lost revenues arising from predation is a necessary substantive element of an abuse. The US case law requires proof, indeed a 'dangerous probability', that the predator will or could recoup its losses. An element of the reasoning lies in the belief that as predation means lower prices, this should not be inhibited without further evidence of a dangerous probability of subsequent exploitation. A further reason lies in the belief that exclusion, while important, must be accompanied by consumer detriment, in this case, in the form of higher prices. I would characterise this as the current orthodoxy among US lawyers and probably economists.

In *Tetra Pak II* the ECJ was asked to find that the possibility of recoupment was a substantive element of abuse, meaning that unless the Commission

could demonstrate this possibility, no abuse would be present. The ECJ
responded that:

> it would not be appropriate, in the circumstances of the present case, to require
> in addition proof that Tetra Pak had a realistic chance of recouping its losses.
> It must be possible to penalise predatory pricing whenever there is a risk that
> competitors will be eliminated.[33]

While this formulation allows room for the future addition of proof
of recoupment to the Commission's burdens,[34] this would be a mistake.
Adopting the view of markets expressed earlier, predation as a strategy
(and there seems to be little doubt that Tetra Pak engaged on a well-
established strategy of exclusion which it thought would add to its long-term
profitability) will serve not only to eliminate immediate competitors but also
to deter others. Its existence will, plausibly, serve to add to the risks of entry
and influence potential entry decisions. If this has the effect of diminishing
the future set of competitors in that market, it also reduces the choices
available to consumers, and everyone else, including the opportunities for
innovators in every sphere in that industry. These possibilities cannot be set
in the balance against short-term predatory prices as, fundamentally, they
cannot be comprehensively identified, still less quantified. They are part of
the competitive process. Making sense of Article 82 in this way explains the
ECJ's reluctance to define predation in terms of subsequent exploitation;
harm to consumers is inferred by the damage to the competitive process
itself. Exploitation is neither a necessary nor a sufficient condition for abuse
to be present.[35]

This is not to say that recoupment is irrelevant. If, as a matter of evidence,
it is *clear*, to the appropriate standard in the assessment of dominance,
that any attempt to raise prices would lead to entry, that is, entry barriers
are low and reputational effects, taking into account the conduct allegedly
abusive, insufficient to deter entry, this suggests to me that the premise, of
a dominant position, should be questioned. So US and EU law are not so
different after all, and even economists can be happy.

By chance, the first case brought by the OFT under the Competition
Act 1998 was partly a predation case.[36] Napp abused its dominant position
by charging predatory prices in the 'hospital' segment of its market, and
charged excessively high prices in the 'community' segment of its market.
The hospital segment was the gateway to competition in the community
segment. Napp argued that taking account of the profits made on the
community segment, its prices in the hospital segment, while low, were
profitable. The circularity of this argument effectively made the OFT's case.
The OFT argued that the exclusionary prices in the gateway segment led

to the abusively high prices in the community segment and went further in arguing that if the hospital pricing was not predatory, it would not pursue the claim of excessive pricing in the community segment. The Competition Appeal Tribunal (CAT) refused this invitation and upheld the vitality of excessive (more properly 'unfair') pricing as an abuse in UK law, as it was obliged to do by reference to the relevant EU competition law. The OFT did not need to argue that evidence of recoupment was necessary, perhaps because of the way Napp advanced its case, which appeared to be a tacit and indirect admission of recoupment.

PRICE DISCRIMINATION

Article 82(2)(c) prohibits 'the application of dissimilar conditions to equivalent transactions, thereby placing other trading parties at a competitive disadvantage'. This is not a charter for simple equality of treatment. First, cost differences would justify differential treatment in almost any circumstance. Second, the reference to 'competitive disadvantage' is vital.

It is established that a dominant firm was entitled to 'compete on the merits'.[37] This suggests that smaller competitors could not have recourse to Article 82(2)(c) as an umbrella protecting them from financial hardship resulting from the superior efficiency of the dominant undertaking. As the ability to offer selective and non-predatory price reductions typically has the effect of offering lower prices to a segment of the market which would otherwise not purchase a product, and is output expanding, any inhibition on this outcome is suspect. Also, it is difficult to advise an incumbent on how to respond to price competition which might be directed towards specific customers or locations. Should specific and targeted responses be made, or should the only response be an expensive general price cut, extending to those customers unaffected by competition and who have already expressed willingness to pay more? If so, surely this would inhibit any price reduction to the disadvantage of consumers? And if this is the right course, would it not encourage entry by an undertaking of (possibly) lesser efficiency than the incumbent? The incumbent is inhibited from competing and the market cannot generate accurate signals about efficient entry.

The growing case law is reasonably clear that an incumbent can indeed 'meet competition' by selectively lowering its prices, though in one of the two cases I am about to discuss, *Irish Sugar*, this defence was declared inadmissible on the facts.[38] This is a development of the case law in *United Brands* and in *Tetra Pak II*, of the right of an undertaking in a dominant position to take reasonable steps to protect its commercial interests.

The case law is also characterised by that paucity or 'wilderness of single instances' I referred to at the outset. In *Hilti*,[39] superimposed on a variety of other practices such as tie-ins, Hilti identified the customers targeted by its competitors and offered them, in a somewhat opaque way, highly preferential treatment and, at the same time, added to the costs of those who had trifled with competitors, by removing volume-related discounts from them. According to the Commission,[40] and endorsed by the ECJ, their pricing policies were illegal. That conduct was designed 'purely to damage the business of, or deter market entry by, competitors, whilst maintaining higher prices for the bulk of its other customers, is both exploitative of these customers and destructive of competition'.

In *Irish Sugar*, border customers were offered selective price reductions in order to thwart imports from the north. This was accompanied by fidelity rebates conditional on the customer purchasing 'all or a large proportion of its retail sugar requirements from it, thus assisting in the foreclosure of the market.' Its target rebates were timed to coincide with the entry of competitors' products in the market. The facts in the case make fascinating reading. There is little doubt, as the court found, that the incumbent's policy was intended to eliminate competition and deter future competition.

Both cases are explicable by reference to the role of competition policy in maintaining a competitive process. The Commission and the European courts found that neither undertaking would have engaged in such practices if it had not been for its market power enabling it to exclude a competitive threat. If successful, both undertakings would have continued to enjoy a virtual monopoly of their respective markets. *Irish Sugar* and some other cases are accompanied by findings of fact that the *direct* motive for the strategy is the exclusion of a competitor.

Perhaps the rationale for the court lies in the ample evidence of wilfulness combined with the potential effect of the selective price reduction on the willingness or ability of manufacturers in Northern Ireland to continue to supply customers in the south in the face of a selective non-predatory price response ruining their business. The court took the view that such competition would no longer be forthcoming.[41] If so, this would have enabled Irish Sugar to increase its prices insulated from future competition.

On whether the judgment would have encouraged inefficient or undisciplined entry, nothing can be said about comparative efficiency unless it is understood that many costs vary with scale. The exporter may not have reached sufficient scale to reap such economies. Its underlying cost schedule may well be below that of the incumbent. Such information would never have been revealed if Irish Sugar had been able to consolidate the totality of its economic power and see off the importer. All that can be said with confidence is that Irish Sugar measured the threat, saw it as significant and deployed its resources accordingly. Perhaps it had formed the view that the importer's costs were indeed lower, a not implausible proposition when it had had 85 per cent of its home market for over ten years. Such an inference can be drawn from all the facts surrounding Irish Sugar's response, which went beyond selective price cuts.

I note that in similar cases the European courts and the Commission have upheld a robust view of selective price discrimination (especially when accompanied by a policy to exclude): I cite the *Compagnie Maritime Belge* case[42] and the *Virgin/British Airways* Decision.[43]

LOYALTY REBATES

Loyalty rebates offered by dominant undertakings, designed to buy fidelity and thereby exclude competitors, or raise their costs, have the same effects as a requirements contract. The familiar tension between lower short-term prices and foreclosure are present here. There is no *per se* prohibition, as the CFI declared in terms in *Irish Sugar*:[44]

> The authorities must appraise all the circumstances, and in particular the criteria and detailed rules for granting rebates, and determine whether there is any tendency, through an advantage not justified by any economic service, to remove or restrict the buyer's choice as to his sources of supply, to block competitors' access to the market, to apply dissimilar conditions to equivalent transactions with other trading parties, or to reinforce the dominant position by distorting competition.

As British Airways and Michelin found to their cost,[45] rebates related to efficiencies are permissible; rebates designed to lock in customers and increase the cost of switching to a competitor are forbidden. The Commission attacked the structure of these schemes, not their existence: they facilitated loyalty not efficiency. Here, the law and practice is evolving. There is uncertainty in how much discontinuity or non-linearity is possible in assessing rebates; whether the level of rebate can exceed likely cost savings, especially scale economies; what should be the length of the rebate period – too long magnifies the foreclosure effect, too short might be ineffective as an incentive; whether the rebate should be confined to incremental sales, or reward all sales. These have to be examined on a case-by-case basis.

The judicial mood is undeniably hostile. A tight loyalty rebate scheme serves to freeze out entry and, if related to aggregate sales, by virtue of the assumed dominance, will offer customers greater benefits than a new entrant could normally match. At least, the entrant, denied scale and other economies, would have to be super-efficient at the outset and blessed with sufficient financial resources to risk entry. I think the judicial instinct displayed here is consistent with the view that, in the absence of compelling reasons to the contrary, entry should be encouraged and that speculation regarding production and allocative efficiency is of secondary importance to plurality, choice and the generation of information that only more players in a market can create. I regard this as well short of 'formalism'.

Again, the analysis is superimposed upon dominance and is only appropriate where economic power is present. The case for rebates and loyalty-inducing devices as an acceptable form of competition in a competitive market is strong, and such devices are widespread. Once dominance is properly attested as present the justification for buying fidelity appears to weaken or disappear. It is noteworthy that some of the trenchant criticism of the *Michelin II* and the *British Airways* judgments focus criticism on the failure to appreciate that each undertaking did indeed face competition and was experiencing falling market shares. What the critics ignore is that this focuses attention squarely on the Commission's finding of dominance not abuse.

CONCLUSION

There is no general theory, nor should there be. Equally, adjudication of Article 82 cases is not conducted in an economics vacuum, one to be abhorred and filled by the enlightenment that only current theories in economics can provide. There is an underlying rationality in the case law which can be explained in terms other than 'ordo-liberalism'. Doubtless this can be explained more clearly by the courts in future and, doubtless, it will be.

Only if there is rivalry and competition can information be generated to match consumers' needs with production over time. Only with plurality can experimentation take place, and mistakes made. Thus the behaviour of a dominant undertaking will be measured by its impact on entry; conduct which cannot be justified as rational but for its capacity to exclude will be condemned. The 'but for' test – as elsewhere in the law – is too simple as test of causation: as the cases show, the desire to exclude, and clear evidence of motive, can be accompanied by other, ostensibly more benign, objectives, unrelated to exclusion. This does not mean that the test is wrong or circular; it is just more difficult to apply. I see no conceptual or intellectual difficulty in assessing motive and effect in the light of the degree of economic power present, and forming a view that the conduct, however justified in terms of short-term profitability or even short-term benefits to consumers, is closely associated with the desire to exclude and owes its profitability by reference to the success of that policy.

The lack of coherent business justification for conduct, the degree of economic power present, the normal conduct of the undertaking (that is, what it once considered to be 'rational'), internal evidence going to an intent to exclude, and the likely situation in the market if the strategy had been pursued uninterrupted, including reputational, are all factors which should be taken into account.

No one said it was easy.

CODA

I obviously hit a nerve of sorts by this lecture because afterwards I received quite a few emails, some congratulatory, some not. The latter were more interesting. Apart from the odd economist's condescension, their tone was unsparing. Some thought I was 'anti-economics' and was guilty of a sort of *trahison de clercs*, letting down the forces of modern economics and siding with my intellectually impaired (judicial) caste. In answer, it is worth repeating that the European courts do not ignore economic analysis if it is well conducted and supported by evidence, and they have strongly criticised the Commission for any past errors and will probably be even more vigorous in the future. I am unrepentant that I do not believe that the courts, or national competition authorities for that matter, can regularly conduct cost–benefit analyses other than on a very superficial basis; that the importance of entry and entry opportunities cannot be overestimated and that the risks and consequences of inefficient entry are lower than those flowing from the protection and consolidation of monopoly. Perhaps one answer is for the Commission to use its powers of sectoral investigation less sparingly – is it fanciful to envisage the establishment of a European Competition Commission which could look at issues in a non-adversarial way, devoid of concerns about penalties and aware of the limitation of markets?

NOTES

1. John Vickers (2004), 'Abuse of market power', *Economic Journal*, June 2005, **115**, F244–261.
2. Though OFT officials still declare in meetings that 'economic theory predicts'.
3. See P. Areeda and D.F. Turner (1975), 'Predatory pricing and related practices under section 2 of the Sherman Act', *Harvard Law Review*, **88** and P.L. Joskow and A.K.

Kleverik (1979), 'A framework for analysing predatory pricing policy', *Yale Law Journal*, **89** (2).
4. John Kay, (2003), *The Truth About Markets*, London: Penguin p. 365.
5. By 'substantive' case law I mean a case that does more than repeat what has been said before.
6. Eleanor Fox, 'The Politics of Law and Economics in Judicial Decision Making: Antitrust as Window' [1986] 61 *NYUL Rev* 554, 558. The notion that economics is not *Wertfreiheit* is not new to anyone privileged to have heard Joan Robinson lecture: see also her *Economic Philosophy* (1962) London: Watts.
7. I refer generally to the works of Kay, Ludwig von Mises, Friedrich Hayek and others on the role of entrepreneurship, including Joseph Schumpeter and Israel Kirzner. This corpus of work is a little distinct from the so-called 'ordo-liberalism' school described by David Gerber, *Law and Competition in Twentieth Century Europe: Protecting Prometheus* (Oxford: Oxford University Press, 1998).
8. I refer to Commissioner Mario Monti's speeches at Fiesole (2003) and Fordham (2003): see DG Comp website.
9. Robert Bork, *The Antitrust Paradox*, (New York: Basic Books, 1978).
10. Letwin, *Law and Economic Policy in America* (Edinburgh: Edinburgh University Press, 1966).
11. *Continental TV Inc GTE Sylvania Inc* 433 US 376 (1977).
12. It was all in Alfred Marshall, of course. See Peter Steiner, '*Sylvania* Economics – A Critique' 60 *Antitrust LJ* 41, 59 (1991).
13. This is not to defend the formalism of that legislation which was potentially capable of rendering lawful many pernicious agreements; I only warn against thinking that too much economic enlightenment happened at once.
14. Case T-374/94 *European Night Services v Commission* [1998] ECR II-3141.
15. *Verizon Communications Inc v Law Offices of Curtis V. Trinko* 540 US 682 (2004).
16. Case C-418/01 *IMS Health v NDC* [29 April 2004]. Note also the important subsidiary theme of the role of specialist regulation: it was held that there was no role for competition law remedies where sectoral regulation had been established. This seems to run contrary to the Commission Decision in *Deutsche Telecom*, OJ L 263 of 14 October 2003.
17. Commission Decision of 24 March 2004, *Microsoft*, C(2004) 900 final.
18. Anon.
19. Case 27/76 *United Brands v Commission* [1978] ECR 207.
20. Case 6/72 *Europemballage Corpn v Commission* (Continental Can) [1973] ECR 215.
21. Case 85/76 *Hoffman–La Roche v Commission* [1979] ECR 461.
22. *Continental Can* (see note 20, above). On a historical note, section 48 of the late Fair Trading Act 1973 required the action or omission, that is, the uncompetitive practices, to be *attributable* to the existence of the monopoly situation, defined as 25 per cent of the relevant market.
23. Case C-333/94 P *Tetra Pak v Commission* [1996] ECR I-5951 (*Tetra Pak II*).
24. *Italian Flat Glass* OJ [1989] L 33/44, [1990] 4 CMLR 535; Case C-396/96P *Compagnie Maritime Belge Transports v Commission* [2000] ECR I-1365.
25. Case T-228/97 *Irish Sugar v Commission* [1999] ECR II-2969.
26. See the summary published after my lecture in the Competition Law Forum's submission to the European Commission on recommendations for key policy objectives, 10 February 2005, British Institute for International and Competitive Law (BICCL).
27. Case 322/81 *Michelin v Commission* [1983] ECR 3461 at point 57.
28. Case 85/76 *Hoffman–La Roche v Commission* [1979] ECR 461.
29. RBB Brief 13, p. 4.
30. Frank Easterbrook, 'Predatory Strategies and Counterstrategies' [1981] 48 *Texas L Rev* 263.
31. Case C-333/94P *Tetra Pak v Commission* (see note 23, above).
32. Competition Commission 2000, *British Energy* ('the market-abuse licence condition'), CC453.
33. Ibid at para 44.

34. As advanced by AG Fennelly in Case C-395/95 P *Compagnie Maritime Belge v Commission*, see para 136 of this Opinion but, as with so much of the Advocate General's Opinion (AGO), not accepted by the court.
35. Eleanor Fox, 'What is Harm to Competition? Exclusionary Practices and Anticompetitive Effect' [2002] 70 *Antitrust LJ* 371.
36. *Napp Pharmaceuticals v DGFT* [2002] CAT 1.
37. OJ 1985 L374/1 at para 81.
38. Case C-62/86 *Akzo v Commission* [1991] ECR I-3359, para 156; *British Sugar/Napier Brown* [1999] 4 CMLR 196 para 31; Case T-228/97 *Irish Sugar v Commission* [1999] ECR II-2969, para 134.
39. Case T-30/89 *Hilti AG v Commission* [1990] ECR II-163.
40. *Eurofix–Banco/Hilti* (1987) OJ L 65/19.
41. One competitor had already gone out of business: *Irish Sugar*, para 222.
42. Case C-395/95 (see note 34, above).
43. [2000] 4 CMLR 999.
44. *Irish Sugar* at para 197.
45. Case T-219/99 *British Airways v Commission,* judgment of 17 December 2003; Case T-203/01 *Michelin v Commission* [2003] ECR II-4071.

CHAIRMAN'S COMMENTS

John Vickers

Introduction

Let me go straight to the business of highlighting points of agreement and disagreement with what Tom has said. In short, I broadly agree with his observations on the current uncertain state of the law, but disagree with some of his comments on economics. I also want to check that Tom's advocacy of 'plurality' would not risk heading down the slippery slope of undisciplined competitor protection. For consumer-orientated competition policy, that would not be the way to go.

Trying to Make Sense of the Law

I agree with Tom that in relation to abuse of dominance:

- the degree of legal uncertainty is currently great;
- there have been relatively few substantive EC cases;
- the EC courts have widened the scope of Article 82; and
- there is a widespread view that some fundamental rethinking is needed.

The widespread view is correct, and that is no criticism of the courts. The courts receive an unrepresentative – and especially tricky – sample of cases, namely those that are appealed (and potentially those initiated as private actions). The cases before competition authorities – like the Competition Directorate of the Commission in Brussels or the OFT – are themselves an unrepresentative sample of the competition law matters generally on which advisers advise and businesses make decisions.

Still, I believe that the competition authorities should take the lead in seeking to clarify the law, subject to correction by the courts from time to time as necessary. The lead can be taken by the way that casework is handled, and by publishing guidance.

The OFT is a new kid on the block as far as abuse of dominance is concerned – only five years ago dominant firms could abuse with impunity as far as UK domestic law was concerned. But since 2000 we have had a number of cases, including infringement decisions upheld on appeal:

- *Napp* (exclusionary, discriminatory and excessive pricing);
- *Aberdeen Journals* (predatory pricing); and
- *Genzyme* (margin squeeze).

And we have made non-infringement findings – for example:

- *BSkyB* (margin squeeze, mixed bundling);
- *British Airways/ABTA* (price discrimination);
- *DuPont* (refusal to supply); and
- *Edinburgh buses* (predatory pricing).

We also issued guidance on a range of issues under the Competition Act, including abuse of dominance. In spring 2004, with the EC modernisation regulation coming into force, we issued revised competition law guidelines, for consultation. We are, as ever, very grateful to all who have responded. Revised OFT guidelines will be adopted soon, except that, in view of the Brussels review of Article 82, on conduct amounting to abuse of dominance we will publish revised guidelines open for further consultation. Needless to say, we are in the meantime very much involved with the Brussels review (as we were with the recent merger review).

In short, the OFT is actively engaged both domestically and as an EC member state authority in the Article 82 debate now under way.

The Issue Is What Sort of Rules, Not Rules Versus Discretion

It is important to be clear on the terms of the debate. Those of us who hope that the law on abuse will develop a better economic basis are *not* arguing for the replacement of rules by discretionary decision making based on whatever is thought to be desirable in economic terms case by case.

I hope that Tom's quotation of John Kay did not suggest otherwise. The economic approach to competition policy may have invited economic engineering in the 1970s, with cost–benefit analyses of alternative industry structures, but does not do so now. Anyway I am not sure that John Kay's advocacy that the purpose of competition policy is to promote pluralism – with its requirement that there be several businesses in each strategic group – would be any less of an invitation. Likewise Tom need not worry about those who see competition law as a matter of applying the economic theory of the optimal allocation of resources. Like witchcraft, they too are frequently suspected but never seen nowadays.

We have got to have rules, for all the reasons Tom gives. Article 82 does not tell dominant firms to go forth and behave socially optimally. It draws a line where *laissez-faire* stops and the special responsibility not to impair genuine undistorted competition begins. The issue, then, is about what sort of rules – and, fundamentally, about what is undistorted competition?

The form-based approach tries to get by with rules without much, or any, economic content. In essence its programme is to have a list of descriptions of behaviour such that if X is on that list then a dominant firm must not do X. The ban on doing X might not apply if the firm can demonstrate that a compelling justification, but from a narrow category, holds. However, that is a risky business and the safe course might be for the firm to avoid X altogether.

The economics-based approach objects to that. First, for many descriptions of behaviour, X is likely to be pro-competitive in a range of economic settings but anti-competitive in others. Without asking some basic questions about economic circumstances, you cannot hope to know whether or not X is anti-competitive in the case at hand. For example, in a case involving discounts, good questions might be:

- How much of the market is affected by the discounts?
- Are scale economies important?
- Do the discounts involve below-cost incremental pricing?

With cartels you do not need to bother with this. No-one could seriously say that hard-core cartels are pro-competitive in some settings though anti-competitive in others. They have no redeeming features. So an effectively *per se* approach makes sense there. But it does not make sense with abuse of dominance. A moment's reflection is enough to show this. Below the threshold of dominance, X is *per se* lawful. How could merely crossing the threshold of dominance make X virtually *per se* unlawful? As Tom observes, the jurisprudence positively calls for conduct to be appraised in all the circumstances, for evidence to be looked at in the round. Economics-based approaches are entirely consistent with this; form-based approaches are not.

The jurisprudence also signals that there is a fundamental question in this whole area. Abuse is by judicial definition distinguished from normal competition, from competition on the merits and from undistorted competition. That is fine, but what are normal competition, competition on the merits and undistorted competition? Put another way, what is harm to competition?

I do not see how form-based approaches can hope to answer this fundamental question (except trivially in terms of whatever is on the list of proscribed behaviours). Economics-based approaches can help to do so, and in specific applications such approaches can indeed be found in the case law – predatory pricing being the prime example.

Predatory Pricing

As Tom notes, the case law on predatory pricing is relatively well developed. It also makes broad economic sense. And it has elements that accord with the underlying principles that I discussed in the Berlin paper that Tom kindly referred to.[1]

But first let me pick up the distinction that he mentioned between economic principles and economic theory. Economic principles are based on the sum of economic learning and experience. The latest research – theoretical and empirical – seeks to *add* to knowledge, and perhaps supersede some prior knowledge, but does not claim to be the *sum* of knowledge. Indeed there is competition between research ideas to improve knowledge. Law and policy should be based on the sum of knowledge – hence principles – not just the latest research. Good research is of great practical importance because over time it leads to better principles and hence better policy.

The economics of predatory pricing is a case in point. The old principle that predatory pricing was irrational so virtually non-existent was defeated by careful analysis of (rather intuitive) reputational and financial issues that showed it to be perfectly rational in a range circumstances. So, as a US Court of Appeals recently put it, the right attitude to allegations of predatory pricing is now one of caution but not incredulity.

The law on predatory pricing is anchored in cost-based tests. (As Tom observes, there are of course great debates about what the cost base should be.) That anchor prevents the protection of competition from drifting into the protection of competitors. It provides some sort of answer to the key question of *whose* exclusion the law against abuse of dominance guards against – the answer being related to competitors *as efficient*, at serving the custom at issue, as the dominant firm.

Despite the negative tone of words like 'exclusion' and 'foreclosure', competition policy cannot sensibly be opposed to all exit (or non-entry) of competitors. Indeed the fundamental issue is to distinguish between exclusion arising from competition on the merits and exclusion arising from dominant firm abuse. The distinction needs a sound economic basis.

Tom went on to discuss whether a showing of likely recoupment should be necessary for a finding of predatory abuse. He concluded that it should not, given the supremacy of entry. I would give more weight to the consumer harm principle than that phrase suggests, and recoupment is directly related to that principle. Still, there are grounds for not having a general requirement to show likely recoupment because dominance plus below-cost pricing plus risk of elimination of competition, without objective justification, usually allows an *inference* of likely recoupment. There is more reason to require a showing of recoupment in US law because unlawful monopolisation, including attempted monopolisation, can be shown without dominance necessarily having been established. It is still a good idea for EC competition authorities to ask themselves whether recoupment is likely, for if not, the firm's dominance may be doubtful.

Where Do We Go from Here?

EC law on predatory pricing has a number of attractive features. It has
less legal uncertainty than exists in relation to other types of abuse, and a
reasonable basis in economic principle. It shows that practical administrability
and economic grounding can go together. More generally, the scope would
seem great for more of both for other abuses. We are not at the frontier
where more economic sense means less legal certainty, and vice versa.

   What we need to do now is to square up to the fundamental question
of what is harm to competition, and to develop practical approaches to
other kinds of abuse that are similarly grounded in economic principle. I
do not have a recipe book but I suggest that promising ingredients are the
as-efficient competitor principle and the consumer harm principle – which
are anyway closely related to each other – with occasional extra insight
coming from the sacrifice principle. Further discussion of those principles
is in my Berlin paper.

Note

1. 'Abuse of market power', speech to the 31st annual conference of the European Association
    for Research in Industrial Economics, Berlin, 3 September 2004, which is in the *Economic
    Journal*, June 2005, **115**, F244–261.

7. The role of economics in merger review

John Fingleton[1]

INTRODUCTION

Economics plays a significant role in merger review in two distinct ways. First, as an input to the political and legislative process of setting policy objectives, it has influenced the formulation of substantive merger law towards competition-based tests. Second, the analysis of economic effects has become a standard element of the determination of merger cases.

In this chapter, I shall examine both of these areas. I shall focus in particular on how merger review has evolved in recent years, and how that evolution has reflected not just economic thinking but also a remarkable exchange of ideas across disciplines, institutions and countries.

SUBSTANTIVE STANDARDS IN MERGER LAW

Public Interest versus Competition Test

The substantive test is a natural starting point for discussing the role of economics in merger review because it determines the ground rules for how economics enters actual cases.

Policy analyses of the merger test have resulted in recent changes in the laws in several EU member states, including Ireland and the UK, and in EU law itself.[2] Despite different starting points (dominance in the EU, public interest in the UK and Ireland), these changes have moved towards a change-in-competition standard. Economics played a significant part in the recent dominance–SLC[3] debate at EU level; that debate was very transparent and is well covered elsewhere.[4]

Instead, I shall focus on the question of whether the test for mergers should be based on competition only or on some wider public interest test in which competition is just one part, alongside criteria such as effects on employment, regional policy, national ownership of assets, and protection of small players.[5] This question is at least as important for merger review as is the dominance–SLC issue, but is not as much discussed.

The move from a public interest to a competition test in EU member states owes a great deal to the decision taken in the 1980s to base the European merger test on a competition-only standard. This decision followed a vigorous debate, and even today there are many who believe that merger policy should be used as an instrument to achieve other policy objectives, even at the expense of safeguarding competition.[6]

The successful implementation of a competition standard at EU level under the 1989 Merger Regulation may help explain why in many countries, the UK and Ireland included, merger decisions under a public interest test had come largely to reflect competition criteria.

Competition experts have an important advocacy role to play in setting out and justifying the underlying economic rationale for a competition test as opposed to a public interest merger test. Such advocacy may be more important precisely when there is agreement on the question within the competition community. It is not just enough to do this when the law is being changed. Even with a competition-only test, the wider public acceptance of the law and its effective implementation relies on its underlying rationale being clearly understood. Otherwise, there may be calls for a dilution or replacement of competition standards.

The main plank of such advocacy is that competition usually operates in the public interest. Greater competition tends to reduce prices and costs, and to increase output, employment and innovation. For example, effects on consumers generally, or on poor consumers, or on government purchases are generally negative if competition is lessened. Similarly, while a competition-neutral merger may result in a small number of specific short-run job losses, the overall effect on long-term employment in the economy should be positive. Conversely, an anti-competitive merger that reduces output will likely reduce short- and long-run employment.

There are two ways in which competition may not coincide with the public interest. First, competition might be in direct conflict with the public interest. If so, some mergers that lessen competition could be in the public interest (for example, national champions). The second case is that the public interest might be wider than competition. This would lead to a very different policy rule, namely to be able to prohibit mergers that did not lessen competition (for example, national ownership).

The two examples I mentioned merit discussion both because they are topical at present in discussions about future European policy and because they frequently rely on mistaken perceptions of competition policy.

Examination of them suggests that neither is a valid example and that in both cases, competition supports the public interest.

National Champions

National champions refer to domestic companies that are strong players on international markets. There is nothing inherently wrong with this, especially when that strength derives from superior efficiency. Although it is not the example that first pops up in the minds of many who use the term, Ryanair may be a nice example of an Irish national champion.

Competition should, in principle, support national champions. Vigorous domestic rivalry should make companies more efficient, innovative and customer focused, and this in turn should strengthen their international competitive position.[7]

But some people argue that merger rules are in conflict with a national champion policy because champions need to have a strong (possibly monopoly) position on the domestic market to make them more effective international competitors. The argument is usually presented in terms of critical scale, but this cannot easily be divorced from the benefit that monopoly profit would convey. While the question should be more germane in smaller more open economies like Ireland where scale is lower, the recent EU debate has centred on larger economies such as France and Germany.[8]

At its essence, this is an argument for domestic protection as an implicit subsidy from monopoly profit on domestic consumers. Unlike most state aid that is funded by taxation, it is less transparent, and more difficult to calculate the cost to the economy. Moreover, the benefits may be illusory: monopolies tend to be inefficient, so that there is no guarantee that granting a monopoly (any more than state aid) will result in better long-term performance. For these reasons, there should be considerable scepticism as to whether restricting competition for national champion reasons would be in the public interest.[9]

The national champion argument dates from a time when domestic capital markets were more isolated and less well developed. External finance may be a better judge of foreign investment than monopoly profits: providing a sort of second look or external check on the investment decision. This variation of the national champion is an argument for improved competition in capital markets.

In any case, the perception of a conflict may reflect a misunderstanding of how markets are defined in merger policy. If the relevant market is international, then domestic scale should not be an issue. Competition authorities routinely approve mergers that result in high shares of domestic production on the basis that consumers are well protected by competition from imports.[10] If the relevant market is domestic, so that domestic sales are produced at home, the argument that domestic scale matters for international competitiveness breaks down.

A third possibility arises where international competition is asymmetric: that is where exports are possible but not imports. Because trade barriers tend to be reciprocal, this scenario is rare. It can arise if the distribution system in one country is blocked to foreign exporters. If so, the public interest may lie not in increasing domestic monopoly power, but rather in using competition policy to tackle the import restrictions that cause the asymmetry.

Tackling cross-border restrictions has been a hallmark of EU policy towards competition and the single market. It is also a reason why domestic competition authorities should be able to advocate the removal of government restrictions because companies who argue a 'world market' in merger cases sometimes ironically use or seek these restrictions to insulate them from foreign competition.

National Ownership

The national ownership argument is in the second category that I mentioned earlier, namely that the competition test does not fully capture the public interest. Proponents argue that in certain cases a country should be able to block a merger that involves foreign takeover of an indigenous firm. This argument is often linked to who makes the decision, that is, an independent agency or a Minister.[11]

A policy of national ownership of this kind is likely to conflict with EU or World Trade Organisation (WTO) membership rules, so that the question may be irrelevant. Even where these rules do not apply or are not enforced, we should question the merits and costs of a merger policy that could block certain mergers where competition is not lessened on ownership grounds.

The possibility of takeover exercises an important discipline on weak management. In sectors that are so concentrated that domestic mergers would be difficult if not impossible, preventing foreign takeover would mean that weak management would have little threat of being replaced. A policy of this kind would tend to restrict inward investment and push up the cost of external finance. Such a policy could have sizeable costs for the economy or sectors concerned.

What might justify such costs? One argument put forward by proponents of a national ownership policy is that foreign owners would not be sensitive to domestic needs, or would not take time to develop personal relationships with customers. But evidence that non-commercial factors dictate business decisions could be more indicative of existing restrictions on competition than the need to restrict competition further.

A second and related argument put forward is that 'good' jobs are preserved in the host country. The fear is that, post-merger, the company is 'truncated' with key functions like advertising, product development and R&D now conducted in another country.

In both cases, it is extremely difficult to assess the credibility of such arguments in terms of market failure. It would be particularly difficult to do so in advance. For this reason, such a policy would be open to widespread abuse by exaggeration. Apart from the costs mentioned above, there is the danger that protection from takeover might be linked subtly to hidden (but perhaps very costly) implementation of some other element of government policy.

We should not overlook the possibility that superior policy tools exist to achieve the same objectives. For example, governments have many instruments to make a country more attractive for good jobs. Indeed, strong competition across all sectors of the economy is one of these tools.[12]

Economic evidence suggests that limiting ownership would, on balance, be extremely costly. There are many good examples, not least of them the City of London, of how a policy of neutrality as to ownership can be successful for the host country. A recent report[13] on Irish enterprise policy pointed out that sectors with foreign capital and ownership contributed more to the high growth rates of the past decade than several indigenous sectors that recorded little or no growth over the period.

Evidence also comes from the contrast between the job creation records of larger EU economies that have different policies. Mario Monti recently observed that neither British national pride nor its employment record has suffered from not flying a nationalist flag.

S'il y a bien une politique qui a été suivie avec constance par le Royaume-Uni en matière économique ces dernières années, c'est la politique de négligence à l'égard du 'pavillon' des entreprises, qu'il s'agisse des entreprises manufacturières ou des services, y compris des services financiers. Or, je doute que la fierté britannique ait souffert de cette politique et je suis convaincu que l'emploi, lui, n'en a pas souffert.[14]

There may be a small number of sectors with very particular national or strategic characteristics where domestic ownership matters more. Examples might be cultural organisations or military suppliers. Even here, a proportional approach that identifies the special objective, and selects the most effective and least costly instrument may not require restricting competition policy.

The media sector is an example where the public interest may not be fully captured by a competition test. Greater competition generally acts in the public interest by promoting plurality and diversity. Indeed, there are many instances where decisions by competition authorities on competition-only grounds have been to the forefront in protecting such values. However, competition may not be sufficient to achieve these objectives in all situations.

Media mergers are the only exception to the application of a competition test for mergers by an independent agency in Irish law. The Statute gives the Authority and the minister independent vetoes over a media merger based on different criteria. If the Authority prohibits a merger on competition grounds, no action can be taken by the minister. Where the Authority does not prohibit on competition grounds, the minister can examine and, if necessary, prohibit it on different criteria.[15] Thus far, this wider test has not been used.[16]

Competition Tests

Competition authorities have an important responsibility to clarify to business and policy makers that merger decisions based on effects on competition make for sound economic policy. We should also demystify what a competition test means. Mistaken perceptions not only lead to political calls for changes or exemptions to merger law, but may also prevent efficient pro-competitive transactions. This clarification should not stop at market definition, but also involve clarifying the approach taken to market concentration and efficiencies, subjects I return to below. In this way, a competition test for mergers can be seen to be in the public interest.

Not every country has a competition test for mergers, and even those that do often have exemptions such as the media example just mentioned. The rise of independent and credible agencies, staffed with competition experts, has meant that merger decisions are primarily taken on competition criteria, regardless of the substantive test and even where there are exceptions. The development of a merger policy that in virtually all instances assesses transactions on the basis of their effects on competition alone is a significant step forward, and an example of the gradual but sustained influence of economics on policy in this area.

THE FRAMEWORK FOR MERGER ANALYSIS

Just as the tests that come from merger law have progressively developed a competition standard, whether by formal law or practice on the ground, so too the analysis of economic effects on competition has come to be a standard element in merger cases.

A thorough exposition of this proposition would examine topics such as vertical and conglomerate mergers, failing firm defences and barriers to entry. It might also develop supporting evidence on impact of the numbers and role of economists trained in industrial organisation that work in competition policy.

Instead I shall focus on three areas that exemplify this trend, namely market definition, the approach to concentration, and efficiencies. I shall then discuss merger guidelines and economic evidence.

Market Definition

Market definition is traditionally the first element in an analysis of competition. The tools of market definition, namely the analysis of substitutability in supply and demand, have changed relatively little. What has changed more is the position of market definition in the overall analysis. Whereas traditionally it was seen as an essential first step in the merger process, it is now seen more as a way of organising information for the rest of the merger analysis.

Substitutability between different products is not always a zero-one choice, but often lies on a continuum. It may not be possible to draw a clearly agreed line between products that are in and out of the market so that some sources of competition may lie outside the resulting defined market. This can particularly be the case with supply substitutes, where potential sources of competitive pressure cannot meaningfully be included in the relevant market.

Some authors[17] have suggested that market definition should be abandoned, and that merger review should focus solely on competitive effects, especially in cases where the analysis of competitive effects exactly mirrors the analysis of market definition. Where a relevant market has different classes of buyers with identifiable characteristics, and where the competitive option available to each class may differ in relative strength, it may make more sense to undertake a different competitive effects analysis for class of customers.[18]

Where there is ambiguity about the market definition, it is important that the decision does not depend heavily on the defined market. Competition authority practice has worked hard towards this end.

The most common approach, especially in contested cases, is to define the market narrowly, but ensure a rigorous analysis of competitive pressure from excluded sources.[19] The recent decision of the UK Competition Commission on supermarkets followed this approach; it defined the market as shops above 1400 square metres, but considered the competitive pressure exerted by shops between 280 and 1400.[20]

An alternative approach is to define the market more broadly, but go on to show that there would be no effect on competition even on the narrow market. Where there may be numerous local markets (for example, retail) but the conditions of competition on each market are broadly similar, agencies may 'define' a national market and, if necessary, complement this with an analysis of any specific local markets that may have different conditions of competition. Such an approach has been used in many non-controversial EU clearance cases, and in retail cases by many agencies.[21]

The choice of approach will be influenced by the importance of concentration in the competitive effects analysis, and undoubtedly how any appeal courts would view this. Where the case law involves implicit or explicit structural presumptions, competition authorities will naturally be more inclined to follow the narrow market definition approach because the resulting concentration will be higher. For example, the US District Court's favourable citation of *Philadelphia National Bank* alongside a reference to a 30 per cent market share in *Oracle Peoplesoft* may have unintentionally reinvigorated elements of a structuralist doctrine.[22]

That brings me neatly to the question of concentration.

Market Structure and the Relevance of Concentration

One of the biggest changes in merger policy has been the move from a heavy reliance on the effect of a merger on market structure (that is, number of suppliers and market shares) towards a focus on the economic effects of a merger.

The previous approach relied on a doctrine known as structure–conduct–performance (SCP). This posited that more concentrated market structures (that is, fewer suppliers) led to less rivalrous behaviour and poorer performance for consumers and the economy in terms of higher prices and lower output. Its application led to legal rules that shifted part of the burden of proof to the parties in concentrated markets.[23] While SCP had an impact on all competition policy, the effect on mergers was particularly severe with mergers where the burden of proof tended to rest with the merging parties. In the US, mergers at extremely low market shares were once prohibited.[24]

Developments in industrial organisation theory in the past 30 years challenged the SCP paradigm, and this new thinking has fed through into policy. The Chicago school critique led by George Stigler and others pointed out that just two competitors could be highly rivalrous. A monopoly could be competitive, if the market was open to entry.[25] Sutton's argument that structure, conduct and performance are jointly determined by underlying tastes and preferences, supported by detailed empirical results, injects further caution against simple rules of causality that focus on market structure.[26]

Concentration remains an important element in merger analysis. For one, it is an extremely useful descriptive tool. Measures such as the Herfindahl–Hirschmann Index[27] (HHI), or simply describing mergers as 3-to-2 or 4-to-3 are important summary indicators that enable us to compare different mergers. There continues to be a strong correlation between prohibited mergers and concentration: 3-to-2 mergers can get approved, but it is rare. At the other end, few 6-to-5 mergers are contested, but it happens.[28]

The important point is that this is a correlation, not a causal relationship. Most people now agree that concentration *alone* can tell us little in a causal sense about the effects of a merger. For this reason, competition authorities generally undertake a full competitive effects analysis, and rely on concentration either as a screen for further analysis, or simply as a summary statistic for the market. The result is that a full competitive effects analysis may lead to some 3-to-2 mergers going unchallenged at the same time that 4-to-5 mergers are challenged and prohibited.

This development cannot be seen in isolation of merger guidelines. As merger analysis has moved from the application of simple, if sometimes mistaken, structural rules towards effects-based outcomes, it is all the more important to give clear guidance on how effects are measured.

Efficiencies

The question of whether and how efficiencies should be considered in merger review has sparked much debate. This attention may be disproportionate given the rarity of merger cases where the outcome depends solely on an efficiencies argument. Even if cases are unlikely to turn on efficiencies alone, it is important that they be capable of being considered along with other factors, especially when merger decisions are taken 'in the round'.[29]

Industrial organisation theory has made a significant contribution to this question. Although Williamson's[30] original insight that efficiency gains from a cost reduction generally outweigh the social loss from a price increase is widely accepted, its relevance to mergers that increase market power is unclear. Whereas the incentive effects of competition force companies to realise cost efficiencies, market power generally results in higher costs rather than higher profits.[31] Where a merger increases market power, the merged entity will thus have every incentive to raise price, but much less, if any, incentive to reduce cost.

This would suggest that a high burden of proof should attach to showing efficiencies in a situation where a merger increases market power. It also helps explain why most jurisdictions are prepared to allow efficiencies provided the 'net price' does not rise. In other words, an efficiency can rarely if ever be used to offset an actual price increase, but it can be used to off-set a margin increase if the lower cost base would result in the final price for consumers being no higher than before the merger.

Efficiencies are more likely to be taken into consideration, and proved by the parties, when competitors remain in the market. The presence of rivals will create incentives to exploit cost reductions, the benefit of which will be all the greater if those rival(s) are in turn stimulated to reduce their costs. In other words, the efficiencies argument works best if rivals are spurred on to greater efficiency via competitive process.

Because the dynamic effects of increased efficiency include effects on non-merging competitors, it may be best considered as a competitive effect rather than as a defence. Price is not the only variable that rivals react with: they can also try to reduce their costs. This approach also avoids the possible pitfall of the efficiencies 'offence': namely focusing on the fact that the efficiencies may harm rivals.[32]

Although the term 'defence' is still used in the US guidelines, practice has evolved so that efficiencies are analysed as part of the competitive effects. Timely and efficient investigation is best facilitated by getting everything about the merger up front, and to consider them together as an integrated package. This may also be more in keeping with the commercial rationale for mergers where the parties are likely to consider their own costs, their rivals' reactions, and barriers to entry simultaneously. This approach is now reflected in the EU Merger Guidelines.[33]

Efficiencies must be merger specific to be considered. Efficiencies that reduce marginal costs may be looked on more favourably than those that reduce fixed costs because they are more likely to be passed on to consumers. Efficiencies that would increase price rivalry would be considered favourably, as would those that arise from more efficient purchasing processes. In contrast, savings due to the integration of administration or head office functions or input price reductions related to buyer power are generally less favourably treated.

It is important to be open to 'demand-side' efficiencies whereby the merger raises the value of the product to consumers. This may require explicit attention to the welfare standard, because both consumer welfare and price could be higher. In other words, a modified 'net price' approach would be required.

The Analysis of Competitive Effects

These and similar changes put the analysis of competitive effects centre-stage, and this is where most of the economic analysis and evidence typically appears.

Two very different competition concerns can arise in a merger. First, there may be a concern that the merged entity will acquire unilateral market power or generate non-coordinated effects.[34] This may include high market shares of the kind associated with a dominant position, but it also includes situations of lower market shares. Mergers of the former kind tend to be rare: in other words there is a self-selection aspect to which mergers come forward. As a result, unilateral effects cases will often arise in situations where the merging parties have a combined market share below 40 per cent. The second concern is with coordinated effects, where the merger would make it easier for the market participants, including the merging party, to coordinate, even tacitly, their prices on the market. In many merger cases, both concerns are present.[35] Both are thoroughly covered in merger guidelines.

Merger Guidelines

The first merger guidelines were produced in the United States in 1968. The evolution of these guidelines over the years traces some of the developments I have outlined above: the revisions in 1982 and 1984 moved away from structuralism, those in 1994 developed unilateral and coordinated effects and the most recent, in 1997, introduced efficiencies. These guidelines were influential not just in the United States, but also in other countries.[36]

In the past few years, several European jurisdictions including the European Commission, France, Ireland and the UK have developed merger guidelines. At the most recent count, at least 26 countries worldwide had merger guidelines, and a recent International Competition Network project undertook a comparative analysis of the guidelines of 12 of these.[37]

Merger guidelines are ostensibly economic documents. They set out the principles and explanations of harm to competition, of pro-competitive factors that would ameliorate or prevent such harm, and explain what evidence the agency will use in evaluating these.

Merger guidelines are hugely important and to be welcomed. They are valuable both to competition authorities and to businesses and their expert advisers. They impose a welcome self-discipline on authorities, and reduce the possibility for new case-specific theories. Business can more easily predict what will be allowed, which in turn may benefit everybody if clearly anti-competitive mergers are stopped at germination. Again, as noted above, this is all the more important given the move away from simple structural presumptions.

Guidelines also help limit the scope of an investigation to clear areas of disagreement, a critical factor in a process with tight time limits. If the parties and the authority can agree on the market definition, or to confine themselves to the question of unilateral effects, much effort, time and expense can be saved. This in turn can help the parties to develop the data and economic analysis to support the deal, often long in advance of notification.

Guidelines also make for greater international consistency of treatment, an increasingly important factor both within the EU network and given the growing number of independent jurisdictions elsewhere undertaking merger review. Because they are not case specific, guidelines encourage countries to follow similar approaches, and to understand their differences where they exist.

It is no coincidence that there is a great deal of congruence between the various guidelines now published. All rely on an enormous amount of learning across institutions, across countries and across disciplines, and I have personally witnessed the enormous efforts at mutual understanding and learning that characterised this process over the past five years. To the extent that this improves both the quality of merger review and the consistency of decisions across countries, it is doubly welcome.

Learning and Institutions

Much of the change in how economics is used in merger review is driven by the deepening of competition expertise, both legal and economic. Law firms, economic consultants, academic institutions, competition agencies and the courts are now populated with an increasing number of ever more experienced and expert individuals. The creation of chief economist posts in many EU agencies in the past few years and the success of the Association of Competition Economics are further indications of the relevance of competition economics.

Courts across Europe have become increasingly expert in competition as the number of cases has grown and as former practitioners have become judges. This is a process that will continue further with Regulation 1 and the new network of European competition judges.

There has been extensive learning across the disciplines of law and economics, across countries and across institutions.

Competition economists or lawyers increasingly have a solid base in the other discipline and engage and discuss issues across disciplines. Often it is more appropriate to speak of a competition expert, rather than a competition lawyer or economist.

Learning across countries has always taken place but has been enhanced considerably by multilateral fora that enable the discussion of substantive law and economics. The work of the International Competition Network (ICN) on comparative merger policy has begun to influence substantive law.[38] Many countries, Ireland included, have relied on OECD work product as a source of better practice when revising merger law. European networks[39] have enabled unprecedented cooperation on cases, ensuring greater consistency, but also much learning from what each other does. International cooperation has been hugely important in the development of merger guidelines.

Learning across private and public institutions is also important. The ability of people to move between competition authorities and the private sector matters a great deal, not only to the level of expertise, but also to the quality of dialogue and the efficiency with which we do our work. A good understanding of each other's views and approaches is important in developing better practices and avoiding costly mistakes.

ECONOMIC EVIDENCE IN CASES

While there is now a great deal of consensus that merger decisions should rest on an economic effects-based analysis, there is less on questions around the standard of proof and evidence required. Guidelines have gone some way to showing what material goes to prove an economic effect, how much of it is needed, and who bears the burden of bringing it forward. But, in part because economic evidence is still relatively new, evidential rules are still developing.

I shall briefly outline some types of evidence that are used and then proceed to discuss the relevance of legal standards to that evidence.

Types of Evidence

Four main types of evidence are commonly used.

First, internal documents of the merging parties that set out their views on competition in the market and written before the merger arose may be more useful than those that are submitted with the notification. 'Hot documents' may show that each party to the merger identifies the other as its main competitor.[40] This should not be decisive: the parties may have overestimated the competition between themselves, or may not be aware of entry or expansion plans by others.

Second, a merger investigation generally solicits the views of customers. When competition is lessened, customers are generally harmed. In contrast, effects on competitors should not matter as they are more likely to benefit from a reduction in competition. Having said that, the views of competitors may be important for understanding how competition in a market works.

The recent retrospective study[41] of mergers by the US FTC shows that 'hot documents' and customer evidence have been critical factors in recent mergers, and particularly for those in less concentrated settings such as 5-to-4 and 4-to-3 mergers.

Third, econometric and other analysis of market data is increasingly used in merger review, facilitated by advances in econometric techniques, greater computing power, and increasing data such as that from supermarket scanners.[42] Analyses of this kind have been used particularly in unilateral effects cases and in cases involving final retail markets.[43] Econometric evidence can be of most use when it points in the same direction as other evidence.[44]

Econometric evidence can also be extremely useful in allaying concerns and especially when economists on both sides find similar results. An example of this is a recent Irish merger in the pharmacy wholesale market.[45] This was a merger between one of three national suppliers and the fourth, a Dublin-only supplier. Different econometric studies of prices done by separate economists for the parties and for the Authority both revealed that prices were if anything higher in the Dublin market, where there were four suppliers, than in the rest of the country with just three. The decision, however, did not rely solely on this evidence, but also on customer evidence, evidence of substantial and varied discounts, and the fact that the target would not have had the ability to enter the wider national market, and so was not a competitive threat on that market.

Econometric evidence of this kind may be less significant in the EU setting than in the US either because the quality of data may not always be as good or because the agencies may have more time to undertake such analyses due to more flexible time limits.

I mentioned 'other analysis of market data' above. This is important, because not all empirical evidence involves econometrics. For example, evidence that market prices are not transparent or that there is substantial variation in discounts may be helpful in reducing concern about coordinated effects.

Fourth, economic models are used as evidence. They will be more useful if:

1. its assumptions are explicitly spelled out and supported by market facts;
2. its predictions are not sensitive to changes in those assumptions, and especially if the assumptions are not supported strongly by market facts; and
3. it is able to explain past market behaviour.[46]

Theories of harm to competition represent essential scaffolding in many cases, but the building itself is often the other evidence in the case.[47] At the end of the day, a strong case will rely on a preponderance of the evidence. If a case relies on only one of the above, then the confidence in that particular evidence will need to be very strong.

The market testing of remedies is another type of evidence that the Irish Competition Authority has used in merger analysis.[48]

Evidence in the Courts

The growth of economic evidence in merger cases has already resulted in some appeal court decisions that speak to the questions of what standard and type evidence is necessary to prove harm to competition. It is beyond the scope of this chapter to review these in detail, but I would like to give two examples.[49]

In *Airtours*, the Court of First Instance overturned a Commission decision based on collective dominance in the UK travel market. The Court did not, as some argue, speak to the proposition that economic models should be avoided because they can produce diverse results. Instead, its criticism was that the market facts did not match the model used.[50]

Airtours is an example of the manner in which the application of new analytic tools of game theory to oligopoly markets with a small number of players has come to affect the legal framework in which coordinated effects are analysed. The analysis of repeated versions of long-established models of static competition[51] enabled better understanding of how a few competitors in a stable market interact over time. This research enabled new insight into cartel formation and stability, where repeated interaction matters significantly.[52] The *Airtours* decision outlines a three-step test that is required to show coordinated effects.[53] This test in turn has found its way explicitly into the European Commission Guidelines on merger analysis.

My second example relates to the welcome development of customer evidence. Two recent US court cases have addressed evidential standards in this area, particularly relating to how that evidence is collected and how it should be interpreted. In *Sunguard*,[54] the court found that the government failed to show that its 50 customer statements were representative of all 7500 customers, or of distinct classes of buyers. In *Oracle Peoplesoft*, the court appeared to require a higher standard for such evidence, namely that the plaintiff show that customers 'could' not find alternative suppliers rather than 'would' not. Similarly, a central question in the Commission's appeal of the decision of the Court of First Instance in *Tetra Laval/Sidel*,[55] currently under review, relates to the standard of evidence required.

The examination of questions of standards of evidence by the courts will require that evidence be developed scientifically, that it be shown to a sufficiently high legal standard, and that the economic theory of harm to competition is rigorously consistent with the market facts. This is important in all competition policy, but especially in mergers where the task is to predict the effect on the market.

The economic analysis of the costs of false positives and false negatives may assist the courts in developing such rules. It is important that standards are not set so high that there could be a significant class of *ex post* anti-competitive mergers that could never satisfy the standard even with the best evidence *ex ante*.

CONCLUSION

Changes in merger policy and the use of economics in mergers have closely followed and reflected developments in underlying economic thinking. Our understanding of competition economics has fortunately not been static.

Economics has had a notable influence on the 'why' of merger policy, leading to the competition tests for mergers as the norm in many countries. This is part of a wider, evidence-based approach to economic policy in which microeconomics instruments are increasingly used to achieve wider economic goals. Here the critical factor is the relationship between competition and productivity growth.

Similarly, the use of economic effects analysis is now well established and common in most jurisdictions. Because it is new, questions relating to the standard of proof and evidence remain. Decisions of the courts will continue to clarify these, and set appropriate standards for economic evidence.

Competition authorities should advocate the use of competition tests implemented with effects-based analysis. While guidelines, speeches and other reasoned decisions are important for advocacy, probably the single most important factor is to ensure that their decisions achieve the highest evidential standards.

This process of change in which new economic thinking is sewn almost seamlessly into the legal jurisprudence enables merger review to achieve its fundamental economic objectives without diminishing legal certainty. While it is true that any change in substantive law can have an initial learning effect, the presence of guidelines and clear procedures does much to limit any such short-run increase in legal uncertainty.

Over the longer term, legal certainty is enormously enhanced if merger decisions reflect sound economic analysis. If it were otherwise, the merger review process would lack the solid foundations necessary to avoid arbitrary and inconsistent decisions. I doubt that an examination of the development of merger case law in both the EU and the US over the past 30 years would negate this proposition.

The publication of merger guidelines and merger decisions not only creates greater transparency and productivity, it also facilitates if not requires essential dialogue across institutions and countries. That merger policy is rooted in solid economic foundations is all the more important in a world where merger decisions on the same or similar transactions are taken by different institutions in different countries.

NOTES

1. The views expressed are my own, and not those of the Competition Authority. I am grateful to Terry Calvani, Damian Collins, Paul Gorecki, Ted Henneberry and Linda Ní Chualladh for helpful comments.
2. Portugal, Austria and Luxembourg have also recently introduced new competition statutes and other EU member states are discussing revisions. The OECD Competition Committee and Peer Review Process have played an important role in facilitating such change more broadly.
3. SLC stands for substantial lessening of competition, and is the legal test in the UK and Ireland and is similar to the new EU test of significant impediment to effective competition.
4. For a concise summary, see Vickers, J., 'Merger Policy in Europe: Retrospect and Prospect' a speech to Charles River Associates (CRA) Members and Antitrust Conference in Washington DC, 11 February 2004 available at www.oft.gov.uk/News/Speeches+and+articles/2004/index.htm. A more detailed account of the economic arguments is given in Fingleton, J. and Nolan, D., 'Mind the Gap: Reforming the EU Merger Regulation', *Mercato Concorenze Regole* 2003 available at www.tca.ie and other papers referred to therein.
5. Criteria under the now repealed Irish Competition Act, 1991 included the level of employment, regional development, rationalisation of operations in the interests of greater efficiency, research and development, increased production, access to markets, shareholders and partners, employees and consumers.
6. For example, speaking in Amsterdam at the 2004 European Competition Day on October 22, Pervenche Berès, President of the ECON Committee of the European Parliament, argued that the short-run impact on employment should be taken into account in merger review. Similar arguments were made in the run-up to the Irish Competition Act 2002, and these are discussed in Fingleton, J., 'Political Economy Insights from Competition Policy in Ireland', in B. Hawk (ed.), *International Antitrust and Policy*, Fordham Corporate Law Institute, Fordham 2001, New York: Juris Publishing, Chapter 21, 2002. More recently, the Report of the Enterprise Strategy Group, Dublin, argued that competition law in Ireland should be modified to allow scale mergers in the food industry.
7. See Porter, Michael E., *The Competitive Advantages of Nations*, New York: Free Press, 1998.
8. The debate in these countries has been more around state aid policy than merger rules. Exemption from competition law is very like state aid in that both involve subsidy, one from consumers and the other from taxpayers. An independent merger policy that does not admit exceptions may lead countries to rely more on state aid.
9. See Kay, John, 'To support the creation of national champions hampers competitiveness', *Financial Times*, 11 January 2005, p. 17.
10. See, for example, the decisions of the Irish Competition Authority in M/03/012 *Smurfit Ireland Limited/Lithographic Universal Limited* 17 July 2003 and E/04/001 *Investigation into a proposed agreement/arrangement in principle whereby Monaghan Middlebrook Mushrooms Limited would acquire 100% shareholding in Carbury Mushrooms Limited*, 26 January 2000. Both decisions are available at www.tca.ie.

11. In advance of the new Irish merger law being introduced, representatives of industry, instead of presenting the national champions argument for political involvement, raised the idea that a minister might want to block a merger that did not lessen competition (as opposed to allowing one that did). In the end, the minister gave up her role in all but media mergers. See Fingleton (2001) (see note 6, above).
12. Almost all businesses are willing to accept all of these arguments when applied to the markets in which they purchase inputs.
13. Report of the Enterprise Strategy Group, Dublin, July 2004.
14. Commissioner Monti was speaking at the French Parliament on 8 June 2004 and also addressed the question of national champions. Roughly this excerpt translates as 'If there is one policy that has been followed consistently by the United Kingdom in economic affairs in recent years, it is the policy of neutrality with regard to the "flag" of companies, regardless of whether they are manufacturing or services companies, and including financial services. However, I doubt that British pride has suffered from this policy, and I am convinced that employment has not suffered'.
15. The Authority is asked to give an opinion on these criteria. For the interested reader, they are:

    (a) 'the strength and competitiveness of media businesses indigenous to the State,
    (b) the extent to which ownership or control of media businesses in the State is spread amongst individuals and other undertakings,
    (c) the extent to which ownership and control of particular types of media business in the State is spread amongst individuals and other undertakings,
    (d) the extent to which the diversity of views prevalent in Irish society is reflected through the activities of the various media businesses in the State, and
    (e) the share in the market in the State of one or more of the types of business activity falling within the definition of "media business" in this subsection that is held by any of the undertakings involved in the media merger concerned, or by any individual or other undertaking who or which has an interest in such an undertaking'.

16. One case, a radio merger, went to a full investigation on competition grounds and the transaction was permitted with remedies. See M/03/033 *Scottish Radio Holdings Limited/ FM104,* 23 February 2004, available at www.tca.ie.
17. The earliest reference I know to this argument is Landes, W.M. and Posner, R.A., 'Market Power in Antitrust Cases', *Harvard Law Review* (March 1981) and the most recent is a 2004 paper by Blumenthal, W. 'Why Bother?: On Market Definition Under the Merger Guidelines', available at www.usdoj.gov /atr/public/workshops/docs/202600.pdf.
18. In M/03/012 *Smurfit Ireland Limited/Lithographic*, the Irish Authority analysed the competitive options available to each class of buyer.
19. An example of this is the recent decision of the Irish Competition Authority in M/04/032 *IBM/Schlumberger,* 28 October 2004. The Authority defined the market narrowly as 'business recovery hotsite services', but the analysis of competitive effects went beyond the players in this relevant market.
20. Competition Commission *Safeway plc and Asda Group Limited* (owned by Wal-Mart Stores Inc); *Wm Morrison Supermarkets PLC; J Sainsbury plc; and Tesco plc.*, September 2003 available at www/competition-commission.org.uk/rep_pub/reports/2003/index. htm.
21. A recent US example is *Royal Caribbean Cruises, Ltd./P&O Princess Cruises plc* and *Carnival Corporation/P&O Princess Cruises plc*, FTC File No. 021 0041 Cruise Lines, where the Federal Trade Commission found that the relevant market was wider than cruises marketed to North Americans but found no competitive effects among cruise line suppliers. See further Coleman, M. and Scheffman, D., 'Empirical Analyses of Potential Competitive Effects of a Horizontal Merger', available at www.ftc.gov.
22. *Philadelphia National Bank* (PNB) was an important tool in the armoury of enforcement officials in days gone by. Once the government showed concentration, the defence had to show that market shares gave an inaccurate account of the probable effects on competition.

Only then did the burden shift back to the government. The US Merger Guidelines and approach of the agencies had moved away from the PNB: the government adopted the burden of showing competitive effects regardless of concentration. See Calvani, T. and Evans, D., 'Regulation of Mergers and Monopolies', *The M&A Lawyer* **17** (2001).

23. See note 22, above.
24. *See United States v. Vons Grocery Co.*, 384 U.S. 270 (1966) in which the Court held unlawful a merger between two grocery chains (third and sixth biggest) that together accounted for 7.5 per cent of sales of retail groceries in Los Angeles.
25. This theory, known as contestability, may be more significant in highlighting conceptually the importance of barriers to entry than in its practical use. Willig, R.D., Panzar, J.C. and Baumol, W.J., *Contestable Markets and the Theory of Industry Structure*, New York: Harcourt, Brace, Jovanovich, 1982.
26. See Sutton, J., *Sunk Costs and Market Structure*, Cambridge, MA: MIT Press, 1991.
27. This is simply the sum of the squares of the market shares of suppliers. A monopoly gives an HHI of 10000, and a market with five equally sized firms gives one of 2000 and so forth. The measure takes account of unequal size distribution in a way that simpler statistics like 3-to-2 may mask.
28. A recent retrospective study by the US Federal Trade Commission on mergers between 1996 and 2003 shows that almost all 3-to-2 mergers were challenged. See www.ftc. gov/opa/2004/02/horizmerger.htm. The data show that several mergers in relatively unconcentrated markets were challenged and Kolasky observes that US agencies challenged more mergers where the combined market share was less than 40 per cent than did the EU Commission. See Kolasky, W.J., 'Coordinated Effects in Merger Review: From Dead Frenchmen to Beautiful Minds and Mavericks', at www.usdoj.gov/atr/public/speeches/11050.htm.
29. In other words, they are based on the overall impact of the merger taking account of competitive effects, barriers to entry and efficiencies. See Competition Authority Merger Guidelines available at www.tca.ie. UK and EU guidelines are similar.
30. Williamson, O.E., 'Economics as an Antitrust Defence: The Welfare Trade-offs', *American Economic Review*, **58**, 1968.
31. This theory is known as X-inefficiency. See Leibenstein, H., 'X-Efficiency Theory', in *The New Palgrave*, London: Macmillan, 1987.
32. There may be specific instances in which harm to rivals via lower costs is coincident with harm to consumers, but the presumption should be otherwise unless there is a clear evidential basis for such harm.
33. See in particular paragraph 82 and footnote 63 OJ C31/5 Guidelines on the assessment of horizontal mergers under the Council Regulation on the control of concentrations between undertakings (2004/C 31/03) of 5 February 2004.
34. This is well covered in the papers on the SLC/Dominance issue cited in note 4, above.
35. Examples include Competition Commission *Safeway plc and Asda Group Limited* (owned by Wal-Mart Stores Inc); *Wm Morrison Supermarkets PLC; J Sainsbury plc*; and *Tesco plc* (see note 20 above), Heinz and Beech-Nut baby foods *FTC v. Heinz*, 116 F. Supp. 2d 190 (D.D.C. 2000), *rev'd* 246 F.3d 708 (D.C.Cir. 2001) *Royal Caribbean Cruises, Ltd./P&O Princess Cruises plc* and *Carnival Corporation/P&O Princess Cruises plc*, FTC File No. 021 0041. This is particularly likely where a merger eliminates a 'maverick' (that is, a supplier with a record or predisposition to different competitive behaviour than other suppliers) from the market.
36. For example, several Irish Competition Authority decisions on mergers in the 1990s cited the US guidelines, and current guidelines used similar HHI thresholds for describing concentration.
37. See www.internationalcompetitionnetwork.org/analysisofmerger.html. The ICN is currently working on a guidelines project jointly chaired by the UK Competition Commission, the UK Office of Fair Trading and the Irish Competition Authority.
38. See www.internationalcompetitionnetwork.org/analysisofmerger.html.
39. The European Competition Authorities, founded in 2001, has established an informal communication system and working groups on specific issues (see www.oft.gov.uk/ECA/

About+the+ECA.htm). The European Competition Network created by Regulation 1/2003 in May 2004 further enhances the ability of the agencies of the 25 member states and the Commission to work jointly on cases.

40. Parties are often reluctant to hand over such documents, and the Irish Authority has had to use its summons powers in a number of instances.

41. See note 28, above.

42. The US courts have established strict rules for expert evidence in competition cases. A good source on this, in the context of econometric evidence in merger cases, is Werden, G.J., Froeb, L.M. and Scheffman, D., 'A Daubert Discipline for Merger Simulation', *Antitrust* magazine, **18** (3), Summer, 89.

43. Perhaps the best-known US case to rely heavily on such evidence was *Federal Trade Commission v. Staples, inc. and office depot, inc.* United States District Court for the District of Columbia 1997 U.S. Dist. Lexis 9322; 1997–2 Trade cas. (cch) p71,867. Studies of this kind are also done by the European Commission (for example, Case Comp/M.1672 *Volvo Scania* Commission Decision of 13.03.2000) and by member states (for example, M/04/02 *Uniphar/Whelehan* July 15, 2004).

44. Although in the context of econometric evidence presented in the trial of an abuse of dominance case, *Masterfoods*, the comments of Judge Keane are relevant. 'I reach that conclusion largely on what has been described as the "commonsense" or "innate characteristics" test ... As to the cross-elasticity of demand criterion, to which much expert evidence was directed, it may be that ... [the] ... econometric study could be said, at least in a negative sense, to confirm the "commonsense" test. Ultimately, however, I think that the acknowledged incapacity of that procedure to embrace all the significant variables which would have to be taken into account significantly reduces its value'. See *Masterfoods Ltd. t/a Mars Ireland v. H.B. Ice cream Ltd.* [1993] ILRM 145, [1992] 3CMLR 830.

45. M/04/02 *Uniphar/Whelehan* July 15, 2004.

46. Simulation models are particularly useful in predicting how the effects of a merger depend on assumptions about unknown variables such as the shape and elasticity of demand. For a detailed discussion, see Werden, G.J. and Froeb, L.M. (forthcoming) 'Unilateral competitive effects of horizontal mergers', in Paolo Buccroosi (ed.), *Handbook of Antitrust Economics*, Cambridge, USA: MIT Press.

47. Kolasky (see note 28, above) points out that many features of detected cartels are not well predicted by theory. For example, known cartels are frequently more stable and involve more participants than theory predicts.

48. The case in question was M/03/033 mentioned in note 16, above. The published decision, available at www.tca.ie outlines the economic testing that was carried out in the market for radio advertising using a 'buy round' analysis.

49. For a detailed and authoritative discussion of the issues of standard of proof and standard of judicial review, as they have applied to EU merger policy, see Vesterdorf, B., 'Standard of proof in merger cases: reflections in the light of recent case law of the Community Courts', paper presented to the Third Annual Merger Control Conference of the British Institute of International and Comparative Law, London, December 2004, http://www.biicl.org/admin/files/Standard_of_proof_Bo_Vesterdorf.pdf.

50. See Bishop, S., 'Alice Through the Looking Glass: The Use and Misuse of Economics in EU Merger Control', *Current Competition Law*, Volume II, 2004.

51. Economists will know these as the Cournot and Bertrand games.

52. For a review of this literature and its impact see Kolasky (note 28, above).

53. Case T-342/99 *Airtours v. Commission* June 6, 2002.

54. *United States of America v. Sungard Data Systems, Inc.*, United States District Court for the District of Columbia, Civil Action No. 01–02196 (ESH), November 14, 2001.

55. Cases T-05/05 and T-80/02 *Tetra Laval BV v. Commission of the European Commission*. While the decision of the European Court of Justice is expected in 2005, the Opinion of Advocate General Tizzano (Case C-12/03P) was published in May 2004.

CHAIRMAN'S COMMENTS

Leonard Waverman

John's analysis is a wonderful survey and a very cogent review of the role of economics and how it has been developing over the last few years. You can see at the end also the warning that as witnesses in important cases, economists must be careful because they have a burden of proof.

I would like to make three points on efficiencies, on convergence and on burden of proof. John states that it is important that efficiencies be considered. Williamson's 1968 paper suggested that efficiency gains from a cost-reducing merger generally outweigh potential price increases. Yet John states that, 'its relevance to mergers that increase market power is unclear'. This is the generic stance of many competition authorities and I simply do not understand it, as an economist. The gain to society from a cost reduction is a gain to society, period. John says that increases in market power may generate 'X-inefficiency'. But surely profit-maximising firms will reduce costs when the opportunities arise. Relying on 'X-inefficiency' to disregard 'efficiencies', seems a bit cavalier. One can see 'X'-inefficiencies and 'externalities' anywhere, maybe we should revoke much use of those words?

This analysis does bring us to the view of whether we use a consumer surplus or a total surplus test. What is the goal of merger policy? Should policy be to make the economy more efficient or is it to make consumers better off? John also suggests that a high burden of proof should attach to showing efficiencies in a situation where a merger increases market power and I want to return to that at the end when I discuss burden of proof.

I also want to talk about convergence and consider how far it has gone. Here John has been one of the important people working on developing the International Competition Network (ICN). So if we are going to have mergers across borders, firms often complain about the high cost of multiple filings and so on. But one of the major costs is really getting it wrong or having some regime that gets it wrong. Firms also have the ability to shop regimes and go to the regime that has the lowest common denominator competition policy. So there is continuous work on convergence. The ICN is established in a number of the countries that are involved in the process, making revisions to laws to increase conformity so that they are more similar. The OECD has played a huge role here, in pushing coordination of policies across countries, not just in filing notifications and in timeframes but also with substantive issues behind merger and competition law generally. There are a number of bilateral agreements and these are growing in number. As economists, we can talk about whether bilateralism is the right approach and whether we go to more of a multilateral approach as in trade policy where bilateral agreements are sometimes viewed as not efficiency enhancing. The ICN has been looking within the EU at convergence and says there is a commonality in things like market definition and in the use of the SSNIP (small but significant non-transitory increase in price) test. But there are variations in treatment of efficiencies; capacity constraints; supply-side effects and the guidelines that John has discussed vary enormously from country to country as does the technical expertise of the agencies. Case law and the decisions and how they are written also vary. For example, whether there is a full decision you can really rely on; in some countries that is not necessarily true. Even within the EU we could go even further, does the agency use the SLC or dominance test (some countries like France have both)? Differences in appeal mechanisms are large across the EU. Differences in legal treatment are also crucial. We are discussing mergers today but in Ireland, cartels are under criminal law and therefore they have to prove beyond reasonable doubt that there is a cartel. Can you have fines in criminal cases? No. And so this difference between criminal and civil law across the EU, is important, as is the difference in fine levels with some jurisdictions having large fines and some that do not. And so we have a lot of issues of convergence that we still have to work on even if we are partly down the road of bringing finer law and finer economics to bear.

Let me end on the burden of proof issue and here I think it is really a substantive issue. Competition policy should be based on competition principles. But do firms have to prove that their merger is in the public interest or do the authorities have to challenge the merger and prove that it is not in the public interest? I take you to the last points John made: the difference of interpretation in the *Tetrapak* case, and the difference between 'could' and 'would'. One change in letters from 'could' to 'would', makes a huge difference in the burden of proof. And I think John was lamenting the fact that in the US this would mean that you could not block mergers which you know were 'bad', *ex ante*, and that you could only get after them, *ex post*. Now is that really a bad position for the US to be in? We do have *ex post* abuse law and economic evidence. What is the evidence that competition authorities get it right, *ex ante*? So it is increasingly important to follow up and to look at whether the decisions do lead to increased welfare for consumers or for total surplus. We do not do enough of that, indeed, we are only just beginning to do it. I think if we did that in a consistent manner then we would come up with a better way of analysing mergers and other issues of competition policy.

Finally, in terms of econometrics and our tasks as economists providing evidence I take you back to Franklin Fisher's book, *Folded, Spindled and Mutilated: Economic Analysis and the US Government v. IBM*, (with J.J. McGowan and J. Greenwood, Cambridge, MA: MIT Press, 1983), which has a chapter in it of the role of the academic economist as expert witness and the problems one has in not being a friend of the court. One says to the client, 'really I give you the truth but truth may be multi-faceted'. I think courts are increasingly going to narrow the ability for economists to say 'on the one hand' and 'on the other hand'.

My last remark is that John started off by talking about 'national champions', and if we look at what he has done in Ireland, I think, in time he will be recognised as the true national champion of competition policy.

Reference

Williamson, Oliver E. (1968), 'Economies as an antitrust defense: the welfare trade-offs', *American Economic Review*, **58** (March), 18–35.

8. Comment on mergers and comparative competition in the water industry

Philip Fletcher[1]

I would like to comment on mergers in the water industry and on comparative competition as I have some past knowledge that may be relevant. I was a very young and green, in the old-fashioned sense of the word, civil servant working in the Private Office of Peter Walker the Secretary of State for the Environment as the regional water authorities were set up at the beginning of the 1970s. I certainly would not claim from that worm's eye view a deep inward knowledge of all the policy considerations. But I can say that the beginning of the 1970s was a time when it was almost an article of faith in the public sector that 'bigger was better'. The Department of Environment was one of the first, one of the only super departments, created especially for that purpose out of three old departments alongside the Department of Trade and Industry. (The DTI though much battered has had a longer survival rate!) It went alongside a substantial reorganisation of local government in the direction of bigger is better. You created bigger entities because there would be economies and efficiency that flowed from them, and a perspective that raised you above the parish pump.

Now again, by coincidence, in 1989 I was Director of Finance in the Department of Environment and my role was to 'ride shotgun' for the Permanent Secretary, who has a particular role as Accounting Officer. This separates him from ministers and makes him or her personally accountable to Parliament for generating proper value for money for the taxpayer. That shotgun role was therefore quite important. It was about ensuring that the Permanent Secretary would be able to sit down in front of the Public Accounts Committee and say, 'I am satisfied that the taxpayer is getting value for money', an article of faith in the privatisation of the public sector utilities.

Now, leaving aside whether I did a good job or not, I do have the answer to the question, 'Well why on earth weren't the regional water authorities broken up before they were privatised?'

First a tribute here to the late Nicholas Ridley MP. He came in as Secretary of State and saw that it was totally unacceptable to have these entities switch from the public to the private sector and continue to carry out an environmental regulation role. So he changed the basis of privatisation. He said we must have a National Rivers Authority because it was unacceptable for those bodies to regulate themselves, and even more unacceptable if they were regulating others operating in the private sector. He was clearly right and it is now not even a matter of debate.

But having done that bit of substantial reorganisation, if the regional water authorities were to be privatised quickly there could be no question of starting to change the structure of these bodies further. There simply was not the evidence or data to float these companies in the market. If you made them significantly smaller they would be too small to float and you would have to do it through trade sales and various other options. So, it is not too surprising that bodies created at the beginning of the 1970s for the different purpose of river basin management were privatised as large entities at the end of the 1980s. It is a bit like Christopher Wren saying 'Well now London has burned down we can create a new London with nice straight lines and properly laid out'. But of course you cannot because property is privately owned. You cannot readily break up London building plots or former regional water authorities. That could still be an issue for the future. We shall see.

On more recent history, listening to some academic commentators, you might almost assume that there have been no mergers. In fact, since my watch began – halfway through the year 2000 – five of the 10 water and water and sewage companies have gone through mergers. Admittedly these have been takeover type mergers. We have had Thames taken over by the still bigger entity, German RWE. Wessex went through the trauma of Enron/Azurix and was then taken over by YTL (Malaysian). We have Northumbrian, having been in the ownership of Suez and now in a different ownership. We have had Southern moving from ScottishPower to its present ownership – the only case to have gone through the Competition Commission in recent times. Welsh Water went in rapid succession from ownership by Western Power Distribution to ownership by a very unusual entity, Glas Cymru, a company limited by guarantee. And you can look at the other five and say none of them has been immune from at the very least speculation about takeover; or significant restructuring over that period.

The same applies to the water only companies, including recently the takeover of South Staffordshire Water (which itself has gone through about three substantially different configurations in the last three years) by Arcapita (previously First Islamic Bank). So it is not as if the water industry has been immune from one of what is normally cited by the City as the major arguments for efficiency through consolidation. This is the threat to the incumbent management that if it fails to perform it will be taken over and will be ejected. That has happened, has been very present in the water industry in recent years.

It is very important to have 22 companies to compare with one another. (It is actually just 23. We have one last tiny company down in Wiltshire which is still regulated properly and still has its price limits just like everybody else. It is a reminder of what the structure used to be like. And it is perhaps a pointer to what it is now like in Germany with some 6000 entities. France and other European partners are not dissimilar.) In the 2004 price review it is no secret to say that comparative competition was a crucial and essential part of the regulatory tool kit. Without it the companies could call almost all the shots.

Comparative competition is essential. Those who say, 'Oh the regulator can surely manage with less than 22, after all 21 would not make much difference' are the siren voices that favour whittling down. I am certainly not saying that Ofwat (Office of Water Services) sets its face against all mergers, but we do say, 'here is some evidence which we will want to think about'. I welcome the fact that politics is taken out of the equation now that the Competition Commission is going to take all decisions on mergers within the sector. I have no doubt, on the strength of my experience on the Southern Water case, that the Commission will treat each case extremely seriously. It will look at all the relevant evidence and will come to appropriately objective conclusions in the light of whatever is put in front of it.

NOTE

1. This contribution by Philip Fletcher was originally a comment on a paper on economies of scale and productivity growth in the water industry. His remarks have been revised slightly because it has not been possible to publish the paper on which he commented.

9. Privatisation and regulation in developing countries

David Parker and Colin Kirkpatrick

INTRODUCTION

Since the 1980s a large number of developing countries have introduced privatisation programmes. While privatisation of competitive enterprises has often led to economic benefits, the privatisation of infrastructure schemes seems to have proved much more problematic (Kikeri and Nellis 2001; Parker and Kirkpatrick 2005). Infrastructure industries, such as transport, energy, water and sewerage supplies and telecommunications, involve some element of natural monopoly in their delivery. The consequence is state economic regulation after privatisation, which in turn requires the development of regulatory capacity in a country. Another permutation is 'competition for the market' under which firms compete for monopoly concessions. Firms bid periodically to operate a service, winning the bid when they offer to achieve the required quality of output at least cost. In principle, provided that the concession contract is complete, in the sense of covering all contingencies during its life, then ongoing regulation is unnecessary. However, contracts are invariably incomplete and require constant monitoring (Guasch 2004). Concession contracts do not, in practice, reduce the need for some form of ongoing scrutiny or regulation.

An essential requirement for economic growth and poverty reduction is the provision of efficient, reliable and affordable infrastructure services. Usually the poor in developing countries suffer from both a high degree of exclusion from access to infrastructure services and the poor quality of those services that they are able to purchase (Clarke and Wallsten 2002). For example, currently 1.1 billion people lack access to safe water supplies and an even larger number lack access to adequate sanitation (Mitlin 2004; World Bank 2004a, p. 219). Infrastructure industries provide essential public services and have an important role to play in meeting the needs of the poor (Willoughby 2003). The case for privatisation lies in the belief that state-owned enterprises (SOEs), which have traditionally been the dominant suppliers of infrastructure services, are a major cause of service failures due to their inefficiency and disregard for consumers. Privatisation is expected to promote more efficient operations, increase investment and service coverage, and reduce the financial burden on government budgets (World Bank 1995). In recognition of the importance of infrastructure reforms in poorer economies, in 2004 the World Bank published a detailed report entitled *Reforming Infrastructure: Privatization, Regulation and Competition.* In it the Bank seemed to reverse its earlier stance and concluded that 'Privatization has been oversold and misunderstood' and that while developing economies have suffered from poor infrastructure performance, 'the structure of ownership has not been the key explanatory variable' (World Bank 2004a pp. 6–7). Rather the report confirmed that 'effective regulation – including the setting of adequate tariff levels – is the most critical enabling condition for infrastructure reform' (p. xii). In other words, privatisation of infrastructure requires effective and efficient state regulation.

However, despite official recognition of the importance of regulation in infrastructure reform, comparatively little consideration has been given to the detailed design of institutional structures and regulatory instruments appropriate to the conditions and capacities that characterise developing countries. In most cases the new regulatory systems that have been created have been modelled on those in Western Europe, the USA or Australia. In particular, donor agencies and consultancies have recommended the creation of 'independent' regulatory offices and the adoption of the price cap form of regulation (Smith 1997). But it is by no means obvious that the advanced economies are appropriate role models. Moreover, there exists no comprehensive audit of the actual performance of regulatory bodies in developing countries.

The objective of this chapter is to review the nature of infrastructure regulation in lower-income economies and to identify areas for future research. The content draws upon research conducted within the Centre on Regulation and Competition based at the University of Manchester and funded by the Department for International Development (DFID).[1] The chapter begins by reviewing the extent of privatisation in infrastructure programmes in developing countries. It then turns to consider two particular issues that are fundamental to economic regulation, namely regulatory governance and the appropriate form of profit control. These two issues have been chosen because regulatory governance lies at the heart of the debate over the merits of 'independent' regulation; while a discussion of price caps versus direct profit regulation highlights the difficulty of designing effective regulatory mechanisms for developing countries.

INFRASTRUCTURE PRIVATISATION IN DEVELOPING ECONOMIES

The 1990s saw a sharp decline in the level of official donor support for infrastructure projects in developing countries. Aggregate flows of aid for the infrastructure sector halved during the course of the decade, to US$8billion in 1999 (Willoughby 2003). This shift away from infrastructure projects reflected the disappointment of donors with the performance of the infrastructure sector. It often appeared to be inefficient, poorly managed, socially and environmentally damaging, and lacking a clear and accountable process of governance to control corrupt practices (World Bank 1994; DFID 2002). However, compared to the decline in official aid, private capital flows for infrastructure investment increased significantly during the decade. This occurred in response to the privatisation of infrastructure in developing countries, a policy encouraged by the main international donor bodies. According to the World Bank's Private Participation in Infrastructure (PPI) database, 26 countries arranged 72 infrastructure projects with private participation in 1984–89, attracting almost US$19 billion in investment commitments. By contrast, in the 1990s 132 low- and middle-income countries pursued private participation in infrastructure – 57 of them in three or all four of the sectors covered in the database, namely transport, energy, telecommunications, and water and sewerage. In total, between 1990 and 2001 governments in developing countries involved the private sector in almost 2500 infrastructure projects, attracting investment commitments of more than US$750 billion. Annual investment commitments for infrastructure projects with private participation grew steadily from 1990, to peak at US$128 billion in 1997. Following the Asian financial crisis of 1997/98, private foreign investment in infrastructure in lower-income economies declined. By 2003 it had returned to a level similar to that in 1994 (Izaguirre 2004).

Private infrastructure projects have taken a number of forms (World Bank 2003, p. 7), namely:

- *Management and lease contracts* The operation and management of an SOE is taken over by a private operator for a given period. The facility remains owned by the public sector and usually government continues to make the investment decisions and retains financial responsibility.
- *Concessions* A private firm takes over the management of an SOE for a given period and assumes the investment risk. Typically, the ownership of the facility reverts back to the public sector at the end of the concession period.

- *Greenfield projects* A private firm or a public–private joint venture builds a new facility and operates it for the period specified in the project contract. The facility may transfer to the public sector at the end of the contract period.
- *Divestitures.* A private firm purchases an equity stake in an SOE during an asset sale.

According to the World Bank, over the 1990–2001 period, divestitures accounted for 41 per cent (US$312 billion) of total private participation in infrastructure projects in developing countries, greenfield projects accounted for 42 per cent, concessions for 16 per cent and management and lease contracts for well under 1 per cent of the total (World Bank 2003, Table 1.3, p. 17).

Among the developing regions, Latin America and the Caribbean accounted for 48 per cent of the cumulative investment in infrastructure (see Figure 9.1). In this region, private participation was often part of a broader sectoral reform programme, aimed at enhancing performance through private operation and competition and generating the financial resources needed to improve service coverage and quality through tariff adjustments (ibid., pp. 2–3). Divestitures and concessions of existing assets predominated, accounting for around 75 per cent of the cumulative investment in private infrastructure projects in Latin America during the period (Figure 9.2). In more recent years, the region's dominance of investment in infrastructure

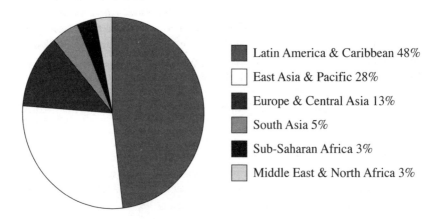

Source: World Bank (2003, Figure 1.6, p. 14).

Figure 9.1   Cumulative investment in infrastructure projects with private participation by region, 1990–2001

has declined, from 80 per cent in 1990 to 40 per cent in 2001, as other areas of the world have opened their infrastructure sectors to private capital.

East Asia and the Pacific countries have been the second-largest recipients of private investment in infrastructure. Over the 1990–2001 period, this region accounted for 28 per cent of cumulative private participation in infrastructure in the developing economies (Figure 9.1). In contrast to Latin America, in Asia the focus has been on the creation of new assets through greenfield projects, which, for example, accounted for 61 per cent of the investment in East Asia in 1990–2001 (Figure 9.2). The Asian financial crisis saw the region's share of annual investment in infrastructure decline from 40 per cent in 1996 to 11 per cent in 1998, before recovering to 28 per cent in 2001.

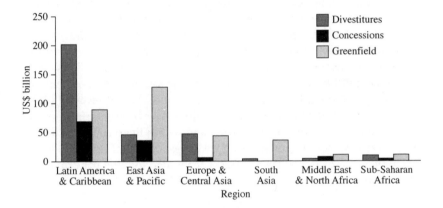

Source: Based on World Bank (2003, Figure 1.7, p. 15).

Figure 9.2 Cumulative investment in infrastructure projects with private participation by type and region, 1990 –2001

Although private activity in infrastructure grew rapidly among developing countries, and particularly in Latin America and Asia, a small number of countries accounted for most of the investment. The 10 countries attracting the largest investment in projects with private participation accounted for 68 per cent of the cumulative investment in 1990–2001 and 47 per cent of the projects. The leading Latin American economies were Brazil, Argentina and Mexico. In Asia, the main economies involved were China, Malaysia, South Korea, the Philippines and India.

Turning to industries, private participation in infrastructure in developing countries has been concentrated in the telecommunications sector, which provided for 44 per cent of the cumulative investment in 1990–2001 (World

Bank 2003, p. 3). Energy, which includes electricity and the transmission and distribution of natural gas, attracted the second-largest share of investment. Electricity accounted for 28 per cent of the cumulative investment in private infrastructure projects during this period. Much of the private investment in electricity has been in greenfield projects with independent power producers implementing build–operate–own (BOO) or build–operate–transfer (BOT) type contracts and investors negotiating for returns to be underwritten in the form of 'take or pay' contracts or sovereign guarantees.

By contrast, private participation in the water and sewerage sector has been very limited, accounting for only 5 per cent of cumulative investments over the decade. The small amount of private involvement in water utilities reflects the inherent difficulties that face privatisation in this sector, in terms of the technology of water provision and the nature of the product, transaction costs and regulatory weaknesses (Kirkpatrick et al. 2004a). Where there has been private participation in water and sewerage, it has often been in the form of transferring vertically integrated water utilities to the private sector through concessions. Of the 233 water projects on the World Bank PPI Project Database, 40 per cent involved concession contracts and these accounted for 64 per cent of the total amount invested (Table 9.1). The private investments in water projects have been concentrated in a small number of developing countries, and within these countries usually the figures have been dominated by a few large contracts (Table 9.2). In the Philippines, for example, five contracts accounted for 38.4 per cent of the total private investment in water services in East Asia.

Table 9.1   Types of private water and sewerage projects in developing countries, 1990–2002

Type	Total investment (US$bn)[*]	%	No. of projects	%
Concessions	22.31	64	93	40
Greenfield investments	7.00	20	75	32
Operations and management (management and lease contracts)	0.18	0.5	46	20
Divestitures	5.48	15.6	19	8

Note: [*] This is the total invested in projects with private participation and not necessarily the private sector's financial commitment.

Source: Calculated using data from the World Bank PPI Project Database, http://rru.worldbank.org/PPI.

Table 9.2   *Largest investments in water services in developing countries,*
1990–2002

	US$bn	No. of projects
Argentina	7.23	10
Philippines	5.87	5
Chile	3.95	13
Brazil	3.17	33
Malaysia	2.75	6
China	1.93	44
Romania	1.04	3
Turkey	0.94	2
Indonesia	0.92	8

Source: Calculated using data from the World Bank PPI Project Database, http://rru.
worldbank.org/PPI.

REGULATION AND REGULATORY CAPACITY

That the institutional context is critical to the outcomes of any regulatory regime is now well recognised. In turn, institutions are credited with having important effects on the trajectory of economic development (North 1990; Lal 1999, ch. 3). Levy and Spiller (1994) focus on regulatory arrangements to sustain private investment and how these vary with the institutional endowment in different countries. That effective privatisation of infrastructure programmes in developing countries requires efficient and effective regulation appears axiomatic. As a consequence, in promoting policy reforms donor agencies such as the World Bank have been criticised for adopting an 'under-socialised approach' (Torp and Rekve 1998, p. 80). Similarly, there is country-level case study evidence which suggests that regulatory bodies may function poorly in a number of low- and middle-income economies. This occurs due to inadequate regulatory skills, regulatory governance weaknesses and the prevalence of regulatory capture by special interest groups, including the ruling elites (for example, Cariño 2002, on the Philippines; Knight-John et al. 2003, on Sri Lanka; TERI 2003, on India; also see World Bank 2004b).

If state regulation is to have the best chance of promoting economic and social welfare it needs to be both *effective* and *efficient:* effective in the sense of achieving its planned goals and efficient in the sense of achieving these goals at least cost. The costs include administration expenses and the costs imposed on the economy in terms of complying with regulations. In terms of effectiveness criteria, while much of the discussion of regulation has focused on improvements in economic and financial performance, distributional issues have strongly influenced public policy towards infrastructure. Most developed countries specify universal access to certain infrastructure services, including telecommunications, water and sanitation and electricity, with the goal of ensuring access for all people at affordable prices. Universal service obligations are typically incorporated in operating licences and concession contracts.

In developing countries, concerns about the accessibility and affordability of infrastructure services are expected to be even more pronounced than in the rich economies. The majority of the population lack access to safe and affordable water services, telecommunications and reliable public transport and energy supplies. Privatisation may hurt the poor when prices have to be increased to make supplies economic, making services even less affordable. Also, as Estache et al. (2002, p. 6) point out, although universal service obligations are politically appealing, they may have limited meaning in the developing country context. This is because they fail to take into account that low-income households often cannot afford the service and hence will not request it. Also, for communities that are not currently served by the formal utility network, service expansion needs to take place on a coordinated and planned basis. In theory these affordability and access concerns can be addressed through financial subsidies. But in practice, subsidies for infrastructure services have often proved to be poorly targeted and regressive in their incidence, not least because the very poor do not receive supplies (Estache et al. 2001; World Bank 2004a, pp. 20–21). Too often the gainers from subsidies and cross-subsidies have been middle- and higher-income groups, especially where, as normal, they control political power.

Considering specifically the actions of regulatory authorities, there is a range of policy instruments that can be used by a regulatory authority to mitigate the potential adverse income distribution effects of infrastructure privatisation, such as requiring continuing cross-subsidies or the introduction of pro-poor pricing schedules, including lifeline tariffs. But the choice of instruments requires a detailed understanding of the social dimensions of infrastructure services in the country or geographical area concerned. Consideration also needs to be given to the unintended costs of using a particular regulatory instrument. For example, cross-subsidies can lead to wasteful consumption and reduced incentives for utilities to extend their services to poorer areas. Also, a number of studies have identified significant administrative costs in identifying households eligible for subsidy and designing tariff schemes that target poverty effectively (for example, DFID 2000a; Estache et al. 2002; World Bank 2004a).

The task of the regulator is to respond to distributive and poverty reduction goals in a way that does not significantly undermine the economic efficiency objective of economic regulation. Balancing the efficiency and effectiveness goals of regulation is particularly challenging in a developing country context because of the large weight that is likely to be placed on social objectives – perhaps in the face of a threat of social unrest and political intervention. The regulator's task is often made more difficult by limitations in regulatory capacity. Many developing countries lack strong regulatory capability in terms of trained personnel and sound laws and law enforcement to sustain regulatory commitment and credibility. Regulatory offices in developing countries tend to be small, undermanned for the job they face and more expensive to run in relation to GDP than in developed economies (Domah et al. 2003). There is a often an acute lack of regulatory staff, especially of economists, accountants and lawyers, trained in regulatory policy analysis and contract design. In a survey of 22 regulators in 13 Asian countries, Jacobs (2004) found the lack of well-trained staff to be a major constraint on good quality regulation. Moreover, the economic and social data needed to evaluate the potential effectiveness of different regulatory instruments is often limited or unavailable.

Given the inevitable trade-offs between social and economic concerns, it is important for government to provide statutory guidance on the extent to which the regulator is responsible for meeting social over purely economic objectives and the regulatory instruments that should be used. This is so because a desire to implement 'pro-poor' regulation measures will probably be perceived by investors as increasing the risk of regulatory discretion. The absence of sufficient safeguards against the misuse of such discretion will increase the cost of capital and impact adversely on services and prices (Smith 2000). As DFID (2000b, pp. 23–5) has commented: 'Effective governments are needed to build the legal, institutional and regulatory framework without which market reforms can go badly wrong, at great cost – particularly for the poor'. This claim is supported by a growing body of empirical evidence which confirms that the quality of the regulatory environment has a significant effect on an economy's performance (Alexander and Estache 1999; Kauffman and Kraay 2002; Jalilian et al. 2003; Kirkpatrick et al. 2004c). More particularly, in the case of infrastructure investments the evidence confirms that privatisation brings greater economic benefits when it is accompanied by an effective regulatory regime (Wallsten 2001; Zhang et al. 2003, 2004; Pargal 2003).

The nature of effective regulatory regimes in advanced countries has now been researched at some length, involving addressing issues of consistency, transparency, accountability, proportionality and effective targeting of regulation (Haskins 2000, p. 60). But there has been much less discussion of appropriate regulatory rules in the context of developing economies and more particularly how the objectives of consistency, transparency and accountability are best achieved – this despite the fact that the threat from regulatory failure is much greater in these economies because of their institutional weaknesses.

One of the main difficulties for privatisation of infrastructure in developing countries lies, therefore, in regulatory governance (Stern and Holder 1999; Minogue 2002) or the legal powers and responsibilities of regulators, including their effective independence from regulatory (including political) capture. The privatisation of utility industries in developed countries has been accompanied by the development of dedicated regulatory offices, to varying degrees independent from government departments. The regulator retains powers to gather information, issue directions and fine or in other ways penalise the firm for regulation infringements. In Western Europe, the USA and Australia, such powers are constrained by legislation and regulated firms have redress through appeal against regulatory decisions to the courts or to another appeals body, such as the Competition Commission in the UK.

Compare this with the economic and legal environment in many developing economies. The differences are stark. The regulatory environment in developing economies is often much less conducive to effective utility regulation than is the case in Western Europe, the USA and Australia (Parker 2002). Regulatory rules and conventions are commonly weak and underdeveloped. Many developing economies lack institutional structures to promote effective information gathering and compliance with the regulatory rules. Corruption and cronyism is often rife, undermining the credibility of any supposed regulatory independence and compromising the objectiveness of any appeal mechanisms. Also, and on a more micro level, regulatory regimes in developing countries frequently suffer from considerable management deficiencies. Specifically, the following are some of the main governance problems in developing countries that can prevent the achievement of efficient and effective regulation:

- Unclear powers – the regulatory 'carrots and sticks' may be ill-defined and their use unpredictable because of political intervention.
- The inability of regulators to commit to some form of 'regulatory contract' to remove inconsistency and unpredictability in regulation. This is so especially in countries with unstable political structures that lead to frequent changes of government and where regulatory practices are not adequately protected by the courts.
- Lack of a developed legal code for regulatory appeals.

- Lack of a developed competition policy to complement sector regulation, which places even greater demands on the sector regulator to police the competitive environment and protect consumers. Today around 100 developing countries claim to have competition laws but in many instances they are wholly or largely ineffective.
- A weak macroeconomic environment, including relatively high inflation and exchange rate weaknesses that impact adversely on the cost base of utilities, complicate rate setting and create disincentives for investors to invest.
- Regulatory and political capture, including the appointment of regulators with links to interested groups, including the regulated industries and the governing elites.

In summary, effective regulatory incentives and regulatory governance regimes need to be in place but both are often either underdeveloped or absent (Spiller 1993; Levy and Spiller 1994; Kauffman and Kraay 2002).

One possible approach to improving regulatory governance in developing countries is to encourage the adoption of some form of regulatory impact assessment (RIA). This is a term used to describe the process of systematically assessing the benefits and costs of both a new regulation before its planned introduction and of an existing regulation to see if it needs to be revised or abandoned (Kirkpatrick and Parker 2004). RIA involves consultation with interested parties before a new regulation is introduced or an existing regulation is revised and its use is recommended within the OECD. By the beginning of 2001, governments in 20 OECD countries were applying it, although the extent of its use varies (Jacobs 1997, 2004; Radaelli 2002). By contrast, there has been little analysis of either the actual use of or potential for using RIA in developing countries. This is despite the considerable interest in measuring the impact of development policy and in the design and implementation of regulation measures (DFID 2000a; World Bank 2001a).

Indeed, there has been an absence of even rudimentary data on the use of RIA-type procedures within governments in developing economies. In an attempt to close this gap in knowledge, a questionnaire survey was undertaken by the Centre on Regulation and Competition in 2003. The questionnaire was sent to 311 government departments and agencies with regulatory responsibilities in 99 developing (including some transition) economies. The questionnaires completed and returned came from 40 countries – a country response rate of 40 per cent – with more than one official in some departments and agencies replying. In total 68 useable questionnaires were returned, giving an overall response rate from officials of 17 per cent. The regulatory activities covered included economic, social and environmental regulation, but with a bias towards economic regulation. The majority of the responses were from regulators of the network utilities, with 25 replies from the energy (electricity, gas, oil and alternative energy) sector, and a further 23 replies from the telecommunications sector. Twenty replies were from other government bodies (Kirkpatrick et al., 2004b).

Respondents claimed that some form of regulatory assessment is being applied in the majority of countries that returned completed questionnaires. However, there were marked regional differences in claimed familiarity with RIA principles. Three-fifths of the replies from Africa reported little or no awareness, whereas the majority of respondents from Asia were fully aware of the concept. Only six of the respondents, however, were familiar with the OECD guidelines on implementing RIA. In four countries respondents reported that guidance on how RIA should be undertaken had been prepared within government. However, these countries included Mexico and South Korea, both of whom are members of the OECD. None of the respondents from Africa claimed that their country had developed guidelines for the conduct of RIA.

The questionnaire answers confirmed that in a number of developing economies there is some understanding of the potential benefits of impact assessment techniques in improving regulatory outcomes. At the same time, however, an understanding of how to apply RIA does not seem deep or widespread, with variations found in knowledge between agencies and government departments even within the same country. The results confirm that there is still an important and urgent need in lower-income economies to improve understanding of how to achieve better regulatory governance. The World Bank (2001b, p. 72) has commented that: 'Better regulation does not always mean less regulation'. But so far, compared to the heavy emphasis that donor agencies have placed on privatisation and the establishment of regulatory agencies in developing countries, they have not been particularly active in promoting systematic methods to improve regulatory governance – as against highlighting the problem (World Bank 2004b). The use of RIA or similar techniques may help to improve regulatory governance internationally, although this is not to underestimate the potential difficulties in introducing effective RIA methods. RIA is not a cure for weak governance – like all reforms the risk is that it will be badly implemented – but it can contribute to improving governance as part of a package of governmental reforms.

In addition to the need for governance reforms in developing countries, there are often weaknesses in methods for regulating firm behaviour and more especially profits and prices. To this we now turn.

REGULATING PRICES AND PROFITS

In developing economies, regulators face a greater dichotomy than in developed countries between promoting economic and social goals because of endemic poverty (Smith 2000). This is important, for what is deemed regulatory ineffectiveness in one context, for instance a failure to remove cross-subsidies that favour the poor but distort allocative efficiency, may not be in another context where poverty reduction is the primary goal of public policy. In developing countries, an industry regulator must pay detailed attention to tariffs so as to balance the need to supply poor households with affordable infrastructure services with ensuring that companies earn sufficient profits to satisfy their investors. This may involve the use of subsidies to suppress tariffs, as for example under so-called output-based aid (OBA), where the payment of a subsidy to an operator is made conditional on the operator having delivered the specified output or other performance measure (Brook and Smith 2003).

There are broadly four main methods of regulating prices and profits in infrastructure industries, namely the use of a price cap, rate of return regulation, a sliding scale regime, which is a hybrid of the first two, and direct state setting of prices. The last may be based on costs of production, equating to rate of return regulation, but is likely to be associated with more arbitrary rules for price setting, reflecting each government's political and social as well as economic priorities. Whatever precise method is used, regulators, whether in dedicated regulatory offices or government departments, are likely to face difficulties arising from the inherent information asymmetries that exist in a regulated environment (Newbery 1999; Parker 2002). In developing countries, such problems are compounded by the weak regulatory governance already discussed and problems in creating effective regulatory incentives (Levy and Spiller 1994).

In recent years the economics of regulation literature has favoured the use of price cap over rate of return regulation because of its greater incentive effects (Armstrong et al. 1994; Weyman-Jones 2003). Also, it seems that price cap regulation has been adopted as the preferred model for utility regulation in a growing number of developing countries. In the Latin American and Caribbean region, for example, a recent study for the World Bank indicated that the price cap method is well established and seemingly preferred to rate of return regulation (Guasch 2001, 2004). However, in the context of developing economies the usual incentive arguments for the use of price cap over rate of return regulation may be less decisive. This is because of the institutional endowment found in many low- and middle-income countries. Even in Western Europe, North America and Australia, price cap regimes have been far from problem free. In developing countries, setting the X-efficiency factor is likely to be particularly problematic and the negotiating process open to regulatory capture. For example, in lower-income economies there is often little scope for effective benchmarking of performance to provide guidance when determining the scope for efficiency gains. In addition, establishing a price cap for a number of years in advance may lack credibility, especially in high inflation economies and those prone to political unrest. One study of almost a thousand utility sector concession contracts awarded between the mid-1980s and 2000 found that 'the adoption of price caps implied higher costs of capital and hence, tariffs, and brought down levels of investment' (Estache et al. 2003). Some 38 per cent of infrastructure contracts using price cap regulation were subject to renegotiation, on average 2.2 years after the award of the contract. This finding is consistent with the view that price caps can create an uncertain environment for international investors. A recent study confirmed that the use of the price cap in Latin America strongly increased the probability of a renegotiation of a concession contract well before the scheduled renegotiation date (Guasch 2004).[2]

In low-income economies with uneconomic prices as the starting point, the movement in real prices will tend to be sharply upwards after privatisation. There may be a lack of credibility on the part of private investors that a country can commit to linking price rises for essential services to the inflation rate. Hence, the application of a price cap is likely to be transitory. Schmalensee (1989) demonstrates that under conditions of uncertainty – which are likely to be found in many developing countries – regulatory methods in which price depends on the actual costs of production generally substantially outperform pure price caps, particularly in terms of maximising consumer surplus. This is so because the more uncertain the environment the higher the price cap will need to be set at the outset to ensure that the regulated firm is willing to invest. This can lead to a higher price–cost margin than where prices are set based on actual costs. Also, efficiency incentives for management are only achieved under a price cap if a firm which is managed inefficiently is allowed to fail and managers lose income. This sanction is largely untested even in the industrialised economies – the recent government rescues of Railtrack and British Energy in the UK suggest that governments are reluctant to allow privatised infrastructure firms to go under even when there have been apparent management weaknesses. The possibility of major utilities being allowed to fail in low-income economies seems to be at least as incredible. The government takeover of failing privatised toll roads in Mexico and the return to the state sector of a number of privatised water ventures in the last few years is some confirmation of this (Esguerra 2002; Guasch 2004, p. 52).[3]

This is not to say that rate of return regulation does not have at least some of the disadvantages associated with price caps. Information asymmetries create problems when operating rate of return regimes too. Moreover, as is well known, whenever the allowed rate of return is set at above the firm's cost of capital the management has an incentive to invest in the firm's asset base. This can lead to overcapitalisation (Averch and Johnson 1962). However, rate of return regulation may have some compensating advantages in the context of developing countries.

First, staff in regulatory bodies are likely to be heavily, if not entirely, recruited from government departments and SOEs and therefore are likely to have experience of setting prices for state industries based on costs. Rate of return regulation can therefore economise on the need to develop new regulatory skills.

Second, rate of return regulation may provide a more secure environment for investors than exists under a price cap regime, where profits can fluctuate significantly. Under rate of return regulation, prices are set to provide a particular level of profitability. The more stable and secure the environment for investors, the greater should be the level of investment funds from both domestic and foreign investors that will be attracted into the industry.

Third, rate of return regulation may have an important role in creating incentives for rapid investment in key infrastructure schemes, at a time when cost minimisation is less of a public policy priority. Crew and Kleindorfer (1996, p. 212) claim this was the case in the USA in the middle of the twentieth century, when there was a perceived need to roll out utility services, such as power, across the country. In developing economies with their need to expand services to populations currently un- or underserved, rate of return regulation may provide important incentives for service expansion. In such an environment, the Averch–Johnson overinvestment critique may lose some of its power, albeit only if the additional investment is socially and economically beneficial rather than simply politically motivated 'gold plating' (which is always a risk).

Finally, rate of return regulation has the advantage of being dependent on actual financial data when setting prices rather than benchmarking and forecasts of costs and revenues over possibly a lengthy future period, as under a price cap (Stelzer 1996). The more accurate the data used when setting prices and profits and the less speculative the basis for the financial settlement, the less scope there may be for regulatory capture. Where prices and profits are based on notional figures there is considerable scope for 'rigging' the result to satisfy the demands of the industry, politicians or other powerful lobby groups. Also, the public are more likely to understand and sympathise with prices based on actual cost increases than prices based on notional forecasts of cost changes and controversial benchmarking exercises.

To assess the actual experiences of developing countries, the questionnaire survey on RIA in 2003 discussed earlier was supplemented by a series of questions on price and profit regulation (Kirkpatrick et al. 2005). Table 9.3 reports the regional distribution of replies to a question on how prices and profits are regulated – usable replies from 36 countries were received to this part of the questionnaire. The results reveal that some form of price cap was being applied in the majority (24) of the countries, although this figure tells us nothing about *how* the price cap was precisely used or the *form* that it took. By contrast, rate of return regulation was used in 17 countries, sliding-scale regulation in seven countries, and direct government setting of prices in 13. In some of the 36 countries more than one of these methods was used, reflecting different approaches adopted for different regulated industries within the same country and sometimes for different segments of the same sector. Other methods of pricing mentioned by respondents were 'adjustment of prices proposed by industrial operators' (negotiation) and 'benchmarking'. It is interesting to note that Asian countries were more likely to use a price cap than rate of return regulation. Also, they seemed to have a lower propensity than the other regions to rely on direct government setting of prices.

Table 9.3   Methods of regulation used (no. of countries)

Region	Price caps	Rate of return regulation	Sliding scale	Government setting prices	Other
Asia	7	4	1	2	–
Africa	7	7	1	5	1
Latin America	5	2	3	4	1
Transition economies	5	4	2	2	–
Total	24	17	7	13	2

Source: Kirkpatrick et al. (2005).

Asked to comment on the operation of price and profit regulation, the difficulty most often cited by officials using a price cap concerned 'information asymmetries'. Respondents in 23 countries mentioned information asymmetry as a serious problem. Other difficulties frequently cited were a 'serious level of customer complaints about rising prices' (17 countries), 'political pressures' (15), 'enterprises providing misleading information' (14, and a further manifestation of information asymmetry in regulation), problems related to 'quality of service' (12) and 'enterprises underinvesting in capital equipment' (10).

Respondents were also asked to comment on difficulties faced when operating rate of return regulation. Again the most cited difficulty related to 'information asymmetries' and 'serious levels of customer complaints about rising prices' (10 countries). Other commonly recorded difficulties involved 'enterprises overinvesting in capital equipment' (9), 'enterprises providing misleading information' (8), 'political pressures' (7), 'excessive rises in the pay of senior management' and problems related to 'quality of service' (6).

Table 9.4 provides a summary of the answers. The figures in parentheses show the percentage of countries in which regulators using either price caps or rate of return regulation reported each difficulty. In particular, it appears that regulators operating price caps complain more about information asymmetries and misleading information from enterprises than regulators using rate of return regulation – respondents in 96 per cent of the countries using price caps reported information asymmetry to be a problem, compared to 59 per cent of countries using rate of return regulation. This suggests that rate of return regulation, while not free from the same problems, is perceived to be more satisfactory in terms of generating accurate information for regulators. It seems also to be the case that the use of a price cap generates a much higher level of customer complaints to regulators than rate of return regulation. This may reflect the fact that rate of return regulation is easier to comprehend and more transparent in the way that it sets prices than a price cap, where calculation of the X factor and 'cost pass throughs' can be highly controversial, especially in the absence of reliable efficiency benchmarking. At the same time, this comes at an apparent cost in terms of both distorting employment levels (both up and down) and overinvestment; the latter result being very consistent with the theoretical literature (the Averch–Johnson effect). However, price caps also seem to be associated with perceived employment distortions and stand accused of promoting *under*investment. This, as discussed earlier, may be particularly undesirable in economies where expanding provision to under-supplied communities is a public policy priority.

The evidence from the questionnaire survey suggests that price caps do cause firms to reduce investment in developing countries, probably reflecting uncertainty about the outcome of 'periodic reviews' when price caps are re-set and the threat of regulatory intervention in pricing policy at other times. Consistent with the existence of uncertainty, price caps seem to be more open to political pressure than rate of return regulation – regulators in 63 per cent of countries using price caps reported this to be a problem, compared with 41 per cent that regulated the rate of return. Again, this

Table 9.4   Reported difficulties faced when operating price caps and rate of return regulation

Difficulties	Price cap	Rate of return regulation
Information asymmetries or inadequate information on the firm's costs and revenues	23 (96%)	10 (59%)
Enterprises providing misleading information	14 (58%)	8 (47%)
Serious levels of customer complaints about rising prices	17 (71%)	8 (47%)
Enterprises earning excessive profits	4 (17%)	4 (24%)
Enterprises over-recruiting labour	4 (17%)	3 (18%)
Enterprises under-recruiting labour	2 (8%)	3 (18%)
Enterprises overinvesting in capital equipment	4 (17%)	9 (53%)
Enterprises underinvesting in capital equipment	10 (42%)	2 (12%)
Excessive rises in the pay of senior management	3 (13%)	6 (35%)
Problems with the quality of service	12 (50%)	6 (35%)
Inability to recruit staff skilled in the management of regulation	4 (17%)	3 (18%)
Political pressures, e.g., ministerial intervention in setting prices	15 (63%)	7 (41%)
Total number of difficulties reported	112	69

Note: Number of countries in which regulators reported a difficulty: figures in parentheses show the percentage of countries in which regulators using price caps/rate of return regulation reported this difficulty. Prices caps are used in 24 countries, while rate for return regulation is used in fewer, 17, countries. The percentage figures standardise for sample size.

Source: Kirkpatrick et al. (2005).

probably reflects the uncertainties surrounding the setting of an optimal X factor to promote maximum efficiency incentives, while at the same time enabling the enterprises to properly fund their operations. Politicians in developing countries are likely to face intense pressure from the public to intervene outside the scheduled price review periods when prices or profits are rising. There is also confirmation that price caps can lead to distortions in the quality of service – regulated firms are incentivised to cut services and hence costs to boost profitability within the cap. This seems to be less of a problem for rate of return regulation, probably reflecting the fact that, under this form of regulation, firms are usually financed to meet agreed output targets. Overall, the results are consistent with the view that transferring price cap regulation from the developed to the developing world is associated with a number of problems. These stem from the particular conditions found in lower-income economies and their existing regulatory capacity.

CONCLUSIONS

There has been much privatisation of infrastructure provision in developing countries over the last decade or so; most low-income countries are reported to have had some form of private participation in at least one infrastructure sector (Izaguirre and Rao 2000). This has, in turn, led to the creation of around 200 regulatory agencies in developing countries (Harris 2003, p. 38). However, as discussed in this chapter, regulatory systems in developing countries tend to remain weak due to failures in regulatory governance. There is evidence of 'uninformed transfer' (Dolowitz and Marsh 2000, p. 17), in which models of regulation are transferred from the industrialised West with insufficient attention to an individual developing country's ability to absorb them given existing regulatory capacity. In the area of regulatory governance, a best-practice model of 'independent regulation' has been transferred without adequate modification to the conditions existing in particular countries. The same applies to the operation of price caps, which requires regulatory conditions that are absent in many developing economies.

Admittedly, some of the evidence detailed above comes from a small-scale questionnaire survey that deserves to be widened and replicated. In particular, the findings may exaggerate the extent to which countries use some form of RIA. The percentage of returned questionnaires was low and countries with no familiarity with RIA may have chosen not to complete the questionnaire. Equally, space has precluded a detailed discussion of reforms in different developing countries. Arguably, a finer grained analysis is needed which recognises that institutional endowments vary across developing economies, just as they do across industrialised ones. Nevertheless, the study has emphasised some of the problems facing regulation of privatised infrastructure services in developing countries.

The results highlight the need for further research both to establish appropriate theoretical models and to develop an improved empirical base on which to build future forms of economic regulation. The approach adopted needs to involve an assessment of the regulatory goals and the weightings attaching to social goals, especially the poverty reduction agenda, as well as economic ones. This will improve understanding of the meanings of regulatory effectiveness and efficiency when assessing the performance of regulation in any particular economy. Also, research needs to involve an assessment of the institutional context within which each regulatory regime is embedded, including an assessment of (a) the political, economic and cultural values that either sustain or frustrate the intended regulation; (b) the scope for, or likelihood of, maintaining regulatory independence in the face of the forces for regulatory and political capture in a country and what countermeasures might be adopted; (c) the extent of regulatory commitment, leading on to an assessment of regulatory credibility; (d) the scope for improving regulatory practice through introducing systematic processes within government to improve regulation, such as the application of RIA; and (e) the potential for real competition, including the creation of an effective competition policy. The last will help to define both the continued need for separate sector-specific economic regulation and the relevant forms it should take. The resulting research should achieve a much better understanding of the appropriate forms of economic regulation for developing countries than exists at the present time.

NOTES

1. The authors of the paper are directors of the Regulation Research Programme in the Centre. We would like to thank DFID for their support. We also thank Dr Yin-fang Zhang of the University of Manchester, formerly our Research Fellow, for her assistance with the research that is reported in this chapter. The scope of the research in the centre is detailed in Cook et al. (2004).
2. There are also other potential problems. For example, in the case of multinational companies investing in regulated infrastructure industries in developing countries, there is scope for moving revenues and costs between countries to maximise tariff increases. Also, in the absence of developed capital markets, there are obvious difficulties in ascertaining the cost of capital so as to estimate required revenues to provide at least a normal return to investors (for a fuller discussion see Kirkpatrick et al. 2005). Admittedly, these difficulties also apply to the other methods of price and profit regulation.
3. Where infrastructure industries are under state control, price cap regimes are likely to be even less effective because SOEs are rarely allowed to fail.

REFERENCES

Alexander, I. and Estache, A. (1999), 'The role of regulatory reform and growth: lessons from Latin America', mimeo, TIPS (Trade and Industrial Policy Strategies) Annual Forum, Washington, DC: World Bank.
Armstrong, M., Cowan, S. and Vickers, J. (1994), *Regulatory Reform: Economic Analysis and British Experience*, Cambridge, MA: MIT Press.
Averch, H. and Johnson, L.L. (1962), 'Behavior of the firm under regulatory constraint', *American Economic Review*, **52**, 1052–69.
Brook, P.J. and Smith, S.M. (eds) (2003), *Contracting for Public Services. Output Based Aid and Its Applications*, Washington, DC: World Bank and International Finance Corporation.

Cariño, L.V. (2002) 'Regulatory governance in the Philippines: a profile', Working Paper no. 44, Centre on Regulation and Competition, Institute for Development Policy and Management, University of Manchester.

Clarke, R.G. and Wallsten, S.J. (2002), 'Universal(ly bad) service: providing infrastructure services to rural and poor urban consumers', Policy Research Paper 2868, Washington, DC: World Bank.

Cook, P., Kirkpatrick, C., Minogue, M. and Parker, D. (eds) (2004), *Leading Issues in Competition, Regulation and Development*, Cheltenham, UK and Northampton, MA, USA: Edward Elgar.

Crew, M.A. and Kleindorfer, P.R. (1996), 'Incentive regulation in the United Kingdom and the United States: some lessons', *Journal of Regulatory Economics*, **9**, 211–25.

DFID (2000a), 'Making markets work better for the poor: a framework paper', mimeo, November, London: Department for International Development.

DFID (2000b), 'Eliminating world poverty: making globalisation work for the poor', Working Paper on International Development, CM. 5006, London: Department for International Development.

DFID (2002), 'Making connections: infrastructure for poverty reduction', London: Department for International Development.

Dolowitz, D.P. and Marsh, D. (2000), 'Learning from abroad: the role of policy transfer in contemporary policy making', *Governance: An International Journal of Public Administration*, **13** (1), 5–24.

Domah, P., Pollitt, M.G. and Stern, J. (2003) 'Modelling the costs of electricity regulation: evidence of human resource constraints in developing countries', mimeo, Risk Regulation, Accountability and Development Workshop, 26 and 27 June, Centre on Regulation and Competition, University of Manchester.

Esguerra, J. (2002), 'The corporate muddle of Manila's water concessions: how the world's biggest and most successful privatisation turned into a failure', London: Water Aid.

Estache, A., Foster, V. and Wodon, Q. (2002), 'Accounting for poverty in infrastructure reform: learning from Latin America's Experience', World Bank Institute, Washington, DC: World Bank.

Estache, A., Gomez-Lobo, A. and Leipziger, D. (2001), 'Utilities privatization and the poor: lessons and evidence from Latin America', *World Development*, **29** (7), 1179–98.

Estache, A., Guasch, J.-L. and Trujillo, L. (2003), 'Price caps, efficiency payoffs, and infrastructure contract renegotiation in Latin America', Policy Research Working Paper 3129, Washington, DC: World Bank.

Guasch, J.L. (2001), 'Contract renegotiation in LAC', mimeo, Washington, DC: World Bank.

Guasch, J.L. (2004), 'Granting and renogotiating infrastructure concessions: doing it right, World Bank Institute Development Studies, Washington, DC: World Bank.

Harris, C. (2003) 'Private participation in infrastructure in developing countries: trends, impact, and policy lessons', World Bank Working Paper No. 5, Washington, DC: World Bank.

Haskins, C. (Lord) (2000), 'The challenge to state regulation', in C. Robinson (ed.) *Regulation without the State ... The Debate Continues*, Readings 52, London: Institute of Economic Affairs.

Izaguirre, A.K. (2004), 'Private infrastructure activity down by 13 per cent in 2003', Policy for the Private Sector 274, Washington: World Bank, September.

Izaguirre, A.K. and Rao, G. (2000). 'Private activity fell by 30 percent in 1999', Public Policy for the Private Sector, note no. 215, Washington, DC: World Bank.

Jacobs, S. (1997) 'An overview of regulatory impact analysis in OECD countries', in OECD, *Regulatory Impact Analysis: Best Practices in OECD Countries*, Paris: OECD.

Jacobs, S. (2004), 'Evolution of East Asian utility regulators: diversity and challenges', mimeo, Jacobs & Associates, Washington, DC.

Jalilian, H., Kirkpatrick, C. and Parker, D. (2003), 'The impact of regulation on economic growth in developing countries – a cross-country analysis', mimeo, Centre on Regulation and Competition, University of Manchester.

Kauffman, R. and Kraay, A. (2002), 'Growth without governance', mimeo, Washington, DC: World Bank.

Kikeri, S. and Nellis, J. (2001), 'Privatization in competitive sectors: the record so far', Private Sector Advisory Services, Washington, DC: World Bank.

Kirkpatrick, C. and Parker, D. (2004) 'Regulatory impact assessment and regulatory governance in developing countries', *Public Administration and Development*, **24**, 1–12.

Kirkpatrick, C., Parker, D. and Zhang, Y.-F. (2004a), 'State versus private sector provision of water services in developing countries: the evidence and a new analysis', mimeo, Centre on Regulation and Competition, University of Manchester.

Kirkpatrick, C., Parker, D. and Zhang, Y.-F. (2004b) 'Regulatory impact assessment in developing and transitional economies: a survey of current practice', *Public Money & Management*, **24** (5), 291–6.

Kirkpatrick, C., Parker, D. and Zhang, Y.-F. (2004c), 'Regulation and foreign direct investment in infrastructure: does regulation make a difference?' mimeo, Centre on Regulation and Competition, Institute for Development Policy and Management, University of Manchester.

Kirkpatrick, C., Parker, D. and Zhang, Y.-F. (2005), 'Price and profit regulation in developing and transition economies: a survey of the regulators', *Public Money & Management*, **25** (2), 99–105.

Knight-John, M., Jayasinghe, S. and Perumal, A. (2003), 'Regulatory impact assessment in Sri Lanka: the bridges that have to be crossed', mimeo, Institute of Policy Studies, Colombo, Sri Lanka.

Lal, D. (1999), *Unfinished Business: India in the World Economy*, Oxford: Oxford University Press.

Levy, B. and Spiller, P. (1994), 'The institutional foundations of regulatory commitment: a comparative analysis of telecommunications regulation', *Journal of Law, Economics and Organization*, **10** (2), 201–45.

Minogue, M. (2002), 'Governance-based analysis of regulation', *Annals of Public and Cooperative Economics*, **73** (4), 649–66.

Mitlin, D. (2004), 'Competition, regulation and the urban poor: a case study of water', in P. Cook, C. Kirkpatrick, M. Minogue and D. Parker (eds), *Leading Issues in Competition, Regulation and Development*, Cheltenham, UK and Northampton, MA, USA: Edward Elgar, pp. 320–38.

Newbery, D. (1999), *Privatization, Restructuring and Regulation of Network Industries*, Cambridge, MA: MIT Press.

North, D.C. (1990), *Institutions, Institutional Change and Economic Performance*, Cambridge: Cambridge University Press.

Pargal, S. (2003), 'Regulation and private sector investment in infrastructure: evidence from Latin America', Policy Research Working Paper 3037, Washington, DC, World Bank.

Parker, D. (2002), 'Economic regulation: a review of issues', *Annals of Public and Cooperative Economics*, **73** (4), 493–519.

Parker, D. and Kirkpatrick, C. (2005), 'Privatisation in developing countries: a review of the evidence and the policy lessons', *Journal of Development Studies*, **41** (4), 513–41.

Radaelli, C.M. (2002), 'The politics of regulatory impact analysis in the OECD countries: best practice and lesson-drawing', mimeo, Bradford: University of Bradford.

Schmalensee, R. (1989) 'Good regulatory regimes', *RAND Journal of Economics*, **20** (3),417–36.

Smith, W. (1997), 'Utility regulators: the independence debate', Viewpoint 127, Washington, DC: World Bank.

Smith, W. (2000), 'Regulatory infrastructure for the poor: perspectives on regulatory system design', mimeo, Washington, DC: World Bank.

Spiller, P. (1993), 'Institutions and regulatory commitment in utilities privatization', *Industrial and Corporate Change*, **2** (3), 421–52.

Stelzer, I.M. (1996), 'Lessons for UK regulation from recent US experience', in M. Beesley (ed.) *Regulating Utilities: A Time for Change?*, London: Institute of Economic Affairs, pp. 189–203.

Stern, J. and Holder, S. (1999), 'Regulatory governance: criteria for assessing the performance of regulatory systems: an application to infrastructure industries in the developing countries of Asia', *Utilities Policy*, **8**, 33–50.

TERI (The Energy and Resources Institute) (2003), Draft Report on Regulation in India for Centre on Regulation and Competition, University of Manchester, New Delhi: Energy and Resources Institute.

Torp, J.E. and Rekve, P. (1998), 'Privatisation in developing countries: lessons to be learnt from the Mozambican case', *Transformation*, no. 36, 73–92.

Wallsten, S.J. (2001), 'An economic analysis of telecom competition, privatization, and regulation in Africa and Latin America', *The Journal of Industrial Economics*, **49** (1), 1–19.

Weyman-Jones, T. (2003), 'Regulating prices and profits', in D. Parker and D. Saal (eds), *International Handbook on Privatization*, Cheltenham, UK and Northampton, MA, USA: Edward Elgar, pp. 496–513.

Willoughby, C. (2003), 'Can public infrastructure institutions be leading agents for pro-poor growth?', mimeo, ADBI (Asian Development Bank Institute) Conference, June, Tokyo.

World Bank (1994), 'Infrastructure for Development', *World Development Report*, Washington, DC: World Bank.

World Bank (1995), *Bureaucrats in Business: The Economics and Politics of Government Ownership*, Oxford and Washington, DC: Oxford University Press and World Bank.

World Bank (2001a), 'Private Sector Development Strategy – Directions for the World Bank Group', mimeo, Washington, DC: World Bank.

World Bank (2001b), *World Development Report*, 2000/2001, Washington, DC: World Bank.

World Bank (2003), 'Private Participation in Infrastructure: Trends in Developing Countries in 1990–2001', Private Sector Advisory Services, Washington, DC: World Bank.

World Bank (2004a), *Reforming Infrastructure: Privatization, Regulation and Competition*, World Bank Policy Research Report, Washington, DC: World Bank.

World Bank (2004b), *Doing Business in 2005: Removing Obstacles to Growth*, Washington, DC: World Bank and Oxford University Press.

Zhang, Y.-F., Kirkpatrick, C. and Parker, D. (2003), 'Electricity sector reform in developing countries: an econometric assessment of the effects of privatisation, competition and regulation', Discussion Paper no. 31, Manchester: Centre on Regulation and Competition, Institute for Development Policy and Management, University of Manchester.

Zhang, Y.-F., Parker, D. and Kirkpatrick, C. (2004), 'Competition, regulation and privatisation of electricity generation in developing countries: does the sequencing of the reforms matter?', mimeo, Centre on Regulation and Competition, Institute for Development Policy and Management, University of Manchester.

CHAIRMAN'S COMMENTS

Colin Robinson

In asking David to examine this subject, we set him a difficult task because there is such variety in the economies, the institutional arrangements, the political structures and the economic policies of 'developing countries' that it is hard to summarise experience with privatisation and regulation in a way that draws out useful lessons. However, using his own research and that of others, David has indeed managed to identify trends in regulation, to show what problems can be caused by the inappropriate transfer of experience gained in the developed world and to suggest ways in which research could help find forms of regulation more suited to conditions in particular developing countries. His analysis is a helpful aid to those of us who are generally more concerned with regulation in Britain, the rest of the EU and the United States as we try to appreciate the very different problems faced by countries at different stages of development.

I shall comment briefly on the two major issues David raises – institutional matters and the form of price and profits regulation.

Institutional Issues

David deals principally with infrastructure privatisation. He questions whether sufficient thought has been given to the design of institutional structures and regulatory instruments for developing countries or whether there has been too ready an acceptance that price cap regulation and independent regulatory offices are the way forward. He is surely right in his emphasis on the importance of institutions. Without appropriate institutions, as Ronald Coase pointed out many years ago, markets cannot flourish. Nor can regulation operate effectively and efficiently without proper institutional capacity which, as David says, is lacking in many developing countries. Regulators in developing countries have a difficult enough task in trying to balance efficiency and distributional objectives. Yet they frequently operate in environments where institutional capacity is severely limited. Many developing countries lack trained people and well-established legal and enforcement systems, information-gathering systems are poor, cronyism and corruption may be serious and regulatory capture may be a major issue. As David notes, 'In summary, regulatory incentives and regulatory governance regimes need to be in place but both are often either underdeveloped or absent'.

He suggests the situation could be improved if governments would introduce 'regulatory impact assessments' (RIAs) and he mentions research which shows that some countries are carrying out such RIAs. The idea of an RIA is to assess *ex ante* the costs and benefits of a new regulation and also to check whether existing regulations should be abandoned. I do not think RIAs have been a great success in this country or, so far as I know, elsewhere. The principal issue, I think, is that since the costs and benefits all lie in the future it is not difficult to come to the conclusion dictated by the assessor's preconceptions. So I would be less sanguine than David about the chances that the widespread adoption of RIAs will improve matters, given the deep-seated institutional problems he identifies.

Price and Profits Regulation

David draws attention to the awkward constraints that face regulators in developing countries where the need to provide poor households with infrastructure services is confronted by the requirement to allow companies to earn enough profits to finance their investments.

He argues that price cap regulation, which is now so much in favour, may not be appropriate for developing countries where setting X, in particular, is a real problem, given institutional conditions. The bargaining process over X may be subject to regulatory capture and price caps, compared with rate of return regulation, may generate an uncertain environment for investors. By comparison, rate of return regulation may make it easier to recruit experienced staff, provide a more secure environment for investors and increase incentives for investment in key infrastructure schemes. Moreover, David argues, data problems are eased because rate of return regulation is dependent on actual financial data rather than forecasts. David mentions research which shows that price caps are now being applied in many developing countries. The research also shows that price cap regulators complain more about information asymmetries and misleading information from regulated companies than do their counterparts who use rate of return. Price caps, he argues, lead to lower investment in infrastructure and to another effect often predicted for price caps – reductions in quality of service to reduce costs and increase profitability.

In thinking about David's conclusions, it is worth going back to the reason why price caps were first introduced. When Britain's regulatory regime was being established, at the time of the privatisations of the 1980s, the US rate of return system was regarded – with good reason – as an awful example to be avoided. Much theoretical work and empirical evidence had demonstrated its poor incentive properties. RPI-X was a way of circumventing these undesirable consequences. But it was not thought of by its authors as the be-all and end-all of utility regulation – which is what it seems to have become. After explaining the disadvantages of the US system and also of periodic efficiency audits, the authors of price cap regulation, Michael Beesley and Stephen Littlechild in a 1982 article continue as follows about the purpose of a cap on prices,

> The purpose of such a constraint is to reassure consumers of monopoly services that the situation will not get worse under privatization. It 'holds the fort' until competition arrives, and is inappropriate if competition is not expected to emerge. It is a temporary safeguard, not a permanent method of control. The 'one-off' nature of the restriction is precisely what preserves the firm's incentive to be efficient, because the firm keeps any gains beyond the specified level ... (Beesley and Littlechild 1983, p. 7)

That strong statement about the temporary nature of a price cap, to 'hold the fort', and about the inappropriateness of price caps when competition is not expected to emerge, makes clear that it is not only in the developing world that price cap regulation has gone far beyond what its authors intended. It is, of course, not uncommon for economic ideas to be applied in circumstances to which they are not really suited. Because economic policy making is so difficult, a new idea tends to be seized on by governments and international institutions and spreads around the world regardless of circumstances. The price cap is one of those ideas that has been taken up as 'the answer' – in its case to the problem of regulating utilities. Even in Britain, its original home, price caps have, in my view, been misapplied. In some utility markets, such as water in England and Wales, whole industries are apparently now being permanently regulated by a price cap even though there is no intention to introduce genuine competition into potentially competitive sectors of the industry and so Beesley/Littlechild 'fort-holding' is, by definition, inappropriate. Relief from the forces of competition will never arrive.

The circumstances in which price cap regulation can usefully be applied seem to me to be as follows. The industry in question should be a utility with a network at its heart. That network (for example, of pipes or wires) should be separated, preferably into a new company. In the rest of the industry, competition should be introduced. In the competitive area, after a brief transitional period there should be no price regulation. In the network, 'natural monopoly' area, regulation should, where feasible, be carried out by a cap on prices.

The reasons why price caps are generally superior to rate of return regulation are, I think, more subtle than generally realised. Price caps are more appealing to economists who think of competition as a process than to those who cling to neoclassical, static versions of competition. Beesley was very keen on the Schumpeterian vision of competition – the 'perennial gale of creative destruction' that in the long run sweeps away the profits of monopolies. Price caps are a pale shadow of Schumpeterian competition. It would be going too far to argue that a periodic price review is similar to the 'perennial gale', but at least it does attempt periodically to sweep away monopoly profits after leaving the monopolists to enjoy them for a period. Thus it gives an incentive to invest which bears some resemblance to the incentives of a competitive marketplace.

So, to conclude, I would be interested to hear what David thinks about the prospects for applying price caps in developing countries in circumstances where they might be expected to work better: that is, after separation of network activities and the introduction of competition into potentially competitive sectors. Of course, both network separation and market liberalisation may be difficult because of poor institutional backgrounds but, if neither is possible so that whole industries – monopoly and potentially competitive sectors alike – become regulated by a price cap, I think I would agree with David that, despite the theoretical advantages of a cap, in practice it probably will not work well. In such inauspicious circumstances, whether price caps or rate of return are used may not matter very much. Neither will yield good results. The basis of the regulatory regime is insecure and there is a high probability that an inappropriate system will become entrenched and indeed grow out of control.

Reference

Beesley, Michael and Stephen Littlechild (1983), 'Privatisation: principles, problems and priorities', *Lloyds Bank Review*, July p. 7.

Index

abuse of a dominant position 138–53
  abuse in general 145–6
  Article 81 141–3
  Article 82 143–5
  chairman's comments 156–60
  loyalty rebates 151–2
  predatory pricing 146–9
  price discrimination 149–52
  rule-based approach 98–9
access charges reviews
  (2000) 8, 16
  (2003) 10–11, 12, 16
  (2008–9) 22
  after Railtrack's going into
    administration 9
  need for government role 15
access requirements, investment in
  local loop facilities 124
accessibility, infrastructure services 194
administration work, Ofgem 80
advertising-funded programming 105,
  107
advocacy, competition tests 162
affordability, infrastructure services
  194
Africa
  gas reserves 46
  price regulation 202
  regulatory assessment 198
  see also North Africa; Sub-Saharan
    Africa
agriculture
  CO_2 and GHG emissions 68
  cost-benefit of reducing cattle stocks
    68–9
Airtours 175
analogue television 104, 108
anti-competitive abuse 146
AOL–Time Warner merger 127–8
appeal court decisions, merger cases
  175

appeal mechanisms, merger reviews 182
Article 81 141–3
Article 82 140, 141, 142, 143–5, 149,
  152
Asia
  gas reserves 46
  price regulation 202
  see also Central Asia; East Asia;
    South Asia
AT&T 122, 124
auction theory, PSB 120

base price, longer-term gas supply
  contracts 38
BBC 104, 114, 134
BBC/Human Capital report (2004)
  110, 111, 112
Beesley Lectures
  (2003) 72
  (2004) 1
Beesley, Michael 213
Belgium, gas trade 33, 34, 35, 37
Bellamy, Christopher 3, 82–93
BG 34
bilateralism, merger reviews 181–2
bottlenecks, telecommunications
  125–30
Bourn, John 81
BP 36, 41, 50
British Gas Board 34
British Railways Board 26
British Wind Energy Association
  (BWEA) 61
Bronner case 126–7, 130
BT 130, 134
Buchanan, Alistair 3, 80–81
bulk contract prices, gas 38
burden of proof, efficiencies, merger
  reviews 169, 182
business lobby, Energy Review (2002)
  75